The Victorian Muse

Selected Criticism and Parody of the Period

A thirty-nine-volume facsimile set essential to the study of one of the most prolific periods in English literature

Edited by
William E. Fredeman, Ira Bruce Nadel, John F. Stasny

A Garland Series

The Gay Science

E.S. Dallas

Volume One

Garland Publishing, Inc.
New York & London
1986

For a complete list of the titles in this series see the final pages of volume two.

This facsimile has been made from a copy in the Library of Congress.

Library of Congress Cataloging-in-Publication Data

Dallas, E. S. (Eneas Sweetland), 1828–1879.
The gay science.

(The Victorian muse)
Reprint. Originally published in 2 v.: London:
Chapman and Hall, 1866.
Includes index.
1. Criticism. 2. Aesthetics. 3. Pleasure. I. Title.
II. Series.
BH39.D344 1986 700′.1 86-9869
ISBN 0-8240-8604-X (set : alk. paper)

Design by Bonnie Goldsmith

The volumes in this series are printed on acid-free, 250-year-life paper.

Printed in the United States of America

THE GAY SCIENCE.

LONDON: PRINTED BY WILLIAM CLOWES AND SONS, STAMFORD STREET
AND CHARING CROSS.

THE GAY SCIENCE

BY

E. S. DALLAS

VOL. I.

LONDON
CHAPMAN AND HALL, 193 PICCADILLY
1866.

PREFACE.

THESE volumes aim at completeness in themselves, but I must ask the reader to bear in mind that they are to be followed by two more. They are an attempt to settle the first principles of Criticism, and to show how alone it can be raised to the dignity of a science. But any one who cares for the discussion is sure to ask at every stage of it—How do your principles bear on the practical questions of criticism? how are they to be applied? I hope to show this ere long; but I venture also to hope that the principles here evolved—even while their application is withheld—may be worthy of attention, may entertain the reader, and may prove to be suggestive.

A few of the following pages have already seen the light in various publications, although they now stand in their places without any acknowledgment of a previous appearance. They are so few in number, and, having been rewritten, are so altered in form, that it would have been difficult, and it seemed to be needless, to introduce them with the usual marks of quotation.

E. S. D.

THE CONTENTS.

CHAPTER I.

INTRODUCTION.

CHAPTER II.

THE SCIENCE OF CRITICISM.

CHAPTER III.

THE DESPAIR OF A SCIENCE.

CHAPTER IV.

THE CORNER STONE.

CHAPTER V.

THE AGREEMENT OF THE CRITICS.

CHAPTER VI.

ON IMAGINATION.

CHAPTER VII.

THE HIDDEN SOUL.

CHAPTER VIII.

THE PLAY OF THOUGHT.

CHAPTER IX.

THE SECRECY OF ART.

INTRODUCTION.

THE GAY SCIENCE.

CHAPTER I.

INTRODUCTION.

I HAVE called the present work the Gay Science, because that is the shortest description I can find of its aim and contents. But I have ventured to wrest the term a little from its old Provençal meaning. The Gay Science was the name given by the troubadours to their art of poetry. We could scarcely now, however, call poetry, or the art of poetry, a science. It is true that the distinction between science and art has always been very hazy. In our day it has been as hotly disputed as among the schoolmen whether logic be a science or an art, or both. Even so late a writer as Hobbes classes poetry among the sciences, for it is in his view the

CHAPTER I.

Meaning of the title.

The term Science.

CHAPTER I. — science of magnifying and vilifying. I hope before I have finished this work to trace

See Chapter IX.

more accurately than has yet been done the dividing line between science and art; but, in the meantime, there is no doubt that poetry must take rank among the arts, and that the name of science in connection with it must be reserved for the critical theory of its processes and of its influence in the world. Such is the sense in which the word is used upon the title pages of the present volumes.

The Gay Science, because the science of pleasure.

Why the Gay Science, however? The light-hearted minstrels of Provence insisted on the joyfulness of their art. In the dawn of modern literature, they declared, with a straightforwardness which has never been surpassed either by poets or by critics, that the immediate aim of art is the cultivation of pleasure. But it so happens that no critical doctrine is in our day more unfashionable than this—that the object

This the doctrine of 3000 years.

of art is pleasure. Any of us who cleave to the old creed, which has the prescription of about thirty centuries in its favour, are supposed to be shallow and commonplace. Nearly all thinkers now, who pretend to any height or depth of thought, abjure the notion of pleasure as the object of pursuit in the noble moods of art. But what if these high-fliers are wrong and the thirty centuries are right? What, if not one of those who reject the axiom of the thirty centuries can agree with another as to the terms of a better doctrine? What if theirs be the true commonplace which cannot see the grandeur of a doctrine, because it comes to us clothed in unclean and threadbare garments? There is no more commonplace thinker than he who fails to see the virtue of the commonplace.

Doubts about pleasure.

Pleasure, no doubt, is an ugly word, and, as representing the end of art, a feeble one; but there is no better to be found. It suggests a great deal for which as yet we have no adequate language. One day it may be that we shall find a different word to express more fully our meaning; but that day will never come until we have first learned thoroughly to understand what is involved in pleasure; and to see what a hundred generations of mankind have groped after when they set before them pleasure as the goal of art. It can be shown that this doctrine of pleasure has a greatness of meaning which the high-fliers little suspect: that it is anything but shallow; and that if it be commonplace, it is so only in the sense in which sun, air, earth, water, and all the elements of life are commonplace. We begin to feel this the moment we attempt to define pleasure. Take any allowable definition. Kant says that it is a feeling of the furtherance of life, as pain is a sense of its hindrance. Such a definition at once leads us into a larger circle of ideas than is usually supposed to be covered by the name of pleasure. Perhaps it is not

Palliated by Kant's definition of it.

CHAPTER I. quite satisfactory, but we need not now be too particular about its terms. What Kant says is near enough to the truth to show that on the first blush of it we need not be repelled by the assertion of pleasure being the end of art. Neither need any one be repelled if this doctrine of pleasure strike the key-note, and suggest the title of the present work, in which an attempt will be made to show that a science of criticism is possible, and that it must of necessity be the science of the laws of pleasure, the joy science, the Gay Science.

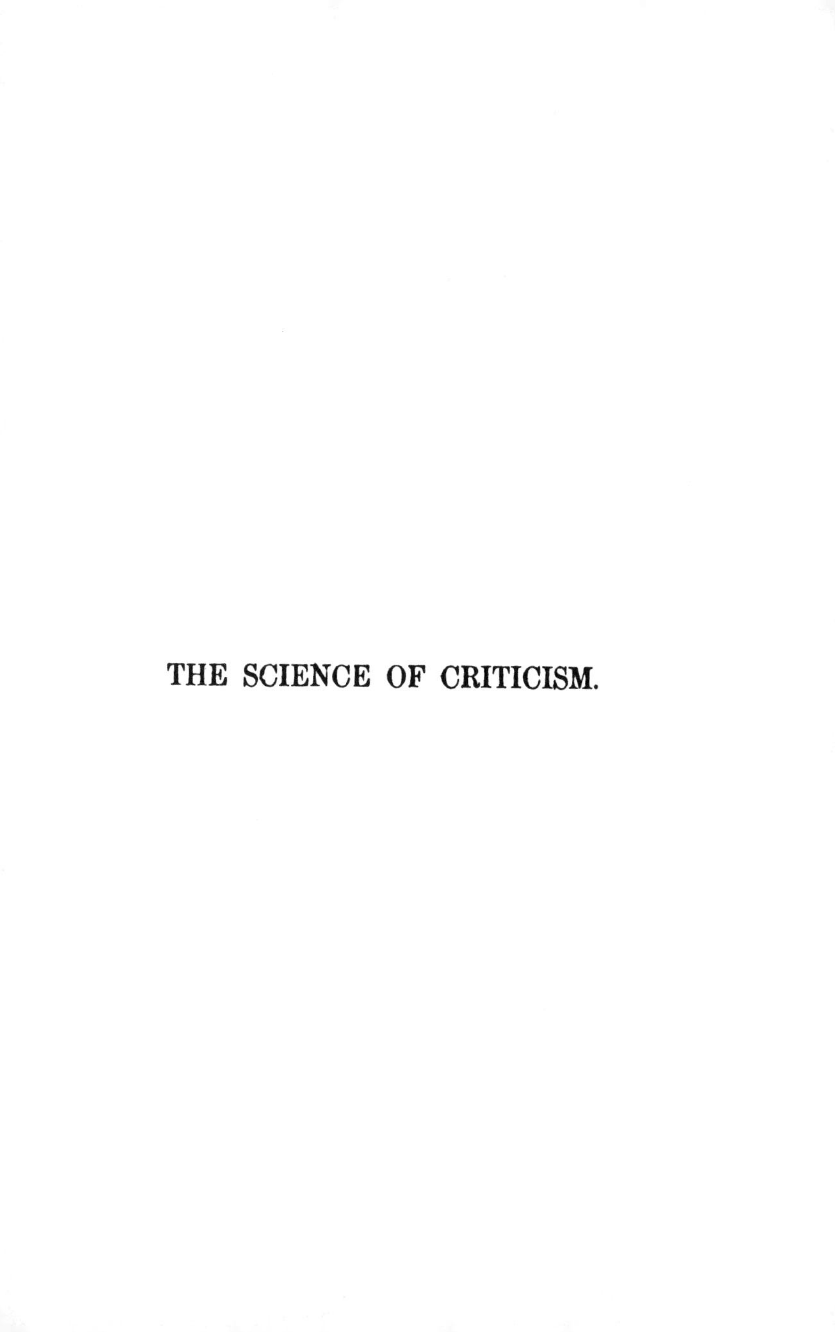

THE SCIENCE OF CRITICISM.

CHAPTER II.

THE SCIENCE OF CRITICISM.

BUT is a science of criticism possible? That is a great question — often asked, and usually answered in the negative. It cannot well be answered in the affirmative, indeed, so long as criticism is undefined. Criticism is a wide word that, according to late usage, may comprehend almost any stir of thought. It is literally the exercise of judgment, and logicians reduce every act of the mind into an act of judgment. So it comes to pass that there is a criticism of history, of philosophy, of science, of politics and life, as well as of literature and art, which is criticism proper. Sir William Hamilton, who never touched criticism proper, was known throughout Europe as the first critic of his day; and Mr. Matthew Arnold has lately been using the word as a synonym not only for science, but even for poetry. Homer,

Criticism in its widest sense.

Essay on Joubert.

CHAPTER II.

Dante and Shakespeare, are in his view critics. Their work is at bottom a criticism of life, and "the aim of all literature, if one considers it attentively, is in truth nothing but that." It may be convenient sometimes to employ the word thus largely; but there is a danger of our forgetting its more strict application to art. Certainly, in the larger, looser sense of the term, a science of criticism, if at all possible, must resolve itself into something like a science of reason—a logic—a science of science. It is needful, therefore, to explain at the outset that there is a narrower sense of the word criticism, and that there is a good reason why it should be specially applied to the criticism of literature and art.

Does not contain within itself the notion of a special science.

Criticism strictly so called,

The reason is, that whereas the criticism of philosophy, truly speaking, is itself philosophy, and that of science science, and that of history history, the criticism of poetry and art is not poetry and art, but is and to the end of time will remain criticism. Kant called his leading work a critique, and he chose that title because his object was not to propound a philosophical system, but to ascertain the competence of reason to sound the depths of philosophy. This, however, as much belongs to philosophy as sounding the ocean belongs to ocean telegraphy. Locke had already done the same thing. He said, that before attempting to dive into philosophy, it would be wise to inquire whether the human mind is able to dive into it, and he would therefore examine into the nature and resources of the thinking faculty. The criticism of the understanding which he thus undertook is Locke's philosophy, just as Kant's critique of reason is the most important part of Kant's philosophy. So in other lines of thought, criticism of philology is a piece of philology, and criticism of history is a contribution to the lore of history. One of the most classical of all histories indeed, that of Julius Cæsar, goes by the name of commentary. But criticism of poetry, it must be repeated, is not poetry, and art lore is not art. The attempt has, no doubt, again and again been made, to elevate criticism into poetry. Witness the well-known poems of Horace, Vida, Boileau, Pope, and others. But criticism that would be poetry is like the cat that set up for a lady and could not forget the mice. Whatever it may be as criticism, it falls short of art. And therefore it is that the name more especially belongs to all that lore which cannot well get beyond itself—the lore of art and literary form.

Is criticism and nothing more.

Now, it must be owned that criticism does not yet rank as a science, and that, following the wonted methods, it seems to have small chance of becoming one. To judge by the names bestowed upon critics, indeed, one might infer that it has no chance at all. Sir Henry Wotton used to say, and Bacon deemed the saying valuable enough to be entered in his book of Apophthegms,

Criticism not yet a science.

What the world thinks of critics and criticism.

CHAPTER II.

that they are but brushers of noblemen's clothes; Ben Jonson spoke of them as tinkers who make more faults than they mend; Samuel Butler, as the fierce inquisitors of wit, and as butchers who have no right to sit on a jury; Sir Richard Steele, as of all mortals the silliest; Swift, as dogs, rats, wasps, or, at best, the drones of the learned world; Shenstone, as asses which, by gnawing vines, first taught the advantage of pruning them; Matthew Green, as upholsterers and appraisers; Burns, as cut-throat bandits in the path of fame; Washington Irving, as freebooters in the republic of letters; and Sir Walter Scott, humorously reflecting the general sentiment, as caterpillars. If poets and artists may be described as pillars of the house of fame, critics, wrote Scott, are the caterpillars. Donne, for not keeping of accent, deserved hanging, said Ben Jonson; and criticism, says Dryden, is mere hangman's work. It is a malignant deity, says Swift, cradled among the snows of Nova Zembla. Ten censure wrong, says Pope, for one who writes amiss. The critic's livelihood is to find fault, says Thackeray. *Non es vitiosus, Zoile, sed vitium*, is the summing up of the wittiest of Latin poets: You are not at fault, Gaffer critic, but fault. Thomas Moore has a fable of which the point is that from the moment when young Genius became subject to criticism his glory faded. Wordsworth describes criticism as an inglorious employ-

The pith of it in Moore's fable.

ment. "I warn thee," says Edward Irving, "against criticism, which is the region of pride and malice."

CHAPTER II.

What critics think of each other.

Nor is this merely the judgment of poets and artists upon their tormentors. The critics have passed sentence upon each other with equal severity. One of the mildest statements which I can call to mind is that of Payne Knight, who opens an essay on the Greek alphabet with the assertion that what is usually considered the higher sort of criticism has not the slightest value. It was but the other day that a distinguished living critic, Mr. G. H. Lewes, found occasion to write—"The good effected by criticism is small, the evil incalculable." Critics have always had a strong cannibal instinct. They have not only snapped at the poets: they have devoured one another. It seems as if, like Diana's priest at Aricia, a critic could not attain his high office except by slaughter of the priest already installed; or as if he had been framed in the image of that serpent which, the old legends tell us, cannot become a dragon unless it swallow another serpent. It is not easy to connect the pursuits of such men with the notion of science. The truth, however, is that criticism, if it merit half the reproaches which have been cast upon it, is not fit to live. It is not merely unscientific: it is inhuman. Hissing is the only sound in nature that wakes no echo; and if criti-

The doom of criticism.

CHAPTER II. cism is nought but hissing, can do nought but hiss, it is altogether a mistake.

Summary of the forms of criticism. It may be hard for the critics to be measured by the meanest of their tribe and by the worst of their deeds; but if we put the meanest and the worst out of sight altogether, and look only to the good, we shall still find that criticism, at its best, is a luxuriant wilderness, and yields nowhere the sure tokens of a science. Take it in any of its forms, editorial, biographical, historical, or systematic, and see if this be not the case.

Editorial criticism. Editorial criticism, whether it takes the course of revising, or of reviewing, or of expounding the texts of individual authors, has, even in the hands of the ablest critics engaged upon the works of the greatest poets, yielded no large results. It is very much to this kind of criticism, at least when it points out a beauty here and a blemish there, that Payne Knight referred, when he declared that it is of no use whatever. A good editor of poetry is, indeed, one of the rarest of birds, as those who have paid any attention to certain recent issues must painfully know. Sometimes the editor is an enthusiastic admirer of his author: in this case he generally praises everything he sees, and edits in the style of a showman. Sometimes he is wonderfully erudite: in this case he rarely gets beyond verbal criticism, and edits on the principle of the miser, that if you take care of the

CHAPTER II.

How unsatisfactory.

halfpence the pounds will take care of themselves. The appearance of one edition after another of the same poets and the same dramatists proves how unsatisfactory was each previous one, and how exceedingly rare is that assemblage of qualities required in a poetical editor —ample knowledge combined with depth of thought, imagination restrained by common sense, and the power of being far more than the editor of other men's work, united with the will to forget oneself and to remain entirely in the background. Perhaps this last is the rarest of combinations. Why should a man, who is himself capable of producing a book, be content with the more humble labour of furbishing up other men's productions? The result is nearly worthless, unless there is some sort of equality, some appearance of companionship and brotherhood between the poet and his editor; but the chances are that only those will undertake the responsibility of editing poetry who are fit for nothing else, who could not by accident write two passable couplets, who could not assume to be the poet's friend, but who, perchance, might lay claim to the dignity of being the poet's lacquey—which Sir Henry Wotton had in his mind when he said that critics are but the brushers cf noblemen's clothes.

An example of it in Shake-

The modern author who has been most read and criticised is Shakespeare. There is a well-

CHAPTER II.

spearian criticism.

known edition of his works in which nearly every line has a bushel of notes gathered from the four winds—from the two and thirty winds. All the wisdom of all the annotators is winnowed, and garnered, and set in array. After all, what is it? That which one critic says, the next gainsays, and the next confounds. On reading a dozen such pages, we close the volume in despair, and carry away but one poor idea, that Shakespearian criticism is like the occupation of the prisoner in the Bastile, who, to keep away madness, used daily to scatter a handful of pins about his room, that he might find employment in picking them up again. Strangely enough, it is not the men of highest intellect that in this way have done the most for Shakespeare. Pope was one of his editors; so was Warburton; Johnson another; Malone too, a very able man. Mr. Charles Knight is correct in saying that the best of the old editors of Shakespeare is Theobald—"poor piddling Tibbald." Whatever be the abstract worth of such editorial researches, their scientific worth is fairly estimated by Steevens, one of the most eager of his race, when he claims the merit of being the first commentator on Shakespeare who strove with becoming seriousness to account for the stains of gravy, pie-crust, and coffee, that defile nearly all the copies of the First Folio.

Its worth estimated by Steevens.

Another example of it

Nor can it be said that there is any more certain appearance of science when the ancient authors are subjected to the same strain of criticism. Witness the famous critics of the Bentley and Porson mould. Giant as he was, Porson had but small hands, that played with words as with marbles, and delighted in nothing so much as in good penmanship. One is astonished in reading through his edition of Euripides, to see how he wrote note upon note, all about words, and less than words—syllables, letters, accents, punctuation. He ransacked Codex A and Codex B, Codex Cantabrigiensis and Codex Cottonianus, to show how this noun should be in the dative, not in the accusative; how that verb should have the accent paroxytone, not perispomenon; and how by all the rules of prosody there should be an iambus, not a spondee, in this place or in that. Nothing can be more masterly of its kind than the preface to the *Hecuba*, and the supplement to it. The lad who hears enough of this wonderful dissertation from his tutors at last turns wistful eyes towards it, expecting to find some magical criticism on Greek tragedy. Behold it is a treatise on certain Greek metres. Its talk is of cæsural pauses, penthemimeral and hephthemimeral, of isochronous feet, of enclitics and cretic terminations; and the grand doctrine it promulgates is expressed in the canon regarding the pause which, from the discoverer, has been named the Porsonian, that when the iambic trimeter, after a word of more than one syllable, has the cretic termina-

In classical criticism.

Porson's preface to the *Hecuba*.

CHAPTER II.

tion, included either in one word or in two, then the fifth foot must be an iambus! The young student throws down the book thus prefaced, and wonders if this be all that giants of Porsonian height can see or care to speak about in Greek literature. Nor was Porson alone; he had disciples even worse. Many a youth of wild temperament wishes for something to break his mind on, like the study of Armenian, which Byron found useful in that way. Let him read Elmsley on the *Medea*. If Porson was a kind of Baal, a lord of flies, Elmsley was a literary dustman. The criticism of detail which both of them studied has an invariable tendency to stray further and further from science, and to become Rabbinical. It ends in teaching Rabbis to count the letters of a sacred book backwards and forwards until they can find the middle one. It ends, as in the last century, in teaching critics to reject false rhymes, and to allow false gods. The motes that people a sunbeam, and are beautiful there, come to eclipse the stars. In the words of Keble:

Elmsley.

> A finger-breadth at hand will mar
> A world of light in heaven afar,
> A mote eclipse yon glorious star,
> An eyelid hide the sky.

Biographical criticism

Balked in the search for science amid the criticism of detail, we next try critics of a higher order, who, not content to examine literary works in and by themselves, examine them in connection with the lives of the authors. The biographical critics are as yet few in number, and their method is of late origin. Johnson (if I must not say Bayle) may be taken as the father of the tribe, though he took to the method rather by chance than from choice, and was never fully alive to its value. It was a great thing, however, to introduce into criticism the personality of an author, and to study his works in the light of his life. It immediately ensured the sympathy of the critics, for Johnson, with all his drawbacks, must be accepted as essentially kind, hearty, and just. Since his time, other writers, in our own and other countries, have made the most of the new method. Their works are of great interest and of lasting value; for whereas editorial criticism is mere analysis, and so far as it is trustworthy contains nothing which was not previously contained in the work revised, in biographical criticism there is somewhat of synthesis; there is a new element added; there is the image of the author's life projected on his work. But, however entertaining or however valuable this may be, it is not science.

The advantages of it.

In so far as a science of human nature is possible, it lies not in the actions of the individual, but in those of the race; not in the developments of a lifetime, but in those of ages and cycles. The biographical critics tell us that Dryden, before he courted the Muse, took a dose of salts; that Anacreon choked on a grape-

But how far from science.

CHAPTER II.

stone; that Æschylus had his bald head broken by an eagle which, high in air, took it for a stone, and dropped a tortoise on it; that Horace was blear-eyed; that Camoens was one-eyed; that two other epic poets were blind of both eyes; that the author of *The Castle of Indolence* used to saunter about his garden, and with his hands in his pockets, bite the sunny sides of his peaches; that John Dennis, the critic, was expelled his college for stabbing a man in the dark (a fact, by the way, unknown to Pope); that Spinoza's darling amusement was to entangle flies in spiders' webs, and to set spiders fighting with each other; that Newton was small enough, when he was born, to be put into a quart-mug, and that if he had any animal taste, it was for apples of the red-streak sort; that Milton married thrice, and each of his wives was a virgin; that Sheffield, duke of Buckingham, married thrice, and each of his wives was a widow. All these details have their significance; but they must be charily dealt with. Too great attention to such matters makes the very worst soil for science, and is apt to reduce a critic to the condition of a parasite. Not that parasitical criticism of this kind is altogether worthless. The latest doctrine of the naturalists is that pearls are the product of a parasite. Still mankind have a wholesome terror of parasites, and usually regard a purely biographical criticism as tending too much to

And how apt to become parasitical.

CHAPTER II.

encourage these animals. The system of biography on biography which now prevails, a biographer getting his life written because he has himself written lives,* reminds one too vividly of that world described by one of our humourists in which

> Great fleas have little fleas
> Upon their backs to bite 'em,
> And little fleas have lesser fleas,
> And so *ad infinitum.*

Historical criticism.

The historical critics take a wider field, and dash at higher game, but usually they have been the least critical of their kind. They have too often been chroniclers rather than historians, bibliographers rather than critics, more bent on recording facts than on determining their value. Even when they reach a higher excellence, and give us histories worthy of the name, their work, if we are to look for science in it, shows at once the fatal weakness of being much too narrow in design. At best, the historian can give us only patches of history; but the historians of literature give us very small patches. The stream of political history has been traced from age to age, and from empire to empire. We can voyage back to Babylon; we can find on the walls of Luxor and Karnac the Hebrew

How far from science.

* On the principle laid down by Sir James Prior, to justify his life of Malone: "He who has expended learning and industry in making known the lives and labours of others, deserves the record he bestows. It forms a debt of honour, if not of gratitude, which literary men are bound to bestow upon each other. The neglect of it is injustice to their class."

CHAPTER II.

faces which we meet in the crowd to-day. But the stream of literary history, though it is equally continuous, has never been thus followed. We take it in small reaches, and the first shallow we come to stops our course. Not only is it thus limited in length of view: it is equally so in breadth. It is needless to dwell on the fact that the history of a nation's poetry has seldom been written with much reference to the national life from which it springs. It is the study of botany apart from geography. What is more remarkable than this, however, is that poetry has been studied and its history written in utter forgetfulness of the kindred arts—music, architecture, painting, sculpture. Moore on one occasion speaks with great contempt of an essay on lyrical poetry written by the author of the *Night Thoughts*, in which not one word is said about music. This is but an exaggerated instance of the separation of the arts, one from another, in the view of criticism. It is precisely as if in relation to the flora of a country, one set of men confined their attention to the monocotyledons, making that a special science, another to the dicotyledons, making that a special science, and a third to the flowerless plants, making that also a science by itself, while none of them gave any thought to any but their own branch of the subject. It seems not yet to have been fully understood that the intellectual flora of a country must be studied

And how limited in its view.

The intellectual flora not studied as a whole.

as a whole; that the arts are one family; that the Muses are sisters; that in their rise and progress there is a concert; that to make out the movements of any one we must watch the movements of all the others in the intricate dance which they lead; and, in a word, that it is only out of comparative criticism, as out of comparative anatomy, and comparative philology, and comparative mythology, that a true science can come.

Comparative criticism.

At present, so far from there being in existence anything which can bear the name of comparative criticism, there is no attempt to produce it, and the very need of it is scarcely acknowledged. The science of language is quite a modern revelation: it was an impossibility until we were able to compare languages together on the grand scale. In like manner the historical criticism of works of art, with a glimmer of science in its method, is out of the question, until we can compare art with art, can see how the rise of one coincides with the setting of another, and can take note of the circumstances under which two or more flourish together. Whether the arts have gained or lost by separation, so that the same man is no longer poet, architect, painter, and sculptor, all in one, is an open question; but for the purposes of science, at least, it would seem that the division of labour and separation of interest have had an evil effect. It was a theory of Leibnitz that the

CHAPTER II.

world is made of monads, each of which has a defined relation to every other, and that the problem eternally before the mind of the Deity is, when the state of any monad is given, to determine what must be the state—past, present, and to come—of every other in the universe. That is, after a sort, the problem which in the universe of art the scientific critic may fairly be called upon to solve. We know from Gibbon that in the darkness of the thirteenth century the orders of a Mogul Khan who reigned on the borders of China told on the price of herrings in the English market. And is it only of such remote influences as rule the price of a herring that we can take account? Surely there is in modern civilization a reason for the fact that our poets of the elder race, as Tasso, delight in no event of nature so much as sunrise, and are continually making proclamation of the effulgence of its coming, while the later ones, as those of the nineteenth century, delight in sunsets, and are never weary of brooding on the glories of an existence that is loveliest at the last. Surely there are some general laws which determine why in ancient times the Doric branch of the great Hellenic family should have been the chief patrons of the lyrical art, while they produced few lyrical artists of renown; and that, as a parallel fact in modern times, England should be the best patron in Europe of musical art, while notwithstanding a

The problem of criticism.

few brilliant exceptions, it is eclipsed by other countries as a begetter of great musicians. Surely, again, there is some general law which necessitated, at one and the same period, in the literatures of two such different countries as England, the head quarters of Protestantism, and Spain, the stronghold of Papacy, of Inquisition and of Loyola, an explosion of superabounding dramatic energy such as in modern times no other literatures can boast of. Surely, once more, there is something in history to account for and to connect together that lust of fame which is rampant in the literature of the Elizabethan era.—in the strains of the greatest poets, Shakespeare and Spenser, as well as in those of the least, Digges and Barnfield —which makes itself felt with such fervour at no other period of our literary progress, and which, indeed, in the whole history of letters, meets with its match but once, namely, among the Roman poets of the Augustan age. These are the things which historical criticism, to be worthy of itself, ought to set forth, which lie within its grasp, and which it hardly ever touches.

Too rarely attempted.

Systematic or scientific criticism.

Not only, however, do the critics—editorial, biographical, and historical—fail us when we go to them for science; but even those who undertake to write of poetry and art systematically give us little or no help. There is in all antiquity only one systematic work of criticism which is of much worth or of any authority, to

In ancient times as represented by Aristotle.

wit—Aristotle's, and that is but a fragment. It might be urged against the scientific character of this famous work that it was built on a too small induction of facts, seeing that the philosopher had only the literature of Greece in his mind. Even, however, with that literature alone before him, he ought not to have committed the mistake which taints his whole work, and has turned what might have been a palace into a cairn, a science into a mere aggregate of facts. His leading principle, which makes all poetry, all art, an imitation, is demonstrably false, has rendered his Poetic one-sided (a treatise not so much on poetry, as on dramatic poetry), and has transmitted to all after criticism a sort of hereditary squint. There is, however, in later criticism a worse fault than the hereditary squint—a fault which belongs to itself, and is not to be found in Aristotle.

In modern times devoted to questions of language.

Among the systematic writers of modern times, from Scaliger downwards, criticism is almost wholly devoted to questions of language. It is true that verbal questions involve much higher ones, for language is the incarnation of thought, and every art has its own speech, every work of art its own voice, which belongs to it as the voice of Esau to the hands of Esau. Epic imagery and verse belong to epic art, the dramatic apparatus of language belongs to dramatic art, and lyrical technicalities belong to the essence of lyrical art with such an indefeasible right of possession as the systematic critics confining

CHAPTER II.

their attention to the language almost wholly, that is, to the body without the soul, little suspect. They have studied figures of speech and varieties of metre, with little care for the weightier points of action, passion, manner, character, moral and intellectual aim. In simile and metaphor, in rhyme and rhythm, they have seen rules and measures, and they have reduced all the art of expression to a system as easy as grammar; but they have not sought to methodise the poet's dream, they have not cared in their analysis to grasp his higher thought. The scope of such criticism will best be seen in the design of a systematic work entertained by one of the chief critics of the last century. Johnson projected a work "to show how small a quantity of real fiction there is in the world, and that the same images, with very [few] variations, have served all the authors who have ever written." It is the similarity of imagery that he thought worthy of chief remark. Situation, incidents, characters, and aims, these are of small account beside similes and metaphors. Johnson's project was conceived entirely in the spirit of systematic criticism, as it has been most approved in modern times. Its analysis of images and phrases is, if not perfect, yet very elaborate. Its analysis of the substance which these images and phrases clothe, is, although not wholly neglected, yet very trivial. And the result is, that as a mere theory of language, as a

Example of what the moderns chiefly understand by a system of criticism.

CHAPTER II.

mere pigeon-holing of words and other technical details, such criticism is unsatisfactory and does not reach the truth, because it has no root, because it forgets the substance and is all for form as form.

Mr. Ruskin's summary of modern criticism as grammar.

No one has more pungently and truthfully described the critical science of what may be termed the Renaissance than Mr. Ruskin. Nearly the whole body of criticism comes from the leaders of the Renaissance, who "discovered suddenly," says Mr. Ruskin, "that the world for ten centuries had been living in an ungrammatical manner, and they made it forthwith the end of human existence to be grammatical. And it mattered thenceforth nothing what was said or what was done, so only that it was said with scholarship, and done with system. Falsehood in a Ciceronian dialect had no opposers; truth in patois no listeners. A Roman phrase was thought worth any number of Gothic facts. The sciences ceased at once to be anything more than different kinds of grammar—grammar of language, grammar of logic, grammar of ethics, grammar of art; and the tongue, wit and invention of the human race were supposed to have found their utmost and most divine mission in syntax and syllogism, perspective, and five orders." *

* Sir Joshua Reynolds's remarks on one of the greatest pictures of Rubens are a fair specimen of the best criticism of his time. We are anxious to learn what so fine a judge as Reynolds

Almost the only systematic criticism of modern times which is not of the Renaissance, and not entitled to this appraisement is that of Germany, which is, if possible, infected with not a worse, but a less manageable, disease. If the criticism of the Renaissance is afflicted with a deficiency of thought, the new epoch of criticism, which the Germans attempted to inaugurate, is charged with a superfecundity of thought tending to overlay the facts that engage it. Mr. Arnold complains of the want of idea in English criticism. "There is no speculation in those eyes." The same complaint certainly cannot be brought

The systematic criticism of Germany.

The defect.

has to say of the Taking Down from the Cross. Observe how instinctively he goes to the grammar of Rubens's treatment. His first thought is for the white sheet.

"The greatest peculiarity of this composition is the contrivance of the white sheet, on which the body of Jesus lies. This circumstance was probably what induced Rubens to adopt the composition. He well knew what effect white linen, opposed to flesh, must have with his powers of colouring; a circumstance which was not likely to enter into the mind of an Italian painter, who probably would have been afraid of the linen's hurting the colouring of the flesh, and have kept it down of a low tint... His Christ I consider as one of the finest figures ever invented; it is most correctly drawn, and, I apprehend, in an attitude of the utmost difficulty to execute. The hanging of the head on his shoulder, and the falling of the body on one side, give such an appearance of the heaviness of death that nothing can exceed it... The principal light is formed by the body of Christ and the white sheet: there is no second light which bears any proportion to the principal; ... however, there are many little detached lights distributed at some distance from the great mass, such as the head and shoulders of the Magdalen, the heads of the two Maries, the head of Joseph, and the back and arm of the figure leaning over the cross; the whole surrounded with a dark sky, except a little light in the horizon and above the cross."

CHAPTER II.

against German criticism. It is all idea. It begins with hypothesis and works by deduction downward to the facts. The most elaborate, the most favoured, and the most successful system in Germany is that of Hegel. To follow it, however, with understanding, you have first to accept the Hegelian philosophy, of which it is a part. It begins by declaring art to be the manifestation of the absolute idea, and when we ask what is the absolute idea, we are told that it is the abstraction of thought in which the identical is identical with the non-identical, and in which absolute being is resolved into absolute nothing. Schelling may not be so wild as this; but he, too, sets out from an absolute idea, and works not from facts to generalisation but from generalisation to facts. The German constructs art as he constructs the camel out of the depths of his moral consciousness. Out of Germany it is impossible and useless to argue with these systems. We can only dismiss them with the assurance that if this be science, then

As in Hegel.

And Schelling.

> Thinking is but an idle waste of thought,
> And nought is everything and everything is nought;

and that between the Renaissance, or grammatical method of criticism, which busied itself too much with forms—the mere etiquette or ceremonial of literature—and the German, or philosophical method of criticism, which wilders and flounders in the chaos of aboriginal ideas, there must be a middle path—a method of criticism

Suggestion of a middle course between the criticism of Germany and that of the Renaissance.

CHAPTER II

that may fairly be called scientific, and that will weigh with even balance both the idea out of which art springs and the forms in which it grows.

Method and value of the most recent criticism.

Recent criticism, even when it eschews philosophy, cuts deeper than of yore, both in Germany and out of it, and cannot be content to play with questions of mere images and verses; but it avoids system. It has never been so noble in aim, so conscientious in labour, so large in view, and withal so modest in tone, as now. In point of fact, philosophy, baffled in its aims, has passed into criticism, and minds that a century back might have been lost in searching into the mystery of knowledge and the roots of being, turn their whole gaze on the products of human thought, and the history of human endeavour. But the philosophers turning critics are apt to carry into the new study somewhat of the despair learned from the old, and, I repeat it, carefully avoid system. The deeper, therefore, their criticism delves, the more it becomes a labyrinth of confusion. Fertile in suggestions, and rioting in results, it is a chaos in which the suggestions, though original, do not always connect themselves clearly with first principles, and in which the results, though valuable, are reft of half their importance by the lack of scientific arrangement. Nor is this all; for we too often see critics toiling in ignorance of each other's

The despair of system.

CHAPTER II.

And want of concert.

work, lauding in one country what is slighted in another, and void of any general understanding as to the division of labour, and the correlation of isolated studies. A fair example offers itself in the criticism of Shakespeare. In England we are most struck with Shakespeare's knowledge of human nature, and power of embodying it in the characters of the drama. We rank this above all his gifts, even above his wondrous gift of speech. Pass over to Germany and note how one of the latest critics there, Ulrici, like a true German, admires Shakespeare chiefly for his ideas. When he is pretty sure that the countrymen of the dramatist will object to some of his criticism — to his fathering spurious plays on Shakespeare, and to his finding in genuine ones the most far-fetched ideas; he says that the English critics are not to be trusted, because they look to the truth of the characters as the chief Shakespearian test. Instead of the truth of the characters, what has he to show? He shows the doctrine of the Atonement preached in one play, the difference between equity and law set forth in another, and in all the plays a shower of puns that continually remind us of the Original Sin of our nature, the radical antithesis between thought and action, idea and reality, produced by the Fall. Go then to France, and see there the well-known writer, M. Philarète Châsles. Frenchmanlike, he regards the plot as all-important in the drama, and says that Lear, Hamlet, and Othello are not

Ulrici.

French criticism.

CHAPTER II.

the creations of Shakespeare, because the story was borrowed. "The admirers of Shakespeare," he says, "praise in him certain qualities which are not his. He is, they declare, the creator of Lear, the creator of Hamlet, the creator of Othello. He has created none of these." Surely the critics of the three nations would gain not a little if they understood each other better, and worked more in concert. Why this conflict of opinion where there ought to be no room for doubt? Why this Babel of voices where all are animated by a common aim? And where the good of criticism if it cannot prevent such misunderstandings?

Glaring example of the impotence of criticism.

The backwardness and impotence of criticism show, perhaps, nowhere so glaringly as in the failure of the most splendid offer of prizes to draw together for competition very high intellectual work. We can get prize oxen and prize pigs that come up to our expectations; but prize essays, prize poems, prize monuments, prize designs of any kind, are notoriously poor in this country, however high we bid. For the Duke of Wellington's monument the offer was about £20,000; and we all know of the disappointment which the exhibition of the designs created. On the other hand, when prizes were offered for the designs of a Foreign Office and an India Office, some admirable drawings were exhibited, but there followed this odd jarring of opinions, that the design to which the judges allotted the

Prize designs a failure.

CHAPTER II. first prize was not adopted by the Government for the building; that the design which took the second prize got really the place of honour in being selected for execution; and that finally Lord Palmerston threw aside all the prize designs, and commissioned the second prizeman to make a wholly new design. Now, what is the meaning of this? Why are prize essays glittering on the surface, and worthless below it? Why are prize poems a mass of inanity, decked out in far-fetched metaphors, and wild personifications? Why is a prize picture quite uninteresting—a conventional display of balanced lights and slanting lines, dull tints and stage simpering? Why is a prize statue about the most unreal thing under the sun? Why has a prize monument never yet been produced that we can think of with perfect pleasure? Why is a prize play so notoriously bad that managers have long ceased to offer rewards for the inevitable damnation?

Why is the prize system a failure in England,

When we know that in Greece it was successful?

The difficulty of answering such questions is the greater because against these disheartening experiences we have to set the fact that under a different system of civilization the offer of prizes produced the most brilliant results. When a Greek drama was acted at Athens it was a prize drama; and we are told that Æschylus won the honour so many times, that Sophocles in the end beat Æschylus, and that Euripides in like manner had his triumphs. The comic dramatist Menander, was drowned in the Piræus, and the story goes (but it is only a story), that he drowned himself in misery at seeing his rival, Philemon, snatch from him the dramatic ivy-crown. Corinna, it will be remembered, won the prize for lyric verse from Pindar himself. Whether it be a fact or not about the poetical contest between Homer and Hesiod, and the prize of a tripod won by the latter, the tradition of such a contest is a voucher for the custom and for the honour in which it was held. At the Pythian games prizes for music and every sort of artistic work were as common and as famous as the prizes for horse-races and foot-races. To realize such a state of things in our time, we must imagine poets, painters, and musicians assembled on Epsom Downs to contend for the honours of the games with colts, the sons of Touchstone and Stockwell, and fillies, the descendants of Pocahontas and Beeswing. Why should that be possible in Greece which is impossible now? Why do we draw the line between jockeys who ride racehorses, and poets who ride their Pegasus—offer prizes for the grosser animals and produce results that have made English horses the first in the world, while the most magnificent offers cannot get a fit monument for the greatest Englishman of the present century?

The explanation to be found in the weakness of criticism.

The explanation is not far to seek: it lies in the uncertainty of judgment, in the waywardness of taste, in the want of recognised standards, in

CHAPTER II.

the contempt of criticism. Good work is not usually forthcoming to the offer of a prize, because when—as in the case of the Foreign and India offices—it does come forth, there ensues a chance medley of opinions, in which there is no certainty that the best work will obtain the reward. The difference in England between a contest of racers and a contest of poets, painters, or essayists, is to be found in this, that the pace of two horses admits of measurement. There is a standard to which all give assent; the race is won by a nose, or a head, or a neck, or a length. There need be no mistake in the comparison; and if the rewards are tempting, we may be pretty sure that the best horses will run, and that the result may be taken as a fair test of merit. If there were any doubtfulness about the test the owners of the best horses would never allow their favourites to run. But in any contest between painters or sculptors, poets or essayists, there is just that dubiety as to the standard of measurement which would prevent the best men from competing.

The standard of judgment.

Influence of school in Greece.

Not so in Greece, and not so in France. It has been well said, that whoever has seen but one work of Greek art has seen none, and whoever has seen all has seen but one. In Greek art, in Greek poems, in Greek prose, there is this uniformity, a uniformity that bespeaks, if not clear science, yet, at any rate, a system of

CHAPTER II.

recognised rules. In architecture, in statuary, in pottery, the uniformity of aim is so palpable, that students have long suspected the existence of strictly harmonious proportions in the various lengths, curves, and angles, which give life and beauty to the pure Pentelic marble, and at length the law which guides these proportions, the rule for example which produces the peculiar curve called the entasis of a Doric shaft, the rule which provides for the height of the Venus of Medici, or of the Apollo Belvedere, the rule which actuates the contour of the Portland Vase, has been detected. Not that these laws will ever enable an inferior artist to produce another Parthenon or another Venus to enchant the world, but that like the laws of harmony in music, they ought to keep the artist within the lines of beauty. Whatever be the practical value of the rules, we see that to every work of Greek art they give the character of a school, and the unity of aim and of habit produced by a school gives us a standard of measurement about which there need be little ambiguity. On a lesser scale, something of the same sort may be seen in France. Frenchmen are surprised at the individuality of English art. Every artist among us seems to be standing on his own dais, and working out of his own head. In France we can see more distinctly schools of art; a genuine approximation of methods, a theoretic sameness of ideals, and we can understand, that

Influence of school in France.

CHAPTER II.

in a country where the influence of school is so apparent, the prize system should be more successful than among us who assert the right of private judgment and our contempt of authority, in no mincing terms. The nation that has three dozen religions and only one sauce, is not likely to have common standards in philosophy, in literature, or in art. Wanting these standards, what faith can we have in our judges? And what wonder that criticism, no matter how deep it goes, should be a byword?

A hopeful sign of our criticism that it has become ashamed of itself.

It is a good thing when criticism knows that it is a byword, and learns to be ashamed of itself. It is not to be cured until it feels itself sick; and there is no more healthy sign of our times than the popularity which has been accorded to the writings of Mr. Matthew Arnold, who has come forward to denounce our criticism as folly, and to call upon the critics to mend their ways. In many most important points it is impossible to agree with this delightful writer. Especially when he attempts to reason and to generalize, he rouses in his readers the instincts of war, and makes them wish to break a lance with him. He is a suggestive writer, but not a convincing one. He starts many ideas, but does not carry out his conclusions. He has power of thought enough to win our attention, charm of style enough to enchant us with his strain; but we are won without conviction, and we are enchanted without being satisfied. The most marked peculiarity of his style, when he has to deal not with facts but with ideas, is its intense juvenility—a boy-power to the *nth*. It would be unjust so to characterize his robust scholarship, and his keen biographical insight. But when he comes to what is more especially called an idea, then his merits and his defects alike are those of youthfulness. There is in his thinking the greenness, the unfitness, the impracticability of youth; there is also in it the freshness, the buoyancy, the indescribable gracefulness, the raging activity of youth. We learn as we read him to have so much sympathy with the fine purpose, the fine taste, the fine temper of his writing, that we forget, or we are loth to express, how much we differ with him whenever he attempts to generalize. In the next chapter I shall have occasion to mention some of his errors. Here the great point to be noticed is, that his outcry against English criticism for its want of science (though that is not the phrase by which he would describe its deficiency) has been received with the greatest favour. At the same time, he does less than justice to English criticism in comparing it with foreign; for if we have faults, so also have the Germans and the French. All alike fall short of science. If we fall short of it in our treatment of idea, they fall short of it in their treatment of fact; and Mr. Arnold would have been much nearer

CHAPTER II. the truth, if he had with even-handed justice exposed the shortcomings of all criticism, instead of confining his censure to criticism of the English school. Be he right or wrong however in this matter, the fact of his having raised his voice against our criticism is in itself important. We may take it for a sure proof that the tide is on the turn, and that a change is working. Mr. Arnold is too sympathetic for a solitary thinker. We may agree with him or differ with him; we may deem his views novel or stale; clear, or the reverse; but of one thing we can have no doubt—that what he thinks, others think also. When such a man complains of the lack of idea in English criticism, we may be satisfied that he is giving form to an opinion which, if it has not before been expressed with equal force, has been widely felt, and has often been at the point of utterance. We may be satisfied also that things are mending. In this case the discovery of the disease is half the cure; the confession of sin is a long step to reform.

Summary of the chapter.

Why criticism is not a science.

In the very act of showing that criticism is not yet a science, something has also been done to show why it has failed of that standard, and why it may be supposed that following another course the dignity of science may not be beyond its reach. Hereafter it will be necessary to point out another great cause of failure in the fact that criticism has hitherto rejected, or at least kept clear of its corner stone; has never attempted to build itself systematically on what nevertheless it has always accepted as the one universal and necessary law of art, the law of pleasure. Meantime, in so far as this discussion has proceeded it will be seen that, if criticism has failed of science, it has been a failure of method. It is only from comparative criticism that we can expect science, but hitherto criticism has been very much lost in details, and has never attempted comparison on the large scale. It is true that all criticism is comparative in a certain sense, for without comparison there is no thought; but it is comparative only within narrow limits, and we have to extend the area of comparison before the possibility of science begins to dawn. The comparison required is threefold; the first, which most persons would regard as in a peculiar sense critical, a comparison of all the arts one with another, as they appear together and in succession; the next, psychological, a comparison of these in their different phases with the nature of the mind, its intellectual bias and its ethical needs as revealed in the latest analysis; the third, historical, a comparison of the results thus obtained with the facts of history, the influence of race, of religion, of climate, in one word, with the story of human development. There is not one of these lines of comparison which criticism can afford to neglect. It must

Failure of method.

What is involved in the new method of comparative criticism.

The comparison threefold.

compare art with art; it must compare art with mind; it must compare art with history; and it must bring together again, and place side by side, the result of these three comparisons.

In what groove of comparative criticism the present work will for the first part run.

But though there is not one of these lines of comparison which it will do to neglect, and there is not one which can be regarded as absolutely of more importance than another, nevertheless it may be that at this or that particular time, or for this or that particular purpose, one line of comparison may relatively be of more value than another; and it would seem that at the stage which criticism has now reached there is nothing so much wanting to it as a correct psychology. Accordingly that is the main course of inquiry which, in the present instalment of this work, an attempt will be made to follow. We want, first of all, to know what a watchmaker would call the movement in art—the movement of the mind, the movement of ideas. Why does the mind move in that way? whither does it move? when does it move? what does it move? Some of these questions are among the most abstruse in philosophy, and so well known to be abstruse, that the mere suggestion of them may be a terror to many readers. I may seem to be calmly inviting them to cross with me the arid sands of a Sahara, and to meet the hot blasts of a simoom. But, indeed, it is a mistake to suppose that a

Nothing so much wanted as a correct psychology.

On the dulness of psychology.

subject which is abstruse must be dull and killing to discuss; and it is quite certain that if this subject of the movement of the mind in art is not made interesting the fault lies with the writer, and not in the subject.

CHAPTER II.

There is a curious picture in the *Arabian Nights* of a little turbaned fellow sitting cross-legged on the ground, with pistachio nuts and dates in his lap. He cracks the nuts, munches the kernels and throws the shells to the left, while by a judicious alternation he sucks the delicate pulp of the dates and throws the stones to his right. The philosopher looks on with a mild interest and speculates on the moral that sometimes the insides of things are best and sometimes the outsides. Now, most of the discussions on mind with which we are familiar are like the pistachio nuts of the gentleman of Bagdad: the shell is uninviting, and the kernel, which is hard to get at, and most frequently is rotten, is the only part that is palatable. But there is no reason why these discussions should not on the outside be as palatable as the date; and if we cannot swallow the stones, still they are not useless, but may be turned to account as seed. The simile is rather elaborate, yet perhaps it is clear; and I shall be glad if in any way it should suggest to my readers that in here inviting them to a psychological discussion I am luring them not to a study which will break their jaws with hard words and their

But that dulness is not necessary.

The subject really as in-

CHAPTER II.

teresting as romance.

patience with the husks of logic, but to one which, if not unfairly treated, ought to be as fascinating as romance:

> Not harsh and crabbed, as dull fools suppose,
> But musical as is Apollo's lute.

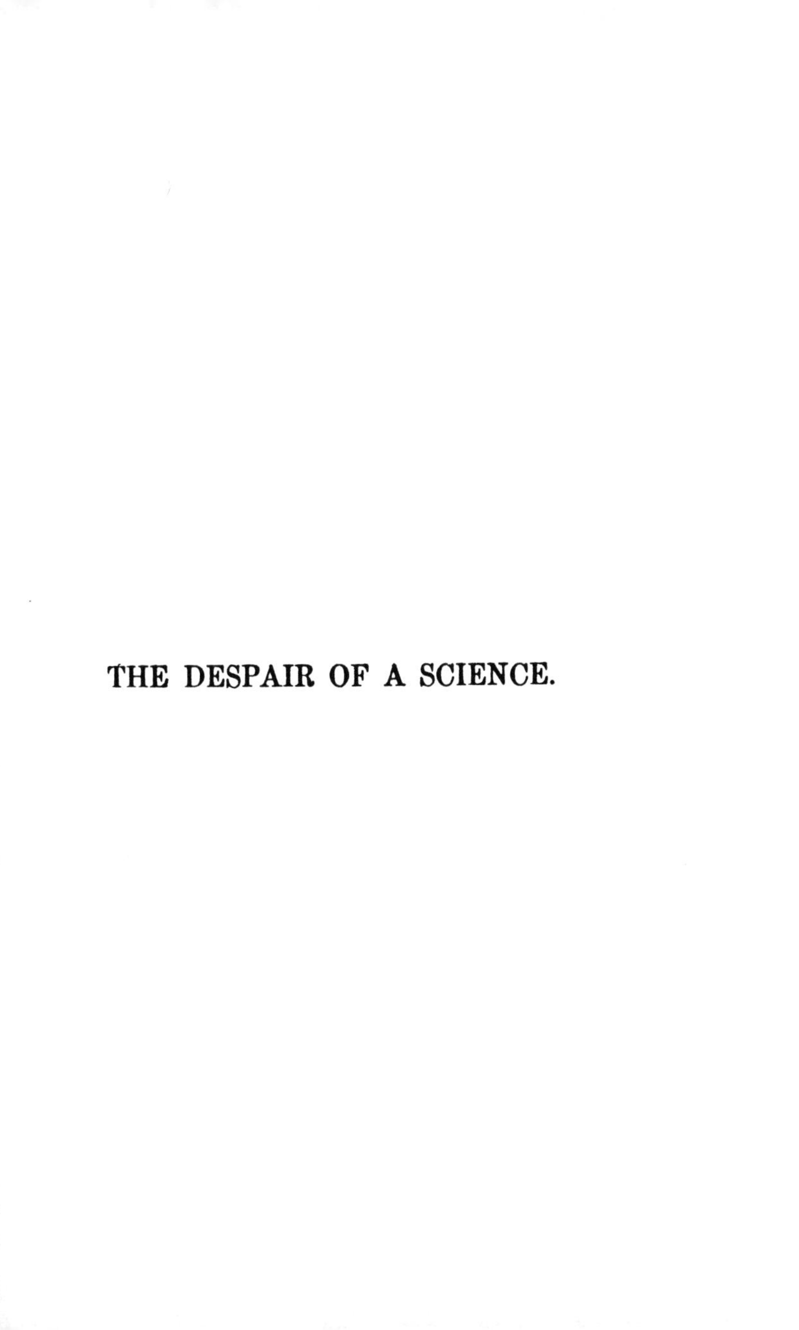

THE DESPAIR OF A SCIENCE.

CHAPTER III.

THE DESPAIR OF A SCIENCE.

CHAPTER III.

IT CAN scarcely be a matter of surprise, that amid the littlenesses of the lower criticism, the confusion and conflicts of the higher, any attempt in our day to work towards a science of criticism is sure to be met with a profound despair. I do not merely mean that the world will have its doubts as to this or that man's ability to approach the science. That is quite fair and natural. The doubt is, whether the science be approachable by any son of man. It is a doubt that cleaves just now to any science which has the mind and will of man for its theme. Methods of criticism are nothing, it may be said, for all methods, including the method of comparative criticism, must fail, when the object is to resolve human work to scientific law. I therefore desire, in this chapter, to make a few remarks on that despair with which nearly all

The despair of critical science not surprising.

CHAPTER III.

Englishmen just now contemplate not merely the science of criticism, but any science of human nature.

What we set before us as the object of science.

Despair of metaphysics has at length bred in us that state of heart which Mr. John George Phillimore exaggerates, but can scarcely be said to misrepresent, when pointing out that what he calls the Queen of Sciences, that is, metaphysics, is utterly ignored among us, he asks what is the substitute for it, and discovers that we give ourselves up to the most intense study of entomology. We believe in insects as fit objects of science; but the mind of man is beyond our science, and we give it up in despair. Mr. Kingsley, who has written one book to show that a science of history is impossible, has written another to show the great and religious advantage at watering-places of studying science in the works of God—that is, in sea-jellies and cockle-shells. The popular science of the day makes an antithesis between God and man. History, politics, language, art, literature—these are the works of man. Animals, vegetables, and minerals—these are the works of God. When the student of natural history discovers a new species, he seems to be rescuing, says Mr. Kingsley, "one more thought of the divine mind from Hela and the realms of the unknown." When a man goes to the sea-side, and, taking the advice of the same author, begins to study natural history, can tell the number of legs on a crab, the number of

Antithesis between the works of God and those of man.

joints on a lobster's tail, names one kind of shell a helix, another kind of shell a pecten—that is called studying the works of God. Or if he goes to some quiet inland village, plucks flowers, dries them in blotting-paper, and writes a name of twenty syllables under each—that is studying the works of God. Or if he analyzes a quantity of earth, can tell what are its ingredients, whether it is better for turnips or for wheat, and whether it should be manured with lime or with guano—that is studying the works of God. And especially is it so if these students set upon the Deity, like a tribe of Mohawks, to hunt out his trail, to pounce upon his footprints, to fathom his designs, to see everywhere the hand, and to acknowledge the finger of God. As though He, whose glory it is to conceal a thing, left finger-marks on his work, the exponents of popular science are always finding the finger of God, and by so doing extol their favourite pursuit, while they tacitly rebut the maxim of Pope, that the proper study of mankind is man. We who have been in the habit of regarding man as the noblest work of God, language as his gift, history as his providence, and genius as heaven-born, are startled to hear the inanimate and irrational creation described as peculiarly the work and the care of the Deity, and seem to listen to an echo of the old heathen dogma—*Deus est anima brutorum*. Amid all this cant of finding God in the material and not in the moral world, and of thence

CHAPTER III.

Popular science in its religious aspect.

The proper study of mankind.

CHAPTER III.

lauding the sciences of matter to the neglect of the science of mind, who but must remember a sermon in which the speaker, it is true, invited his audience to consider the lilies of the field and to behold the fowls of the air, but only that he might drive home the question—Are ye not much better than they?

Misanthropy of the antithesis between the works of God and those of man.

This antithesis between the works of God and the works of man, which we find in the science of our time, seems to have begun in a misanthropical vein of thought belonging to a considerable portion of the poetry of the nineteenth century. Byron, of all our recent poets, would be most easily accused of this misanthropy; but it is not of Byron that we have to complain: it is of Wordsworth and his incessant harping on the opposition between nature and humanity. It was from Wordsworth's region of thought that the petty controversy arose, many years ago, as to the materials of poetry. Bowles contended that poetry is more immediately indebted for its interest to the works of nature than to those of art; that a ship of the line derives its poetry not from anything contributed by man—the sails, masts, and so forth; but from the wind that fills the sails, from the sunshine that touches them with light, from the waves on which the vessel rides—in a word, from nature. The essence of this criticism is misanthropy; it is such misanthropy as abounds in Wordsworth; it is misanthropy which Byron fought against manfully, and with which he was

Wordsworth to some extent answerable for it.

incapable of sympathising. We can trace this misanthropy downwards to Mr. Ruskin, at least so long as he was under the influence of Wordsworth. In his earlier criticism he was always quoting that poet; his whole mind seemed to be given to landscape painting, and he conceived of art as the expression of man's delight in the works of God. He has long outgrown the Wordsworthian misanthropy, and has learned to widen his definition of the theme of art; but still in his eloquent pages, as in the strains of Wordsworth, and as in the tendency to landscape of much of our poetry and painting, the men of science will find some sanction for the hollow antithesis which sets the works of God against those of man.

How it shows itself in Ruskin.

It would be unjust not to remember in behalf of this one-sided devotion to physical science—a devotion to it that confines the very name of science almost entirely to the knowledge of matter and material laws, and denies it to the knowledge of man and mental laws—that among all the intellectual pursuits of the present century, the science of things material can point to by far the most splendid results. What more dazzling in speculation than the discovery of Neptune? What more stimulating to curiosity than the researches of Goethe, Cuvier, and Owen? What more enticing to the adventurer than the geological prediction of the gold fields of Australia? In chemistry we have well-nigh

Something to be said for the one-sided devotion to physical science which now prevails.

The feats of science.

CHAPTER III.

realised the dream of alchemy, and pierced the mystery of transmutation. Photography is a craft in which Phœbus Apollo again appears upon the earth in the mortal guise of an artist, and to the powers of which no limit can be set. In meteorology, the wind has been tracked, storms and tornados have been reduced to law. In electricity we seem to be hovering on the verge of some grand discovery, and already the electric spark has been trained to feats more marvellous than any recorded of Ariel or Puck. Optics now enables us to discover the composition of the sun, and to detect the presence of minerals to the millionth part of a grain. Seven-league boots are clumsy beside a railway; steam-ships make a jest of the flying carpet. Think, too, of the immense public works which modern science has enabled England to complete. The Crystal Palace rose like the arch of a rainbow over the trees in Hyde Park; the tubular bridge spans the Menai Straits, high enough for "the mast of some great ammiral" to pass beneath: innumerable bridges, tunnels, canals, docks, dazzle the imagination. A thousand years hereafter poets and historians may write of our great engineers and scientific discoverers, as we now speak of Arthur and his Paladins, Faust and the Devil, Cortes and Pizarro. Why should not those who figure in "the fairy tales of science" obtain the renown which is rightfully theirs?

And the great public works which it has produced.

The results they have achieved are all the more

CHAPTER III.

The recent origin of the sciences,

wonderful, if we take into account the comparatively recent origin of our sciences. It is little more than two hundred years since there was only one man of scientific note in England—William Harvey; when Sydenham was but beginning to practise; when Barrow was studying the Greek fathers at Constantinople; when Ray was yet unknown; when Halley was yet unborn; when Flamsteed was still teething; when Newton was a farmer-boy, munching apples as he drove to market on Saturdays; when Hooke was a poor student at Oxford, assisting Boyle in his manipulations; when Boyle lived in seclusion at the apothecary's, and was chiefly remarkable for associating with men whose names begin with W—Wallis, Willis, Wilkins, Ward, and Wren. None of the founders of the Royal Society had then emerged from obscurity, and the Royal Society was a small club that met in secret and called itself the Invisible College. Two centuries have brought a marvellous change. Science came into England with tea, with tea-drinking it spread, and it is now imbibed as universally. It has so commended itself by great achievements that at length every one of the sciences has a society for itself, all the great cities of the United Kingdom have scientific societies, and there is such a rage for science throughout the country and in every class, that, not unlike the tailors of Laputa, who, abjuring tape, took altitudes and longitudes with a quadrant, the London tailors profess to cut

And their present development.

CHAPTER III.

their shirts scientifically, and in the ardour of science baptize their masterpiece Eureka.

Different fate of the mental sciences.

Meanwhile, amid this rush of the intellectual current all in one direction, it fares ill with mental science; it fares ill with all the sciences that may more strictly be called human, including that of criticism. As a scientific object, the shard-borne beetle is of more account than man: the cells of the bee and the cocoons of the silkworm, than all the efforts of human genius, all the wonders of human handiwork. Philosophy, I have said, has filled us with despair, and despair of philosophical methods has spread to despair of all that philosophy touched, and regarded as peculiarly its own. Nor is this the only form in which despair of a human science in general, and a critical science in particular, shows itself. These are days in which the forms of literature are opposed to the elaboration of system; and as the essence of science is system, here is another foundation for despair to build upon. Then, again, there are moralists who are eager to keep clear the great doctrine of the freedom of the will; who are afraid to regard human actionas in such wise governed by law, that it is capable of scientific calculation; and here is another ground of despair. Lastly, there are persons who, unable to see the practical use to which a science of criticism (but I ought to speak more generally, and say a science of human nature) may be turned, are apt to pass upon it a

Various points of view from which is produced the despair of any science of human nature.

CHAPTER III.

sentence of condemnation, which on the other hand they do not pronounce on the merely physical sciences, when they are unable to perceive immediately the practical value of any material discoveries; and thus again is engendered another form of despair. Let me say a few words upon each of these passages of despair.

Philosophical despair of mental science.

And first, of the philosophical despair that now attaches to the scientific treatment of all those subjects which philosophy used to handle. Mr. G. H. Lewes has written a very clever and learned book on the history of philosophy, in which he always insists that the chief problems of metaphysics are insoluble. This work is so brilliant that it has been much read and pilfered from; and for practical purposes it is the best history of philosophy that the English reader can consult; but it is burdened with the fallacy that because what is called metaphysics is impossible, therefore any attempt at a science of the mind must be vain. Does it follow that because metaphysical methods have failed, therefore scientific methods must fail also? Now the despair of a mental science which Mr. Lewes entertains he also entertains, as it would seem, for all the branches of that science, criticism included. He says that "philosophy has distorted poetry, and been the curse of criticism." Most of us will agree with him, if by philosophy he means metaphysics. We all find the greatest difficulty

What Mr. Lewes says of philosophical criticism.

CHAPTER III.

in understanding what are called the philosophical critics, and when we get at their meaning it looks very small. They are afraid to be clear, lest they be deemed shallow; or they love to think themselves profound, because they are unable to plumb their own ideas.

A philosophical critic—Wagner

A fair specimen of the philosophical critic is Richard Wagner, who has invented the music of the future. Whatever may be thought of his music, he has a considerable reputation as a musical critic. Discoursing on art, in the most approved philosophical method, he defines poetry in terms which it is beyond me to translate, and so I make use of Mr. Bridgeman's translation. "If we now consider," he says, "the activity of the poet more closely, we perceive that the realisation of his intention consists solely in rendering possible the representation of the strengthened actions of his poetised forms through an exposition of their motives to the feelings, as well as the motives themselves, also by an expression that in so far engrosses his activity as the invention and production of this expression in truth first render the introduction of such motives and actions possible." This is the jargon of philosophy, and it is the curse of criticism. If this is what Mr. Lewes condemns, who in this country will contradict him? But sometimes it is not clear whether, when this author speaks of philosophy, he means simply philosophy as it used to be understood, or also includes under that name

The jargon of philosophy.

Distinction between philosophy and science

genuine science, because it is the science of mind as distinct from body. The name of philosophy has been especially allotted in this country to mental science—to psychology; and it seems a hard thing to say that in this sense philosophy has been the curse of criticism. In point of fact, the great fault of criticism is its ignorance—at least its disregard of psychology. It is true that mental science has not yet done much for us in any department of study; but it must not be forgotten that the application of scientific methods to the mind and action of man has been even more recent and more tardy than their application to the processes of nature, and that the time has not yet come to look for ripe fruit, and to curse the tree on which it is not found. Any science of a true sort, mathematics apart—any science that is more than guessing, or more than a confused pudding-stone of facts—is now but two centuries old. The most advanced of the sciences that relate specially to human conduct is the science of wealth, and political economy is but a century old. The other sciences that take account of human action are still in their infancy; and to despair of them is but to despair of childhood.

The great want of criticism—psychology.

Science as applied to mind too recent to be accused of fruitlessness.

Sir Edward Lytton expresses despair of a different kind. He sees the futility of system; he knows that from time to time the most perfect systems have to be remodelled, and give way to new schemes. Hence, in one of his most lively

The despair of system.

CHAPTER III.

Expressed by Sir Edward Lytton.

essays, he bepraises the essay, and seems to condemn system as pedantic. Sir Edward Lytton has always shown such a faculty for construction, that in his heart of hearts he can scarcely despise system; but as some of his remarks may lead a hurried reader to take an opposite view, a word or two of explanation may be necessary.

Systems soon forgotten.

It is true, that systems are soon forgotten and pass out of sight. What survives of Plato, for example, in modern thought? A few fragments that have not always even a relation to his system.

Take Plato for an example.

Take one of Plato's favourite ideas—that poets should be excluded from the model republic because they dispense falsehood, and because they are seekers of pleasure. Here is a view of poetry that survives, and that derives importance from the great name of Plato. The world remembers the conclusion at which he arrived; it has forgotten the process by which he arrived at it. He condemns art as false, because when a painter paints a flower he takes a copy not of the thing itself. The flower is not the thing itself, but the earthly copy of the thing which, according to his system, exists as an idea in the Divine mind. The picture of the flower, therefore, is the copy of a copy, and must be untrue. Nobody would now accept this reasoning, but people accept the conclusion. So, again, art is bad because pleasure is its chief end, and, as the gods feel neither pleasure nor pain, the end of art is not godlike. Here, again, nobody would accept the reasoning,

CHAPTER III.

but the conclusion would be accepted by a Puritan, who would rely on Plato's authority. And thus it is—the system falls to pieces, while fragments of it stand fast for ever quite independent of the system. Contemplating such a result, the essayist is inclined to ask what is the good of system, and suggests that it may be enough to put forth oracles in disjointed utterance. It is good not to overrate system; it is good to see that its use is but temporary. Still in our time, in which, through the extension of periodical literature, detached essays have assumed unwonted importance, there is a tendency to fly system altogether and so to underrate it.

The forms of current literature very adverse to system.

System is science. Science is impossible without the order and method of system. It is not merely knowledge: it is knowledge methodised. It may be true that over the vast ocean of time which separates us from Plato nothing has come to us from that mighty mind to be incorporated in modern thought but a few fragments of wreck. Yet these fragments would never have reached us if they had not at one time been built into a ship. When the voyager goes across the Atlantic he may be wrecked; he may get on shore only with a plank. But he will never cross the Atlantic at all if he starts on a plank, or on a few planks tied together as a raft. "Our little systems have their day," says the poet, and it is most true, but in their day they have their uses. There is a momentum in a system which does

Value of system.

CHAPTER III.

not belong to its individual timbers, and if we admire the essay, it is not necessary to undervalue more elaborate structures.*

Despair of mental science that springs from moral views.

Despair of yet another kind is expressed by those who, from a moral point of view, do not like to think of human conduct as obedient to scientific rule. Such men as Mr. Froude have so strong a sense of the freedom of the will, and of the incalculable waywardness with which it crosses and mars the best laid plans and the most symmetrical theories, that they will not hear of such a thing as a science of history. Mr. Froude's lecture on that subject is not published, and appears only in the records of the Royal Institution;

Expressed by Mr. Froude.

but it is perhaps the most eloquent of all his compositions, and it is full of wise suggestions. Its general conclusion, however, must be firmly resisted by those who, admitting the freedom of the

* Mr. Grote has lately been quoting a passage from Professor Ferrier on this point, as to the value of system, which is exceedingly well put. I quote the same passage, but with some slight differences of omission and admission: "A system of philosophy"—or what is, in Ferrier's meaning, the same thing, a system of science—"is bound by two main requisitions—it ought to be true and it ought to be reasoned. If a system is not true, it will scarcely be convincing; and if it is not reasoned, a man will be little satisfied with it. Philosophy, in its ideal perfection, is a body of reasoned truth. A system is of the highest value only when it embraces both these requisitions, that is, when it is both true and reasoned. But a system which is reasoned without being true, is always of higher v lue than a system which is true without being reasoned. The latter kind of system has no scientific worth. An unreasoned philosophy, even though true, carries no guarantee of its truth. It may be true, but it cannot be certain."

CHAPTER III.

will, still hold to the possibility of reducing human conduct on the large scale to fixed law. Mr. Froude argues that because we are not able to predict the changes of history, therefore history cannot fairly be regarded as a science; and his argument, though levelled against a science of history, goes to deny the possibility of any science of human nature. In point of fact, however, we can predict a good deal in human history, as, for example, by the aid of political economy, a science which is barely a century old; and Mr. Froude's reasoning, if it were sound, would oust geology from the list of the sciences, because it does not enable us to predict what changes in the earth's surface are certain to take place in the next thousand years.

The gist of his reasoning.

It is only in the exact sciences that knowledge reaches the prophetic strain, and all the sciences are not exact. Mr. John Stuart Mill points out that though the science of human nature falls far short of the exactness of astronomy as now understood, yet there is no reason why it should not be as much a science as astronomy was, when its methods had mastered only the main phenomena, but not the perturbations. This is precisely the view to be taken of that part of the science of human nature which, for the purposes of the present inquiry, may be called the Gay Science—the science of the Fine Arts, including poetry—only it might be expressed more strongly. The most certain thing in

All the sciences are not exact.

The exactitude of art.

CHAPTER III.

human life is its uncertainty. We are most struck with its endless changes, and cannot be over-confident that we shall ever reduce these to the unity of science. But art is crystalline in its forms, and the first, the deepest, the most constant impression which we derive from it is that of its oneness. I have already quoted the saying, that he who sees only one work of Greek art has seen none, and that he who sees all has seen but one. This is most true; and the Greek gave expression to the same thought in the legend of the brothers Telecles and Theodorus of Samos. Far apart from each other, the one at Delos, the other at Ephesus, carved half of a wooden statue of the Pythian Apollo, and when the two were brought together, they tallied as if they had been wrought in one piece by one hand. Shelley has even gone further, and has spoken of single poems, an *Iliad* or a *Lear*, as parts of one vast poem—episodes "in that great poem which all poets, like the co-operating thoughts of one great mind, have built up since the beginning of the world." If this be the character and position of art, it cannot be unreasonable to suppose that a science of it is within our reach, and that of all the sciences which have to do with human nature, it ought to be the most exact.

Illustrated in Shelley's conception of poetry.

Despair produced by the modesty of science.

Lastly, there is a despair engendered by the very modesty of science. A science of criticism, if it be worthy of the name, cannot pretend either to

CHAPTER III.

make art an easy acquisition, or to do away with all diversity of taste and opinion. The Miltons will evermore think that Dryden is but a rhymer; Dryden will still foretell that cousin Swift will never be a poet; Handel will always jeer at the counterpoint of young Glück, and Schumann make light of the music of Meyerbeer.* What then is the use of criticism? The fact, however, is, that no science in the world can insure its followers from error, or make its students perfect artists. Chemistry, with all its exactitude, does not save its professors from making a wrong analysis. The votaries of geology are still wrangling about some of its main principles; and were they agreed, it does not follow that they would be able to apply those principles rightly to the various regions of the earth. Political economy, the most advanced of the sciences that have man for their subject, is not all clear and steadfast, and daily the nations bid defiance to its clearest and most abiding truths. Why then should a critical science, if there is ever to be one, do more than all other sciences in leading its

The impotence of science.

* Mr. Paley, in his late edition of Euripides, the best that has yet been produced, calls attention to a delicious remark of Professor Scholefield's: "Quod ad ipsum attinet Euripidem, non sum ego ex illorum numero, qui nihil in eo pulchrum, nihil grande, nihil cothurno dignum inveniant." I am not, he says, of those who see in Euripides nothing fine, nothing great, nothing that belongs to high art. If it be remembered that Euripides was Milton's favourite poet, the innocence of Scholefield's remark will appear all the more inimitable.

CHAPTER III.

disciples into a land free from doubt? It is the law of all human knowledge, that the more the rays of the light within us multiply and spread, the increasing circle of light implies an increasing circumference of darkness to hem it round. Increase the bounds of knowledge, and you inevitably increase the sense of ignorance; at all the more points in a belt of surrounding darkness do you encounter doubt and difficulty. It is absurd, therefore, to suppose that any science can abolish all doubts and prevent all mistakes. Moreover, as a science of criticism cannot make perfect judges, so neither can it make faultless poets. The theory of music has never made men musical, and all the discoveries of the critic cannot make men poetical. Few sayings about art are more memorable than that of Mozart, who declared that he composed as he did because he could not help it, and who added, "You will never do anything if you have to think how you are to do it." Art comes of inspiration—comes by second nature. Nevertheless, it comes according to laws which it is possible to note and which imperatively demand our study. It is not long since people regarded the weather as beyond the province of science, and treated the labours of Fitzroy either as useless, because they did not enable him to foretell but only to forecast, or as impious, because it was argued that if we can forecast the weather, it must be idle to pray for rain.

The more science the greater sense of ignorance.

The impotence of criticism no more than the impotence of other sciences.

CHAPTER III.

It is curious to see how exacting we are in our demands for knowledge, and how we learn to underrate it altogether if in any respect it disappoints our expectations. Criticism is nought, people think, because it does not make poets perfect, and judges infallible. So it has happened that chemistry was despised when it failed to turn lead into gold, that astronomy was neglected when it failed to prognosticate, that the Bible is said to be in danger because we do not find in it the last new theory of science.

> Hang up philosophy :
> Unless philosophy can make a Juliet,
> Displant a town, reverse a prince's doom,
> It helps not, it prevails not : talk no more.

How Mr. Matthew Arnold vaunts criticism.

On this point as to the modesty of science, it is necessary to be very explicit, because he who is in our day the most hearty in denouncing the weakness of our criticism, Mr. Matthew Arnold, is also the most imperious in vaunting the office of the critic; and there is a danger lest from his unguarded expressions it should be supposed that criticism promises more than it can perform. Mr. Arnold, for example, tells us that the main intellectual effort of Europe has for many years past been a critical one; and that what Europe now desires most is criticism. What he means by this it is not easy to make out. For on the one hand, he assures us that Homer, Dante, and Shakespeare, are to be regarded as critics, and that everything done

But his meaning is not quite clear.

CHAPTER III.

As for example in what he says of M. Sainte Beuve.

in literature is at root criticism; from which it would appear that there can be nothing specially critical in the intellectual movement which is now in progress. On the other hand, we stumble once and again upon the statement that the first of living critics is M. Sainte Beuve. Now, we know M. Sainte Beuve as an indefatigable, a clever, and well-informed writer—a man of good judgment, and in France of great literary influence. But when we are told in succession that the great intellectual movement of our age is critical, and that the first of living critics—therefore, the leader of this intellectual movement, is M. Sainte Beuve, who is not greatly puzzled to know what so dainty a writer as Mr. Arnold can possibly mean? Is it a proof of our English want of insight that with all the vivacity of his Monday chats, we on this side of the water fail to see in M. Sainte Beuve the prophet of the age—a great leader of thinking—the enlightener of Europe? He is a brilliant essayist, a man of great knowledge; his taste is unimpeachable; and he dashes off historic sketches with wonderful neatness. But for criticism in the highest sense of the word—for criticism in the sense in which Mr. Arnold seems to understand it—for criticism as the mastery of dominant ideas and the key to modern thought—as that one thing which Europe most desires—we should scarcely go to the feuilletons of M. Sainte Beuve.

Once more we return to another form of the statement that the intellectual movement of our time is critical. Mr. Arnold identifies criticism with the modern spirit; and then he tells us that the modern spirit arises in a sense of contrast between the dictates of reason and of custom, the world of idea and the world of fact. We live amid prescriptions and customs that have been crusted upon us from ages. When we become alive to the fact that the forms and institutions of our daily life—the life individual and the life national, are prescribed to us not by reason but only by custom, that, says Mr. Arnold, is the awakening of the modern spirit. The truth is, however, that what he describes as the peculiar spirit of modern thought—that is, nineteenth-century thought — is the spirit of every reforming age. It was, for example, the spirit of Christianity as it showed itself at first in the midst of surrounding Judaism. It was the spirit that actuated the protest against the mummeries of Romanism in the sixteenth century.

His statement that the modern spirit is essentially critical.

From these and other illustrations of what he understands by criticism, it would seem that Mr. Arnold has allowed himself, in the graceful eagerness of a poetical nature, to be carried headlong into generalizations that are illusive. But the general effect of his expressions is to spread abroad an inflated idea of criticism—what it is, what it can do, what is its position

The wrong conclusions which may be drawn from Mr. Arnold's generalizations.

CHAPTER III.

in the world. People will not stay to examine patiently whether Mr. Arnold makes out his case or not. They will but carry away the general impression, that here is a man of genius and of strong conviction, who speaks of criticism as just now the greatest power upon earth. They will, therefore, expect from it the mightiest effects; and grievous will be their disappointment at the modesty of its actual exploits.

General view of the advantage of a science of criticism.

Though a science of criticism may not accomplish all that people expect of it, is it necessary to show that it is to be coveted for its own sake? If men will criticise, it is desirable that their judgments should be based on scientific grounds. This is so obvious, that instead of dwelling on the worth of critical science in and for itself, I would here rather insist on its value from another point of view—as a historical instrument. Some late philosophers, Cousin in particular, have sought for a clue to the world's history in the progress of metaphysical ideas. They believe that the history of philosophy yields the philosophy of history. They may be right, though it is awkward for the facts, or at least for our power of dealing with them, that the philosopher is ever represented as before his age. While he lives his thought is peculiar to himself, and his kingdom is not of this world: it is not till long years after his decease that his thought moves

On the interpretation of history through philosophy.

The interpretation of history through criticism.

mankind and his worldly reign begins. It would seem, however, that if it were possible to establish a critical science, the method which the French and Germans have adopted, of interpreting history through the history of philosophy, might with advantage be varied by the interpretation of history through the history of art. There is this wide difference between philosophy and art, that whereas the former is the result of conscious effort, the latter comes unconsciously, and is the spontaneous growth of the time. Now, supposing we had a critical science, and knew somewhat of the orbits and order of the arts, their times and seasons, we should have a guide to history so much safer than that furnished by the course of philosophy, as a spontaneous growth is less likely to deviate from nature than any conscious effort. It is said that philosophers have in their hands the making of the next age; but at least poets and other artists belong to the age they live in. In their shady retreats they reflect upon the world the light from on high, as I have seen an eclipse of the sun exquisitely pictured on the ground, while the crowds in Hyde Park were painfully looking for it in the heavens with darkened glasses. Through the leaves of the trees the sun shot down his image in myriads of balls of light that danced on the path below; and as his form was altered in the sky, the globes of light underfoot changed also their aspect, waning

CHAPTER III.

into crescents, and the crescents into sickles, and the sickles into nothingness, until once again as he recovered his beams the sickles reappeared, and grew on the gravel walk into crescents, and the crescents into perfect orbs. There were myriads of eclipses on the ground for the one that was passing in the sky.

On the right of praising the moral sciences.

Every man lauds his own pursuit. He who is deep in helminthology, or the science of worms, will tell us that it is the most interesting and useful of studies. But I can scarcely imagine that when putting in a word for a science of human nature, and for criticism as part of it, and when claiming for that science the place of honour, I am fairly open to the charge of yielding to private partiality. At all events, in mitigation of such a charge, let it be remembered that man too has the credit of being a worm, and that he may be entitled to some of the regard of science, were it only as belonging to the subject of helminthology. We may give up any claims which the science of human nature has to precedence over all the other knowledges, if we can get it recognised in popular opinion as a science at all, were it but as a science of worms. And for criticism, as a part of the science of human nature, it may be remembered that Sir Walter Scott was pleased to describe the critics as caterpillars, and that, therefore, they may have a special claim to be regarded in this marvellously popular science of worms. Or if

Summary of the argument.

this way of putting the case may seem to be wanting in seriousness, then in all seriousness, let me insist that the despair of the moral sciences which now prevails, is founded on mistake; that the neglect of them gives a hollowness to our literature; and that all criticism which does not either achieve science, or definitely reach towards it, is mere mirage. As the apostle declared of himself, that though he could speak with the tongues of men and of angels, and had not charity, he was become as sounding brass, or a tinkling cymbal; so we may say of the critic, that though he have all faith, so that he can remove mountains, and have not science, he is nothing. There are men like Iago, who think that they are nothing if not critical, but the critic is nothing if not scientific.

Aim of the present work.

Of the following attempt I am not able to think so bravely as to challenge for it the honours of a science. Any one, indeed, who will read this volume through, will see that it is a fight for the first principles and grounds of the science. I put my work forward, not as a science, but as a plea for one, and as a rude map of what its leading lines should be. Even if it should fail here, however, it may be at least as useful as the unlucky ship that grounded at the battle of Aboukir, and did for a waymark to them that followed. I have the greater confidence, however, in laying the present theory before the reader, inasmuch as glimpses and

Not a science, but a plea for one, and a map of its leading lines.

tokens of it are found in the pages of many of the best writers; and I believe that it will thus stand the test given by Leibnitz to ascertain the soundness of any body of thought that it should gather into one united household, not by heaping and jumbling together, but by reconciling, proving to be kindred, and causing to embrace opinions the most widely sundered and apparently the most hostile.

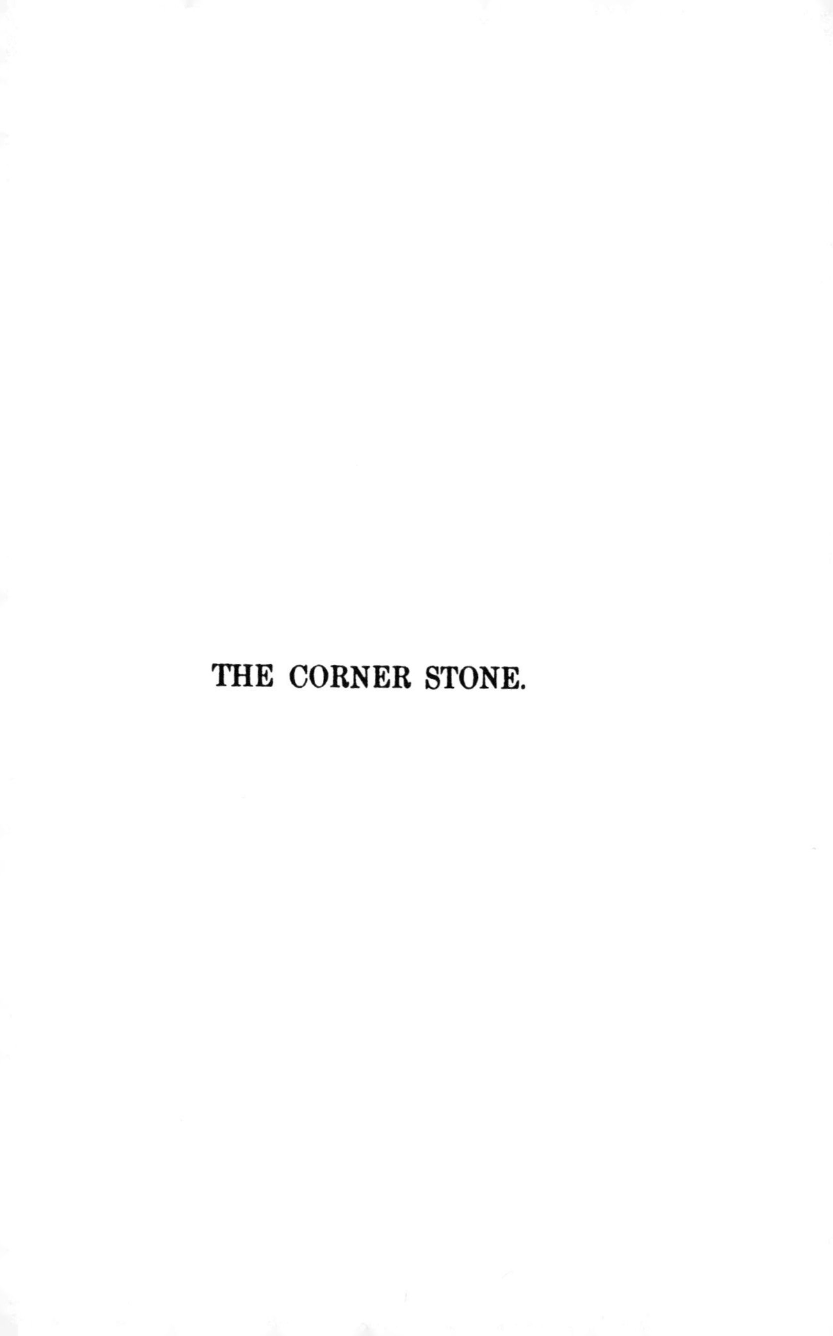

THE CORNER STONE.

CHAPTER IV.

THE CORNER STONE.

THOUGH foundation stones are laid with silver trowels and gilded plummets, amid music and banner, feasting and holiday, in the present chapter, which has to do with the basis of the Gay Science, there will be found nothing of a gala. It embodies the dull hard labour of laying down truisms—heavy blocks which are not to be handled in sport, but which it is essential that we should in the outset fix in their places. If I seem to labour at trifles, I must ask for some indulgence; because, although, when fairly stated, the main doctrine of this chapter will forthwith pass for a truism, in the meantime it is not acknowledged even as a truth. What is here maintained to be the only safe foundation of the science of criticism, however obvious it may appear to be, has never yet been fully accepted as such, and has never yet been built upon. There are some

CHAPTER IV.

Object of this chapter to prove a truism.

CHAPTER IV.

Truisms sometimes require demonstration.

truisms which it may be necessary to hammer out. Euclid felt the necessity of demonstrating point by point, that two sides of a triangle are greater than the third, whereupon Zeno laughed and said that every donkey knows it without proof. The donkey will not go round two sides of a field to get to his fodder if, peradventure, he can go in a straight line. The object of this chapter is to uphold the wisdom of the ass. There is a straight line for criticism to take, and criticism never has taken it, but always goes round about.

A science of criticism implies that there is something common to the arts.

A science of criticism, embracing poetry and the fine arts, is possible only on the supposition that these arts all stand on common ground; and that, however varied may be the methods employed in them, their inner meaning and purpose is the same. No critical canon has a wider and more undoubting acceptance than that which assumes the sisterhood of the arts. We may ignore it in practice, or we may be at a loss to explain the precise meaning of it; but the close relationship of the muses is one of the oldest traditions of literature, and one of the most familiar lessons of our school-days. The family likeness of the arts is so marked, that language cannot choose but describe one in terms of another. Terence, in one of his prologues (*Phormio*), refers to the poets as musicians. "Music," says Dryden, "is inarticulate poetry." Thomas

On the admitted relationship of the arts.

Fuller has at least twice in his works, once (on the *Holy and Profane State*) when speaking of artists generally, and again (in his *Worthies*), when writing of Dr. Christopher Tye. defined poetry as music in words, and music as poetry in sounds. Other writers dwell on the similarity of the poet and the limner. Simonides, among the Greeks, is the author of the famous saying which comes down to us through Plutarch, that poetry is a speaking picture, and painting a mute poetry. Horace, among the Latins, puts the same idea into three words—*ut pictura poesis.* Whether as expressed by the Greek or by the Latin poet, the sense of the connection between poetry and painting came to be so strong and over-mastering in modern criticism, that at length men like Darwin in England, and Marmontel in France, learned to see in the similarity of the two arts, the elements of a perfect definition of either; and Gotthold Lessing, the first great critic of Germany, had to write a work in which, taking the representations of Laocoon in poetry and in sculpture for an example, he proved elaborately that after all there is a difference between the arts, and that each has its proper limits. The underlying unity of the arts is one of the common-places of criticism, which D'Alembert concentrated in one drop of ink, when, in the preface to the French Encyclopædia, he comprised under the name of poesy all the fine arts, adding, at the same time, that they might also

The arts so like that they have been treated as identical.

CHAPTER IV. be included under the general name of painting. Goethe has strikingly conveyed a like thought in one of his verses which has been translated by Carlyle—

As all nature's thousand changes
But one changeless God proclaim,
So in art's wide kingdom ranges
One sole meaning still the same.

Wherein consists the unity of art.

What is this one meaning, still the same, of which we hear so much and know so little? What is the bond of unity which knits poetry and the fine arts together? What is the common ground upon which they rest? What are we to understand by the sisterhood of the muses? Whenever the philosopher has encountered these questions, as the first step to a science of criticism, he has come forward with one of two answers. All attempts to rear such a science are based on the supposition either that poetry and the fine arts have a common method, or that they have a common theme. Either with Aristotle it is supposed that they follow the one method of imitation; or with men whose minds are more Platonic, though Plato is not one of them, it is supposed that they are the manifestations of one great idea, which is usually said to be the idea of the beautiful. All the accredited systems of criticism therefore take their rise either in theories of imitation or theories of the beautiful. It is not difficult, however, to show that both of the suppositions on which these

Two answers to this question usually given.

And both false.

systems rest are delusive, and that neither is calculated to sustain the weight of a science. Before we can arrive at the true foundation of the science, it is necessary to clear the ground from the silt and ruins of false systems which encumber it.

The Aristotelian doctrine that art has a common method, that of imitation.

We begin with the Aristotelian system, which has obtained the widest acceptance, and which is the only one of great repute that now exists, though it exists only in name. Aristotle attempted to build a science of criticism on the doctrine that poetry and the fine arts have a common method. Poetry is an imitation, said the philosopher. Not only are the drama, painting, and sculpture imitative, but so is a poetical narration; so, too, is music, and so is the dance. Imitation is the grand achievement which gives to the arts their form and prescribes their law. It is the manifold ways and means of imitation that we are to study, if we are to elevate criticism into a science.

This the corner stone of ancient criticism.

Although this theory is so narrow that the science established on it took the form very much of an inverted pyramid, it ruled the world of letters till within a late period. It is the corner stone of ancient criticism: it is the corner stone of all modern criticism that takes its inspiration from the Renaissance. It was accepted in the last century with undoubting faith as an axiom, and the most astonishing conclusions were built upon it, as some divines draw the

CHAPTER IV.

And how implicitly accepted.

most dreadful inferences from dogmas to which they have learned to attach a disproportionate value. Thus a troop of French critics worked their way to the principle of *la difficulté surmontée*. The chief excellence of imitation was said to consist in its difficulty, and the more difficult it became the greater was its merit. Hence the pleasure of verse, because it throws difficulties in the way of imitating speech. The English critics, not to be behindhand, started off on like vagaries. One of them showed conclusively that since the pleasure of poetry is derived from imitation, the pleasure is double when one poet imitates another; that if that other has borrowed from a third, then the pleasure becomes threefold; and that if it be the imitation of a simile, which in itself includes a double imitation, then again the pleasure is multiplied. Milton is, in this respect, greater than Virgil, says the sapient critic, for whereas the Roman poet imitated Homer directly, the English one has the glory not only of imitating him directly, but also of imitating him at second or even at third hand, through Virgil and others.

I do not give these illustrations of the theory of imitation as proofs of its fallacy. It would fare ill with most doctrines if they were to be judged by the manner in which the unwary have applied them. The illustrations I have given are proofs only of the simplicity of faith with which the theory of imitation came to be accepted in the last century as if it were one of the prime truths of religion, or one of the axioms of reason, worthy of universal empire at all times, in all places, under all circumstances. It was a good thing of which the critics could not have too much; it was wisdom on which it was impossible to lay too great a stress. Gradually the theory wore itself out, and has fallen out of account. But it died hard, and held its ground so lustily, that, even in our own time, critics whom we should not reckon as belonging to the school of the Renaissance, but to the more original schools of Germany, have given their adhesion to it. Jean Paul Richter adopted it vaguely as the first principle of his introduction to Æsthetic, while Coleridge says distinctly that imitation is the universal principle of the fine arts, and that it would be easy to apply it not merely to painting, but even to music.

How it held its ground, and how hard it died.

The theory is as false as any can be which puts the part for the whole, and a small part for a very large whole. Music, for example, is not imitative. When Haydn stole the melody to which he set the eighth commandment, the force of musical imitation could no further go. If the same composer, in his finest oratorio, attempts to reflect in sound the creation of light, and to indicate by cadence the movements of the flexible tiger; if Handel in descanting on the plagues of Egypt gives us the buzz of insect life, and indicates by the depths of his notes the depths of

Falsehood of the theory.

As shown in music.

CHAPTER IV.

the sea in which the hosts of Pharaoh were drowned; or if Beethoven, in the most popular of his symphonies, tries to give us the song of the cuckoo, the lowing of herds, and the roar of the storm, these imitations are over and above the art, and are confessedly foreign to it. As music is not imitative, so neither is narration. Words represent or stand for, but cannot be said to imitate ideas. Plays, pictures, and statues—in one word, the dramatic arts, are imitative; but to say that imitation is the universal principle of the fine arts, is simply to reduce all art to the canon of the drama.

Limits of the theory.

Scaliger's objection to it unanswerable.

It is impossible to get over the objection to the theory of the Stagyrite, urged centuries ago by the elder Scaliger. If poetry, he said, be imitative in any sense which applies to every species of it, then in the same sense also is prose imitative; if the fine arts are imitative in any sense which applies to all alike, in the very same sense also are the useful arts imitative.* In point of fact, Plato declared in so many words, by the

* I remember in my college days hunting through half a dozen libraries for a mediæval book, the title of which — *Ars Simia Naturæ* – excited my curiosity. I expected to find in it a middle age anticipation of Schelling's Philosophy. My friend, Professor Baynes, had been already on this track, and with some laughter exploded on me the information that the book I was hunting for could have nothing to do with the fine arts, though it might have much to do with the black. I mention this as one more illustration of the fact that if the fine arts are imitative, they are not peculiarly so. The same thing has been said of the useful arts; the same also of the black.

mouth of the prophetess Diotima (in the *Banquet*), that the exercise of every inventive art is poetry, and that any inventor is a poet or maker; from which it might appear that Bechamel and Farina, as the creators of sauces and perfumes, or Bramah and Arnott, as the inventors of locks and smokeless grates, take rank beside the bard who sang the wrath of Achilles, and the sculptor who chiselled that grandest statue of a woman, the Venus of Milo. Thus the foundation of critical science is laid in a definition which is not the peculiar property of art. Coleridge himself, without foreseeing the consequences of his admission, and without drawing Scaliger's conclusion, went much further than Scaliger in the view which he took of the nature of imitation as applied to the fine arts. He declared that the principle of imitation lies at the root not merely of the fine arts, but also of thought itself. The power of comparison is essential to consciousness—the very condition of its existence; we know nothing except through the perception of contrariety and identity; we cannot think without comparing; and so the imitations of art, he said, are but the sublime developments of an act which is essential to the dimmest dawn of mind. It would be a pity to ruffle the feathers of this wonderful suggestion, which took Coleridge's fancy because it looked big; but it may be enough to point out that it yields with a charming simplicity all we

Coleridge's defence of it unavailing.

CHAPTER IV.

need contend for. It allows that in the sense in which imitation may be described as the universal law of art, it may also be described as the universal law of thought itself, and therefore of science, which is, in Coleridge's own language, the opposite of art. In a word, it is not peculiar to art, and is incapable of supplying the definition of it. Certainly it has never yet, in the science of criticism, yielded a result of the slightest value. For in truth, although imitation bulks so large in Aristotle's definition of poetry, it sinks into insignificance, and even passes out of sight, in the body of his work. He makes nothing of it; his followers less than nothing. Notwithstanding Richter's, notwithstanding Coleridge's adhesion to it, the theory of imitation is now utterly exploded.

The other theory which displaced the Aristotelian.

The Aristotelian theory ruled absolute in literature for two millenniums. No other theory was put forward to take its place, as the foundation of critical science, till within the last hundred years or so. It satisfied the critics of the Renaissance—that is, the old order of critics who based their thinking on the settled ideas and methods of classical literature, and revelled in systems that were little beyond grammar. There came a time, however, when the need of a deeper criticism began to be felt. The old criticism that through the Renaissance traced a descent from Aristotle, dealt chiefly with the forms of art. A new criticism was demanded that should search into its substance. It arose in Germany. Not satisfied with the old grammatical doctrine that the arts have a common form or method, the philosophical critics of Germany tried to make out that they have a common theme—a common substance, and chiefly that this theme, this essence, is the idea of the beautiful. It is always an idea. They are not agreed as to what the idea is; but they are nearly all agreed that it is the manifestation of some one idea. I repeat from Goethe:

Arose in Germany

That art has a common theme.

As all nature's thousand changes
But one changeless God proclaim,
So in art's wide kingdom ranges
One sole meaning still the same.

Much of what might be said on this subject must be reserved for the next chapter, in that part of it which has to do with the German school of critics and their chief contribution to criticism. In the meantime it may be enough to point out that whereas innumerable attempts have been made to analyze the grand idea of art which is generally supposed to be the idea of the beautiful, and out of this analysis to trace the laws and the development of art, it cannot be said that in following such a line of research any real progress has been made. We cannot point to a single work of authority on the subject. In countless works that represent the thought of the last hundred years, we shall find references to the one grand idea of art, the beautiful;

Remarks on this conception of Art.

That art is the manifestation of the beautiful.

but when we come to inquire what is the nature of the beautiful, we can get no satisfactory answer, and can hear only a clatter of tongues. It is for this very reason that the theory of the beautiful, as the common theme of art, subsists. If it were less vague, it would be more opposed. With all its vagueness, however, two facts may be discovered which are fatal to it as a foundation for the science of criticism. The first is the more fatal, namely, that it does not cover the whole ground of art. The worship and manifestation of the beautiful is not, for example, the province of comedy, and comedy is as much a part of art as tragedy. The beautiful, most distinctly, is one of the ideas on which art loves to dwell; but it is not an idea which inspires every work of art. Moreover, on the other hand (the second fact I have referred to), is it to be supposed that to display beauty is to produce a work of art? *La belle chose que la philosophie!* says M. Jourdain, not untruly; but are fine systems of philosophy to be reckoned among the fine arts? Horace, long ago, in a verse which has become proverbial, expressed the truth about the position of beauty in art. *Non satis est pulchra esse poemata*, he said: *dulcia sunto.* It is not enough that a work of art be beautiful; it must have more powerful charms.

Two facts fatal to it.

That art is the manifestation of the true.

Convinced that the idea of the beautiful is inadequate to cover the whole field of art, critics have suggested other ideas as more ample in

CHAPTER IV.

their scope. It is said, for example, by some, that art is the reflex of life—of life, not in its fleeting forms, but in its hidden soul; of facts, therefore, which are eternal symbols, and of truths which are fixed as the stars. It will be found, however, that if we thus take the idea of the true as the theme of art, and attempt to build upon it a science of criticism, it is open to precisely the same objections as there are to the idea of the beautiful when placed in a similar light. Music is an art, but in what sense are we to say that its theme is eternal truth, or that Mendelssohn's concerto in D minor is a reflex of the absolute idea? In what sense are the arabesques of the Alhambra eternal truths or reflections of the eternal essence? The idea of the true is not the theme of all art, and it is not peculiar to works of art to take the true for a theme. Still the same objections apply to yet another definition of the artistic theme. "Art," says Sir Edward Lytton finely, "is the effort of man to express the ideas which nature suggests to him of a power above nature, whether that power be within the recesses of his own being, or in the Great First Cause, of which nature, like himself, is but the effect." This is a happy generalisation which goes a great way; but it is surely not enough to say that it is the object of art to exhibit ideas of power. Ideas of power, ideas of truth, ideas of beauty—it will not do to bind art as a whole, or poetry as a part of it, to the

Open to the same objection.

Also that art is the manifestation of power.

CHAPTER IV.

service of any one of these groups. There is no one word relating to things known that in its wide embrace can take in the theme of all art, and if it could comprise the theme of all art, it would not be the property of art alone. The subject of art is all that can interest man; but all that can interest man is not the monopoly of art.

The subject of art is all that can interest man.

Wherein then does the unity of the arts reside?

If the unity of the arts does not lie in the possession either of a common method which they pursue, or of a common theme which they set forth, wherein does it consist? Manifestly the character of an art is determined by its object; and though the critics have made no use of the fact, yet it is a fact, which they admit with very few exceptions, that poetry and the fine arts are endowed with a common purpose. Even if poetry and the arts could boast of a common method and a common theme, still every question of method and the choice of theme must be subordinate to the end in view. The end determines the means, and must therefore be the principal point of inquiry. If, then, we inquire what is the end of poetry and the poetical arts, we shall find among critics of all countries and all ages a singular unanimity of opinion—a unanimity which is all the more remarkable, when we discover that, admitting the fact with scarcely a dissentient voice, they have never turned it to account—they have

Their common purpose.

This common purpose an admitted fact.

practically ignored it. It is admitted that the immediate end of art is to give pleasure. Whatever we do has happiness for its last end; but with art it is the first as well as the last. We need not now halt to investigate the nature of this happiness which poetry aims at, whether it is refined or the reverse, whether it is of a particular kind or of all kinds; it is enough to insist on the broad fact that for more than two thousand years pleasure of some sort has been almost universally admitted to be the goal of art. The dreamer and the thinker, the singer and the sayer, at war on many another point, are here at one. It is the pleasure of a lie, says Plato; it is that of a truth, says Aristotle; but neither has any doubt that whatever other aims art may have in view, pleasure is the main—the immediate object.

Some explanation of this doctrine of pleasure.

Here, however, care must be taken that the reader is not misled by a word. Word and thing, pleasure is in very bad odour; moralists always take care to hold it cheap; critics are ashamed of it; and we are all apt to misunderstand it, resting too easily on the surface view of it as mere amusement. There is in pleasure so little of conscious thought, and in pain so much, that it is natural for all who pride themselves on the possession of thought to make light of pleasure. It is possible, however, in magnifying the worth of conscious thought, to underrate the worth of unconscious life. Now

CHAPTER IV. art is a force that operates unconsciously on life. It is not a doctrine; it is not science. There is knowledge in it, but it reaches to something beyond knowledge. That something beyond science, beyond knowledge, to which art reaches, it is difficult to express in one word. The nearest word is that which the world for thirty centuries past has been using, and which sky-high thinkers now-a-days are afraid to touch—namely, pleasure. There is no doubt about its inadequacy, but where is there another word that expresses half as much? If art be the opposite of science, the end of art must be antithetical to the end of science. But the end of science is knowledge. What then is its antithesis—the end of art? Shall we say ignorance? We cannot say that it is ignorance, because that is a pure negation. But there is no objection to our saying—life ignorant of itself, unconscious life, pleasure. I do not give this explanation as sufficient—it is very insufficient—but as indicating a point of view from which it will be seen that the establishment of pleasure as the end of art may involve larger issues, and convey a larger meaning than is commonly supposed. What that larger meaning is may in due course be shown. In the ninth chapter of this work I attempt to state it, and stating it to give a remodelled definition of art. In the meantime, one fails to see how, by any of the newfangled expressions of German philosophy, we

Drawn from the antithesis between art and science.

See Chapter ix.

can improve upon the plain-spoken wisdom of the ancient maxims—that science is for knowledge, and that art is for pleasure.

CHAPTER IV.

But if this be granted, and it is all but universally granted, it entails the inevitable inference that criticism is the science of the laws and conditions under which pleasure is produced. If poetry, if art, exists in and for pleasure, then upon this rock, and upon this alone, is it possible to build a science of criticism. Criticism, however, is built anywhere but upon the rock. While the arts have almost invariably been regarded as arts of pleasure, criticism has never yet been treated as the science of pleasure. Like the Israelites in the desert, who after confessing the true faith went forthwith and fell down to a molten image, the critics no sooner admitted that the end of art is pleasure, than they began to treat it as nought. Instead of taking a straight line, like the venerable ass which was praised by the Eleatic philosopher, they went off zigzag, to right, to left, in every imaginable direction but that which lay before them. Art is for pleasure said the Greeks; but it is the pleasure of imitation, and therefore all that criticism has to do is to study the ways of imitation. So they bounced off to the left. Art is for pleasure said the Germans; but it is the pleasure of the beautiful, and therefore all that criticism has to do is to comprehend the beautiful. So they bounced off to the right. In

The necessary inference as to the nature of criticism.

But how the critics have turned aside from that inference.

One and all.

Greeks.

And Germans.

CHAPTER IV.

the name of common sense, let me ask, why are we not to take the straight line? Why is it that, having set up pleasure as the first principle of art, we are immediately to knock it down and go in search of other and lesser principles? Why does not the critic take the one plain path before him, proceeding instantly to inquire into the nature of pleasure, its laws, its conditions, its requirements, its causes, its effects, its whole history?

Why they thus turned aside from the straight road.

This turning aside of criticism from the straight road that lay before it into by-paths has been owing partly to the moral contempt of pleasure, but chiefly to the intellectual difficulty of any inquest into the nature of enjoyment, a difficulty so great, that since the time of Plato and Aristotle it has never been seriously faced until in our own day Sir William Hamilton undertook to grapple with it. Whenever I have insisted with my friends on this point, as to the necessity of recognising criticism as the science of pleasure, the invariable rejoinder has been that there is no use in attempting such a science, because the nature of pleasure eludes our scrutiny, and there is no accounting for tastes. But the rejoinder is irrelevant. All science is difficult at first, and well-nigh hopeless; and if tastes differ, that is no reason why we should refuse to regard them as beyond the pale of law, but a very strong reason why we should seek to ascertain the limits of

CHAPTER IV.

difference, and how far pleasure which is general may be discounted by individual caprice. It is not for us to parley about the difficulties of search, or the usefulness of its results. Chemistry was at one time a difficult study, and seemed to be a useless one. Hard or easy, useful or useless—that is not the question. The question is simply this : If there is such a thing as criticism at all, what is its object? what is its definition? and how do you escape from the truism that if art be the minister, criticism must be the science of pleasure ?

The fact remains that the doctrine of pleasure is not allowed its rightful place in criticism.

Whatever be the cause of the reluctance to accept this truism, the fact remains that the doctrine of pleasure has not hitherto been put in its right place as the corner stone of scientific criticism, entitling it to be named the science of pleasure, the Joy Science, the Gay Science ; and I set apart the next chapter to explain and to enforce a principle which is of the last importance, and which, but for the backwardness of criticism, would now pass for an axiom, the most obvious of old saws. If art be the minister, criticism must be the science of pleasure, is so obvious a truth, that since in the history of literature and art the inference has never been drawn (except once in a faint way, to be mentioned by and by), a doubt may arise in some minds as to the extent to which the production of pleasure has been admitted in criticism as the first principle of art.

And we proceed to

It is worth while, therefore, to begin this dis-

CHAPTER IV. — the proof of what that place should be.

cussion by setting the authorities in array, and showing what in every school of criticism is regarded as the relation of art to pleasure. I proceed, accordingly, to take a rapid survey of the chief schools of criticism that have ruled in the republic of letters, with express reference to their opinion of pleasure and the end of art.

THE AGREEMENT OF THE CRITICS.

CHAPTER V.

THE AGREEMENT OF THE CRITICS.

CHAPTER V.

Survey of the schools of criticism.

I PROPOSE in this chapter to show that the end of art has in all the great schools of criticism been regarded as the same. Speaking roundly, there are but two great systems of criticism. The one may be styled indifferently the classical system, or the system of the Renaissance. It belongs to ancient thought, and to the modern revival of classicism; and it chiefly concerns itself with the grammatical forms of art. The other is more distinctly modern; it first made way in Germany, and, philosophical in tone, chiefly concerns itself with the substantial ideas of art. But these divided systems may be subdivided, and perhaps the plainest method of arranging the critical opinions of past ages is to take them by countries. It will be convenient to glance in succession at the critical schools of Greece, Italy, Spain, France, Germany, and England. And from this survey,

Their divisions.

CHAPTER V.

it will be seen that if criticism has never yet been recognised as the science of pleasure, poetry and art have always been accepted as arts of pleasure. In our old Anglo-Saxon poetry, the harp is described as "the wood of pleasure," and that is the universal conception of art. There may in the different schools be differences in the manner of describing the end of art; but there is none as to the essence of the thing described.

All the schools teach one doctrine as to the end of art.

The Greek school of criticism.

I. Homer, Plato, and Aristotle are the leaders of Greek thought, and their word may be taken for what constitutes the Greek idea of the end of poetry. The uppermost thought in Homer's mind, when he speaks of Phemius and Demodocus, is that their duty is to delight, to charm, to soothe. When the strain of the bard makes Ulysses weep, it is hushed, because its object is defeated, and it is desired that all should rejoice together. Wherever the minstrel is referred to, his chief business is described in the Greek verb to delight. What the great poet of Greece thus indicated, the great philosophers expressed in logical form. That pleasure is the end of poetry, is the pervading idea of Aristotle's treatise on the subject. To Plato's view I have already more than once referred. He excluded the poets from his republic for this, as a chief reason, that poetry has pleasure for its leading aim. In another of his works he defines the pleasure, which poetry aims at, to be that which a man of virtue

As represented by Plato, and Aristotle accepted the one doctrine.

CHAPTER V.

Plato's reasoning about pleasure.

may feel; and he may therefore seem to be inconsistent in his excluding the artist, who would create such enjoyment, from his model fold. Plato is not always consistent, and from his manner of dialogue it is often difficult to find out whether any given opinion is really his own or is only put forward to make play; but in this case the inconsistency may be explained by reference to another dialogue (*Philebus*), in which he has an argument to show that the gods feel neither pleasure nor pain, and that both are unseemly. The argument is, that because pleasure is a becoming—that is, a state not of being, but of going to be—it is unbecoming. He starts with the Cyrenaic definition of pleasure as a state not of being, but of change, and he argues that the gods are unchangeable, therefore not capable of pleasure. Pleasure which is a becoming, is unbecoming to their nature; and man seeking pleasure seeks that which is unseemly and ungodlike. Think of this argument what we will, the very fact of its being urged against poetry in this way, brings into a very strong light the conviction of Plato as to the meaning of classical art. And what was Plato's, what was Aristotle's view of the object of art, we find consistently maintained in Greek literature while it preserved any vitality. We find it in Dionysius of Halicarnassus; still later we find it in Plutarch.

Although every school of criticism has maintained substantially the same doctrine, each has

CHAPTER V.

The prominent consideration in Greek criticism.

its own way of looking at it, and it is interesting to note how from time to time the expression of the doctrine varies. In the Greek mind the question that most frequently arose in connection with the pleasure of art was this, Is it a true or a false pleasure? It is the question which every child asks when first the productions of art—a tale or a picture—come under his notice. But is it true? And so of the childlike man; the first movement of criticism within him concerns the reality of the source whence his pleasure is derived. The Greeks especially raised this question as to the truth of art. Is the pleasure which it affords, the pleasure of a truth or that of a lie? The question naturally arose from their critical point of view, which led them to look for the definition of art in its form. They defined art as an imitation, which is but a narrower name for fiction. It will be found, indeed, throughout the history of criticism, that so long as it started from the Greek point of view, followed the Greek method, and accepted the Greek definition of art, that this question as to the truth of fiction was a constant trouble. And when the Greek raised his doubt as to the truth of art, let it be remembered that he had in his mind something very different from what we should now be thinking of were we to question the truthfulness of this or that particular work of art. A work of art may be perfectly true in our sense of the word, that is to say, drawn to

Is the pleasure of art true?

the life, but it cannot escape from the Greek charge that it is fiction. **CHAPTER V.**

Treatment of the question. The first suggestion of the Greek doubt, as to the reality of the foundation of pleasure in art, emerges in the shape of a story told about Solon, which does not consort well with dates, but which as a story that sprung up among the Greeks, has its meaning. **Story of Solon.** It is said that when Thespis came to Athens with his strolling stage, and drew great crowds to his plays, Solon, then an old man, asked him if he was not ashamed to tell so many lies before the people, and striking his staff on the ground, growled out that if lies are allowed to enter into a nation's pleasures, they will, ere long, enter into its business. Plutarch, who relates this anecdote, gives us in another of his works the saying of the sophist Gorgias in defence of what seemed to be the deceitfulness of the pleasure which art aims at. **The saying of Gorgias.** Gorgias said that tragedy is a cheat, in which he who does the cheat is more honest than he who does it not, and he who accepts the cheat is wiser than he who refuses it. Many of the Greeks accepted the cheat so simply that, for example, they accused Euripides of impiety for putting impiety into the mouth of one of his dramatic personages. **How the artists tried to deceive.** And not a few of their painters undertook to cheat with the utmost frankness. Apelles had the glory of painting a horse so that another horse neighed to the picture. Zeuxis suffered a grievous disappointment when, having painted

CHAPTER V.

a boy carrying grapes, the birds came to peck at the fruit but were not alarmed at the apparition of the boy. There are other stories of the same kind, as that of the painted curtain, and yet again that of the sculptor Pygmalion, who became enamoured of the feminine statue chiselled by himself.

So far there is nothing peculiar in the working of the Greek mind.

Let it be observed that in the working of the Greek mind so far there is no marked peculiarity. In all young art there is the tendency to realism; in nearly all young criticism there is a difficulty of deciding between the truth of imitation and the truth of reality. When Bruce, the African traveller, gave the picture of a fish to one of the Moors, the latter saw in it not a painting but a reality, and, after a moment of surprise, asked: "If this fish at the last day should rise against you and say: Thou hast given me a body, but not a living soul,—what should you reply?" In keeping with this tone of mind, the Saracens who built the Alhambra, and in it the fountain of the lions, deemed it advisable to inscribe on the basin of the fountain: "Oh thou who beholdest these lions, fear not. Life is wanting to enable them to show their fury." In Italian art, not only in its earlier stages, but even in its period of perfect development, we find the same phenomenon. I might quote whole pages from Vasari to show how an artist and a critic of the Cinque Cento thought of art. He says that one of

CHAPTER V.

Raphael's Madonnas seems in the head, the hands, and the feet to be of living flesh rather than a thing of colour. He says that the instruments, in a picture of St. Cecilia, lie scattered around her, and do not seem to be painted, but to be the real objects. He says of Raphael's pictures generally that they are scarcely to be called pictures, but rather the reality, for the flesh trembles, the breathing is visible, the pulses beat, and life is in its utmost force through all his works.

How the love of illusion showed itself for example in Italian art.

In Italian art also it may be well to note a tendency to confound fact and fiction, which may explain something of the same tendency as it showed itself among the Greeks. Let me ask—What is the meaning of the two Dominicans who are introduced kneeling in the picture of the Transfiguration? Many another picture might be mentioned in which a similar treatment is adopted, and especially by the painters before Raphael, as Dominic Ghirlandajo, and men of that stamp. But everybody knows the crowning work of Raphael, and that, therefore, may serve best for an illustration. What are we to make of the two Dominicans? If, instead of the two bald-pated, black-robed monks, the artist had placed on the Mount of Transfiguration a couple of wild bulls feeding or fighting, they would puzzle one less than his two monks. Why is their monastic garb intruded among the majestic foldings of celestial

CHAPTER V.

draperies? The Saviour went up to the mount with Peter, James, and John, alone; he was transfigured before them; he appeared in company with Moses and Elias; he charged the disciples that they should tell it unto none till the Son of Man were risen from the dead. And yet Raphael introduces on the scene two modern monks to share the vision! Not only is the Gospel narrative thus violated; there is a still stranger anomaly. The three disciples are lying down, blinded with the light and bewildered in their minds. The Dominicans are kneeling upright and looking on. Raphael has deliberately introduced into his picture—the spectator. He has torn aside the veil which separates art from nature—the ideal from the real; and we, even we, the living men and the real world, are absorbed into the picture and become part of it, so that if that be indeed a picture and a dream, then are we also pictures and dreams; and if we are indeed certainties and realities, then also is that wondrous scene a certainty and a reality. The old Geronimite in the Escurial said to Wilkie, as he stood in the Refectory gazing on Titian's picture of the Last Supper:

Wilkie's story of the Geronimite.

"I have sat daily in sight of that picture for now nearly threescore years; during that time my companions have dropped off, one after another. More than one generation has passed away, and there the figures in the picture have remained unchanged. I look at them till I sometimes think that they are the realities, and we but the shadows." And that is the mood of mind which the introduction into a picture of the modern spectator in modern costume is calculated to awaken. The Italians, when, on the canvas of Ghirlandajo, they looked on the well-known figures of Ginevra di Benci and her maidens, as attendants in an interview between Elizabeth and the Virgin Mary, found themselves projected into the picture and made a part of it.

Further illustration of the love of illusion in Greek and other forms of art.

Now, this method of confounding fact and fiction, in order that fiction may appear to rise to the assurance of fact, was not peculiarly Italian, but existed in full force among the Greeks. It was an essential feature of their drama. The most marked characteristic of the Greek drama is the presence of the chorus. The chorus are always present,—watching events, talking to the actors, talking to the audience, talking to themselves,—all through the play, indeed, pouring forth a continual stream of musical chatter. And what are the chorus? The only intelligible explanation which has been given is that they represent the spectator. The spectator is introduced into the play and made to take part in it. What the Greeks thus did artistically on their stage, we moderns have also sometimes done inartistically and unintentionally, but still to the same effect. We have had the audience seated on the stage, and sometimes, in the most

CHAPTER V. ludicrous manner, taking part in the performance. When Garrick was playing Lear in Dublin to the Cordelia of Mrs. Woffington, an Irish gentleman who was present actually advanced, put his arm round the lady's waist, and thus held her while she replied to the reproaches of the old king. The stage in the last century was sometimes so beset with the audience, that Juliet has been seen, says Tate Wilkinson, lying all solitary in the tomb of the Capulets with a couple of hundred of the audience about her. We should now contemplate such a practice with horror, as utterly destructive of stage illusion; and yet we must remember that it had its illusive aspect also, by confounding the dream that appeared on the stage with the familiar realities of life.

From all this, however, it follows that if the Greeks made a confusion between fact and fiction, art and nature, they were not peculiar in so doing. What is peculiar to them is this, that they gave a critical character to their doubt as to the limits of truth in art. It was fairly reasoned. If it showed itself sometimes as a childish superstition, sometimes as the mere blindness of a prosaic temper, and sometimes as an enjoyment of silly illusions, it also at times bore a higher character and rose to the level of criticism. The Greeks were the first to raise this subject of the truth of art into an important critical question which they transmitted to after times.

What is peculiar to the Greeks.

CHAPTER V.

Plato's manner of stating critically the doubt as to the truth of pleasure.

This is not the place to enter into a discussion whether they were right or wrong, and whether fiction be or be not falsehood. That discussion will be more fitly handled when we come to examine the ethics of art. Here we need only record and confront the fact that the objection to the pleasure of art which most frequently puzzled the Greek thinkers, was that it appeared to be mixed up with lies. Plato, as I have already said, exhausted his dialectical skill in showing the untruthfulness of art. He condemned it as an imitation at third hand. He meant, for example, that a flower in the field is but the shadow of an idea in the mind of God; that the idea in God's mind is the real thing; that the blossom in the meadow is but a poor image of it; and that when a painter gives us a copy of that copy, the picture stands third from the divine original, and is, therefore, a wretched falsehood. Plato's statement as to the truth of art is thus grounded on his theory of ideas, and when that theory goes, one would imagine that the statement should go also. It is a curious proof of the vitality of strong assertion, that his opinion (but it would be more correct to say the opinion to which he gave currency) abides with all the force which his name can give to it, while the theory of ideas from which it sprung and derived plausibility, has long since gone to the limbo. It is incredible that mankind should find enduring pleasure in a lie. There cannot

The doubt survives apart from the reasoning on which it rests.

CHAPTER V. be a more monstrous libel against the human race than to say that in the artistic search for pleasure, we have reality and all that is most gracious in it to choose from; that we look from earth to heaven and try all ways which the infinite beneficence of nature has provided; that nevertheless we set our joy on a system of lies; and that so far the masterpieces of art are but tokens of a fallen nature, the signs of sickness and the harbinger of doom.

Aristotle's statement of the counter doctrine.

As Plato took one side of the question, Aristotle took the other, and in the writings of the latter we have the final conclusion and the abiding belief of the Greek mind upon this subject of the truth of art. The view which he took was concentrated in the saying that poetry is more philosophical than history, because it looks more to general and less to particular facts. We should now express the same thing in the statement that whereas history is fact, poetry is truth. Aristotle does not set himself formally to answer Plato, but throughout his writings we find him solving Plato's riddles, undoing Plato's arguments, and rebutting Plato's objections. Many of his most famous sayings are got by recoil from Plato. Thus his masterly definition of tragedy, which has never been improved upon, and which generation after generation of critics have been content to repeat like a text of Scripture, is a rebound from Plato. And the same is to be said very nearly of Aris-

To be found in the ninth chapter of his *Poetics*.

totle's doctrine concerning the truth of art. It is so clear and so complete that it has become a common-place of criticism. It asserted for the Greeks, in the distinctest terms, the truthfulness of art; it showed wherein that truthfulness consists; and, as far as criticism was concerned, it at once and for ever disposed of the notion that art is a lie. Greeks like Gorgias could see vaguely that if art be a cheat, it may, nevertheless, be justifiable, as we should justify a feint or other stratagem in war. It was reserved for Aristotle to put the defence of art on the right ground—to deny that it is a cheat at all—and to claim for it a truthfulness deeper than that of history.

The lesson of Greek criticism.

This, then, is one of the earliest lessons which the student of art has to learn. The first lesson of all is that art is for pleasure; the second is that the pleasure of art stands in no sort of opposition to truth. We in England have especial reason to bear this in mind, for we are most familiar with the doctrine that art is for pleasure, as it has been put by Coleridge; and it is not unlikely that some of the repugnance which the doctrine meets in minds of a certain order may be due to his ragged analysis and awkward statement. He rather prided himself on his anatomy of thought and expression, but he hardly ever made a clean dissection. Mark what he says in this case. He says that the true opposite of poetry is not prose, but science,

How it has been perverted by Coleridge.

CHAPTER V.

and that whereas it is the proper and immediate object of science to discover truth, it is the proper and immediate object of poetry to communicate pleasure. This is not right. Coleridge has defined science by reference to the external object with which it is engaged; but he has defined poetry by reference to the mental state which it produces. There is no comparison between the two. If he is to run the contrast fairly, he ought to deal with both alike, and to state either what is the outward object pursued by each, or what is the inward state produced by each. He would then find that, so far as the subject-matter is concerned, there is no essential difference between poetry and science, it being false to say that the one possesses more of truth than the other; and he would define the difference between the two by the mental states which they severally produce—the immediate object of science being science or knowledge, while that of poetry is pleasure. To say that the object of art is pleasure in contrast to knowledge, is quite different from saying that it is pleasure in contrast to truth. Science gives us truth without reference to pleasure, but immediately and chiefly for the sake of knowledge; poetry gives us truth without reference to knowledge, but immediately and mainly for the sake of pleasure. By thus getting rid of the contrast between truth and pleasure, which Coleridge has unguardedly allowed, a difficulty

The true doctrine.

is smoothed away from the doctrine that the end of art is pleasure, and that of criticism the analysis of pleasure. His statement has an air of extraordinary precision about it that might wile the unwary into a ditch. All his precision goes to misrepresent the pure Greek doctrine.

CHAPTER V.

The Italian school of criticism.

II. From Greece we pass over into Italy, as the stepping-stone to modern Europe; and it matters not whether we speak of old pagan Italy, whose critical faith was most brightly expressed in the crisp verses of Horace; or of christianised Italy, which at the revival of letters stood forward as the earliest school both of art and of criticism in modern Europe. Everybody will remember how Horace describes a poem as fashioned for pleasure, and failing thereof, as a thing of nought, that belies itself, like music that jars on the ear, like a scent that is noisome, like Sardinian honey bitter with the taste of poppy. Among the great critics of the moderns, Cæsar Scaliger stands first in point of time, and he takes the same view as the old Greek philosophers. After denying the Aristotelian doctrine of imitation as the one method of art, he says that poetry is a delightful discipline by which the heart is educated through right reason to happiness—happiness being with him another name for perfect action. Next to Scaliger stands another Italian critic, Castelvetro, who wrote a commentary on

As represented by Scaliger, Castelvetro, Tasso, and others.

CHAPTER V.

Aristotle's *Poetics*, in which he fearlessly opposed the master, when he thought it right to do so. He, too, saw in enjoyment the end of poetry, and maintained the doctrine so uncompromisingly, that some of the French critics long afterwards took him to task for it. But Scaliger and Castelvetro were a sort of antiquarians, and might be said to lean too much towards ancient literature. Tasso was more distinctly a modern, and has left us, with his poems, a number of critical discourses. In these he states unflinchingly that delight is the immediate end of poetry, and the whole of the Italian school of criticism goes with him. The doctrine is firmly stated in Vida's famous poem.

What is peculiar in their view of art.

It is less interesting, however, to know that the Italians, as well as the old Romans, maintained the universal doctrine concerning art than to ascertain with what limitations they maintained it. Here we come to another great lesson. If the first of all lessons in art is that art is for pleasure, and the second is that this pleasure has nothing to do with falsehood, the third is that art is not to be considered as in any sense opposed to utility. The ancient Romans and the modern Italians were never much troubled with what vexed the too speculative Greeks—the seeming untruthfulness of art pleasure; their more practical genius brooded over its seeming carelessness of profit. Scaliger describes the Italians of

CHAPTER V.

his day as bent on gain; and in most of their statements of the end of art they take heed to link together the two ideas of pleasure and profit; pleasure taking the precedence, no doubt; but pleasure always with profit. In the Latin language, indeed, the verb to please or delight signifies at the same time to help or be of use, and the two ideas became inseparable in all criticism traced back to Rome. See how sturdily Horace insists upon the twin thoughts:

> Aut prodesse volunt, aut delectare poetæ,
> Aut simul et jucunda et idonea dicere vitæ.

And again, how in one of his neatest and best-known phrases, he steadily keeps in view the need of mingling wisdom with pleasure:

> Omne tulit punctum, qui miscuit utile dulci,
> Lectorem delectando, pariterque monendo.

That the pleasure of art must be profitable.

Scaliger among the moderns faithfully reflects this Roman view, and never refers to the pleasure for which and in which art lives, without limiting the idea of pleasure by associating it with moral discipline and gain. Castelvetro leant more to the Greek view, and put all thought of profit as connected with art in a secondary position. Tasso, however, perfectly caught the spirit of the Latin doctrine; and as he puzzled over the Horatian line in which poets are said to set their hearts either on doing good, or on giving pleasure, he asked himself whether it is possible that art should have two ends, the one of pleasure, and the other of

How Tasso puzzled over the doctrine worthy of particular attention.

CHAPTER V.

profit? He came to the conclusion that art can have only one end in view—pleasure; but that this pleasure must be profitable. The strain of criticism thus originated flows through all modern literature that owns to Italian influence. In one form or another, we come upon it in Spanish, in French, in German writers; and we find it very rife in England during those Elizabethan days when our literature was most open to Italian teaching. Philip Sidney, for example, says that the end of poesy is to teach and delight; while in another passage he adds that to delight "is all the goodfellow poet seems to promise."

How the Italian doctrine is to be understood.

In these Horatian, in these Italian maxims, the true wheat has to be threshed from a great deal of straw, and winnowed from a good deal of chaff. Deep at the root of them lies the conviction which takes possession of every thoughtful mind, that nothing in this world exists for itself, can in the long run be an end to itself, can have an ultimate end in its own good pleasure. In pursuing this line of thought, however, a man soon finds that he is apt to argue in a circle—such a circle as one of our subtlest poets suggests in saying—

Wherein it goes too far.

Sydney Dobell.

> Not well he deems who deems the rose
> Is for the roseberry, nor knows
> The roseberry is for the rose.

So, therefore, when we hear men like Victor Hugo crying aloud in our day that the end of art is not art, but the cause of humanity, we can only answer that there may be a sense in which this is correct enough, as there is also a sense in which science may be said to exist not for itself, but for human advancement; still that we are now talking of immediate ends; and that as the end of science is science, even if we are wholly ignorant of the practical use to which it may hereafter be turned, so the end of art is its own good pleasure, even if we fail to see the direct profit which this pleasure may bring. And thus the laureate sings—

CHAPTER V.

> So, lady Flora, take my lay,
> And if you find no moral there,
> Go, look in any glass and say,
> What moral is in being fair?
> Oh, to what uses shall we put
> The wildweed flower that simply blows?
> And is there any moral shut
> Within the bosom of the rose?

How far it is true.

Again, there is a core of truth in the Horatian maxim that art should be profitable as well as pleasing, since it always holds that wisdom's ways are ways of pleasantness, that enduring pleasure comes only out of healthful action, and that amusement as mere amusement is in its own place good, if it be but innocent. There is profit in art as there is gain in godliness, and policy in an honest life. But we are not to pursue art for profit, nor godliness for gain, nor honesty because it is politic. There are minds, however, so constituted that nothing seems to be profitable to them, except it comes in the form either of knowledge or of

CHAPTER V. direct utility. Those of a didactic turn are fond of dwelling on the idea of poet and artist, to which Bacon refers when he points out that the Greek minstrels were the chief doctors of religion; to which Thomas Occleve bore witness when he saluted Chaucer—"O universal fadre of science;" which Sir Thomas Elyot entertained when he said that poetry was the first philosophy; which Puttenham had in view when he devoted one of his chapters to showing that the poets were not only the first philosophers of the world, but also the first historiographers, orators, and musicians; which Sir John Harington contemplated when he described poetry as "the very first nurse and ancient grandmother of all learning;" which La Mesnardière stuck to when he discovered that Virgil was useful as a teacher of farming, Theocritus for his lessons of economy, and Homer for the knowledge which he displays of wellnigh every handicraft. "Sonate, que me veux tu?" cried Fontenelle, as he heard a symphony, and thought of those who see a deep meaning and a useful purpose in all works of art; but he might have found enthusiasts to answer him, and to show him philosophy in a jig, theology in a fugue, like that sage who discovered the seven days of creation in the seven notes of music. Divines opposed to dancing, from Saint Ambrose to the Rev. John Northbrooke, have yet had much to say in favour of what they call spiritual dancing, such

Some of the absurdities to which it led.

as that of King David; Sir Thomas Elyot discovered all the cardinal virtues in the various figures of a dance; and the dancing-master Noverre treated of his steps as a part of philosophy. These are, of course, vanities on which it is needless to comment. Nor need we waste time on those who apply to art the utilitarian test. The inhabitants of Yarmouth in 1650 begged that Parliament would grant them the lead and other materials "of that vast and altogether useless cathedral in Norwich" towards the building of a workhouse and the repairing of their piers. Thomas Heywood, who has been described as a sort of prose Shakespeare, gave a rather prosaic proof of the utility of the drama from the effect produced by a play acted on the coast of Cornwall. The Spaniards were landing "at a place called Perin," with intent to take the town, when hearing the drums and trumpets of a battle on the stage, they took fright and fled to their boats. When men condescend to talk of the utility and profit of art in this sense, one is reminded of those religions which gave their followers first the pleasure of worshipping the god, and then the advantage of eating him:

> The Egyptian rites the Jebusites embraced,
> When gods were recommended by the taste;
> Such savoury deities must needs be good
> As served at once for worship and for food.

Pleasure an indefinite term very

Once more, pleasure is an indefinite term, which is so often connected in our minds with

CHAPTER V.

forbidden gratifications, that it may be necessary, not in logic, but in practice, to fence it from misapprehension. When we sound the praises of love, it is taken for granted that we mean pure, not unhallowed, passion; when we vaunt the excellence of knowledge, it is understood that we are referring to knowledge which is neither vile nor vain; but pleasure—people are so frightened at pleasure that when we speak of it as the proper end of art, it has to be explained that we are thinking of pleasure which is not improper, and it has to be shown that if art, in the pleasure which it yields, fail to satisfy the moral sense of a people, it is doomed. It may amuse for a little, but it has within itself a worm that gnaws its life out. Be the pleasure however good or bad, lofty or mean, there are some who object to it as such. We have seen how Plato could not away with pleasure, because the gods, whose nature is unchangeable, have no experience of it. Mr. Ruskin is the modern critic who has the strongest objection to pleasure as the end of art. In a lecture delivered at Cambridge he said that all the arts of life end only in death, and all the gifts of man issue only in dishonour, "when they are pursued or possessed in the sense of pleasure only." Since no one thinks of pleasure as the only end of art, it may be supposed that his objection to the doctrine maintained in this chapter is not so strong as it appears to be. In another passage, however, he states his view more distinctly.

Margin notes: apt to be misunderstood. — Ruskin's protest against pleasure as the end of art may be considered here, pleasure being regarded as immoral, and therefore unprofitable.

CHAPTER V.

"This, then, is the great enigma of art history: you must not follow art without pleasure, nor must you follow it for the sake of pleasure." It must be admitted that there is some reason for this objection. Mr. Ruskin has here, in fact, touched on one of the most curious laws of pleasure. It will be found that when we begin to talk of pleasure, at once we fall into seeming inconsistencies and contradictions. It is only by a concession to the exigencies of language that we can speak of pleasure as obtained from any conscious seeking. Not to forestall what has to be said of pleasure in the proper place, it may be enough here to illustrate the present difficulty about it by quoting what Lord Chesterfield says of wit. "If you have real wit," he says, "it will flow spontaneously, and you need not aim at it; for in that case the rule of the Gospel is reversed, and it shall prove, seek and ye shall not find." So pleasure is spontaneous, and comes not of any conscious seeking. But there is such a thing as unconscious seeking; and all great art has in it so little of wary purpose that it does not even pursue pleasure with a perfect and sustained consciousness. If you strive after wit, as Lord Chesterfield says, you will never be witty; and if you hunt after pleasure, as Mr. Ruskin says, you will fail of joy. And yet, after his kind, with what may be called an under-consciousness, the man of wit intends wit, the man of art intends pleasure, and both attain their ends. Mr.

Answered by reference to Lord Chesterfield's saying about wit.

CHAPTER V.

Ruskin himself has defined art as the expression of man's delight in the works of God. Why is delight expressed except for delight? There is not only no objection to saying that art is the expression of delight, but also the statement of that fact is essential to the true conception of art. It is, however, an advance upon the Italian doctrine of pleasure, which will more properly be handled in the sequel, when in the course of travel we come to Germany.

The Spanish school of criticism not very original, but still authoritative.

III. Next in order after the Greek and Italian schools of criticism comes the Spanish, which took its cue mainly from the Italian, and originated little that can be accepted for new. That it should adopt the universal doctrine of criticism, and represent art as made for pleasure, is but natural. Montesquieu put forth a wicked epigram, that the only good book of the Spaniards is that which exposes the absurdity of all the rest. It is unfair, however, because a book like *Don Quixote* is never quite solitary in its excellence; and though the Spaniards have the name of being echoes in art and timid in criticism; though they were fettered by the Inquisition, and got such men among them as Cervantes and Lope de Vega to hug their chains as if they were the jewelled collars and the embroidered garters of some splendid order of chivalry—bound down and ground down, they showed the native force of genius in masterpieces of art which, for their kind, have never been surpassed, and in touches of criticism that still hold good.

It held to the one doctrine.

Now, the Arragonese and Castilian poets, at a very early period, adopted the Provençal conception of poetry as the Gay Science. And not only was that conception of poetry entertained by the Spanish races at a time when they were light of heart, and spoke of their own lightheartedness as an acknowledged fact; they kept it when, to all the world, and to themselves, they grew sombre, grave and grandiose. A Spanish Jew of the fifteenth century, even if he were a converted one, is not the sort of person whom one would select as the type of joyousness, and the expounder of the gay art. Juan de Baena, a baptized Jew, secretary and accountant to King John II. and a poet of some mark, published a famous Cancionero, or collection of the poets, in the preface to which he has never enough to say of the delightfulness and charm of poetry. He mingles this view, it is true, with some stiff notions, as that the poet who can produce so much pleasure must be high-born, and must be inspired of God, but his idea throughout is, that the art is for pleasure. Other Spanish critics follow in the same track, as Luzan, who, however, takes most of his ideas on criticism from the Italians. He refers at considerable length to the Italian discussion as to the end of poetry—is it pleasure? is it profit? is it both? and if both, how can any

CHAPTER V.

art have two ends of co-ordinate value? Like the Italians, he came to the conclusion that the two ends must be identified—that the pleasure must profit, and that the profit must please.

But it had its own special view.

But the Spaniards had their own point of view just as the Greeks and the Italians had theirs. The Greeks raised a question as to the truth of the pleasure created by art; the Italians raised a question as to its profitableness; and these two inquiries practically exhausted all discussion as to the morality of poetry and art. The Spaniards raised another question, which is more purely a critical one. Art is for pleasure, but whose pleasure? Not that this question had been wholly overlooked by the Italians. On the contrary, some of the French critics, that in the days of the Fronde and of the Grand Monarch buzzed about the Hôtel Rambouillet, were wild and withering in the sarcasms which they poured on the poor old Italian, Castelvetro, for venturing to assert that poetry is to delight and solace the multitude. But the Spaniards, having a noble ballad literature that lived amongst the people, and was thoroughly appreciated by them, were prepared to maintain a similar doctrine more strenuously—a doctrine the very opposite of that which would describe art as caviare to the general, and confine the enjoyment of it to the fit and few.

That art is for the people.

Gonzalo de Berceo is the first known of Spanish poets. There were poets before him,

CHAPTER V.

but their works are anonymous. He lived in the thirteenth century, and he begins one of his tales in this characteristic manner:—"In the name of the Father, who made all things, and of our Lord Jesus Christ, son of the glorious Virgin, and of the Holy Spirit, who is equal with them, I intend to tell a story of a holy confessor. I intend to tell a story in the plain Romance in which the common man is wont to talk with his neighbour; for I am not so learned as to use the other Latin. It will be well worth, as I think, a cup of good wine." What the unlearned Gonzalo thus simply expressed, Cervantes and Lope de Vega, some three centuries later, uttered with more critical precision. The view of Cervantes will be found in *Don Quixote* in those two chapters in which the canon and the priest discourse together on the tales of chivalry, and on fiction generally. They complain that the tales of chivalry, intended to give pleasure, have an evil effect in ministering to bad taste. But the canon, who has no mean opinion of the approbation of the few as opposed to the many, tells us distinctly that the corruption of Spanish art, which, he laments, is not to be attributed to the bad taste of the common people, who delight in the meaner pleasures. "Do you not remember," he says, "that a few, years since, three tragedies were produced which were universally admired, which delighted both the ignorant and the wise, both the vulgar and the refined; and that by those three pieces

How this doctrine showed itself in Berceo, in Cervantes, and in Lope de Vega.

How Cervantes discussed it in *Don Quixote*.

CHAPTER V.

the players gained more than by thirty of the best which have since been represented." His hearer admits the fact. "Pray, then, recollect," returns the canon, "that they were thus successful, though they conformed to the rules of high art; and, therefore, it cannot be said that the blame of pursuing low art is to be ascribed to the lowness of the vulgar taste."

Lope de Vega.

Lope de Vega, however, was still bolder than Cervantes. It will be observed that, according to Cervantes, you must follow the recognised rules of high art, and you may be quite sure that they will please the people; but in the chapter from which I am quoting (the 48th), while he bestows the highest praise on Lope de Vega, he expresses a regret, that, in order to please the public, he had yielded to the demands of a depraved taste, and had swerved from the rules of art. Lope's conception of his duty is the converse of this, and is quite logical. "Tales have the same rules with dramas, the purpose of whose authors is to content and please the public, though the rules of art may be strangled thereby." Terence propounded a like doctrine in the prologues of two of his plays. In the prologue to the *Andria* he reminds his audience that when the poet first took to writing he believed that his only business was to please the people; and in that to the *Eunuch*, he says, that if there be any one who strives to please as many, and to offend as few good men as possible, it is the poet. But

The same view expressed by Terence.

Terence was merely a comedian, and Lope de Vega is, to the best of my knowledge, the first serious writer who stated ruthlessly the doctrine of pleasure with all its logical consequences. He has been well backed, however, both by comic and serious writers. Molière, when his *School for Wives* was attacked, and proved to be against the rules, wrote a little piece in defence of it in which he entrusts his cause to the logic of a certain Durante. One great point in Durante's pleading is expressed as follows:—"I should like much to know whether the grand rule of all rules be not to please, and whether a stage piece that has gained this end has not taken the right way. Will you have it that the public are astray, and are not fit to judge of their own pleasure?" In English we have expressed the same view in the well-known couplet of Johnson's—

CHAPTER V.

By Molière.

By Johnson.

> The drama's laws, the drama's patrons give,
> And those who live to please, must please to live.

There is a difficult question here involved. It is indeed the first difficult question that meets the critic. Tasso played with it a little. He saw that the end of poetry is to please; he saw also that to the Italians the romances of Ariosto and other poets gave greater pleasure than the epics of Homer; and putting these two facts together, he saw an inference before him, from which he shrank back in dismay. It was left for the French critics to sound the abysses of such an inference, and to turn it to account as a

A difficult question here involved.

CHAPTER V.

critical warning. In the meantime the Spanish writers scarcely see the difficulty that lies ahead, and are content to insist on the wisdom of pleasing the multitude. Cervantes says, Please the multitude, but you must please them by rule. Lope de Vega says, Please the multitude even if you defy the rules.

An opposite doctrine supposed to have been held by Milton.

The view thus set forth invites misapprehension, but it has not a little to say for itself. Never have words of such innocent meaning had such baneful effects upon literature as those in which (if I may be allowed to anticipate) Milton expressed his hope that he would fit audience find though few. It might be all well for Milton who had fallen, as he himself expresses it, on evil days and evil tongues, who lived almost as an outcast from society, who saw around him universal irreligion and unblushing licence, to hint a fear that he might not command an audience attuned to his sacred theme, and ready to soar with him to heavenly heights; but his example will not justify those who would wrest his words into a defence of narrow art—of art that fit audience finds though few, or, as we might otherwise phrase it, in an opposite sense, that fit welcome finds though small. If the effect of Milton's phrase were simply to soothe the feelings of the disappointed poets who write what nobody will read, it would be a pity to deprive them of such comfort; but the fact is, that poets of rare ability often in our bookish times brood over the same idea, content themselves with a small audience, adapt themselves to the requirements of a coterie, and in imagination make up for the scantiness of present recognition by the abundance of the future fame which they expect. It may be remembered that Wordsworth, in a celebrated preface, enters into elaborate antiquarian researches, to show that the neglect which he suffered from his contemporaries was only what a great poet might expect, and that the most palpable stamp of a great poem is its falling flat upon the world to be picked up and recognised only by the fit and few.

And certainly held by Wordsworth.

Now, in art, the two seldom go together; the fit are not few, and the few are not fit. The true judges of art are the much despised many—the crowd—and no critic is worth his salt who does not feel with the many. There are, no doubt, questions of criticism which only few can answer; but the enjoyment of art is for all; and just as in eloquence, the great orator is he who commands the people, so in poetry, so in art, the great poet, the great artist will command high and low alike. Great poetry was ever meant, and to the end of time must be adapted, not to the curious student, but for the multitude who read while they run—for the crowd in the street, for the boards of huge theatres, and for the choirs of vast cathedrals, for an army marching tumultuous to the battle, and for an assembled

On the fit and few as judges of art.

CHAPTER V.

nation silent over the tomb of its mightiest. It is intended for a great audience, not for individual readers. So Homer sang to well greaved listeners from court to court; so Æschylus, Sophocles, and Euripides wrote for the Athenian populace; so Pindar chanted for the mob that fluttered around the Olympian racecourse.

Does a printed as distinguished from a written literature, make any difference?

The discovery of the alphabet and the invention of printing have wrought some changes. A read is different from a heard literature, but the change is not essential. In modern, as compared with ancient literature, we find Dante compelling the attention of every house in Italy, by describing its founders in hell fire; we find Tasso writing verses that are still sung by the gondoliers of Venice; we find Chaucer pitching his tale for the travellers who bustle through the yard of an inn; we find Shakespeare doing all in his power to fill the Globe Theatre; we find our own laureate sending forth a volume that sells by the myriad, by the myriad to be judged. Few English critics have been more fastidious than Johnson, and yet what was his opinion as to the pleasure which Shakespeare created? "Let him who is yet unacquainted with the powers of Shakespeare," he says, "and who desires to feel the highest pleasure that the drama can give, read every play from the first scene to the last with utter negligence of all his commentators. When his fancy is once on the wing, let him not stop at correction or explanation. Let him read on through brightness and obscurity, through integrity and corruption; let him preserve his comprehension of the dialogue, and his interest in the fable; and when the pleasures of novelty have ceased, let him attempt exactness, and read the commentators." In a word, the highest pleasure which the drama can give is a pleasure within reach of the many, and belongs to them without the help or the wisdom of the learned few.

The democratic doctrine of art will be displeasing to some.

There is an aristocracy of taste to which such conclusions as these will be repugnant. And at first sight, indeed, it appears odd that an aristocratic people like the Spaniards should thus frankly accept a low-levelling democratic doctrine of taste—should regard the domain of letters as essentially a republic; while on the other hand, as we shall presently see, the French who are now known to us as the most democratic people in Europe, established the theory of art as caviare to the general. The truth is, that the French theory of art was established by the French noblesse and courtiers when the people were among the most downtrodden in Christendom, and had no rights that were respected; while again the Spanish idea of art arose among a race whose very peasantry had some ancestral pride, were, so to speak, but a lower rank of peers, and were divided by no impassable gulf from the haughtiest Don. Those

Expressed by saying that all great art is gregarious.

who dislike the republican tinge of the Spanish view may see, at least, this much truth in it—that all great art is gregarious. The great artist is never as one crying solitary in the wilderness; he comes in a troop; he comes in constellations. He is surrounded by Paladins, that with him make the age illustrious. He belongs to his time, and his time produces many, who if not great as he, are yet like him. Nothing is more marked in history than the phenomenon of seasons of excellence and ages of renown. Witness the eras of Pericles, Augustus, the Medici, Elizabeth, and others. What means this clustering, this companionship of art, unless that essentially the inspiration which produces it is not individual but general, is common to the country and to the time, is a national possession? And how again can this be if the pleasure of art is not in the people, and the standard by which it is to be judged is not in their hearts? In one word, the pleasure of art is a popular pleasure.

The French school of criticism.

IV. It would be too much, however, to say that the Spanish view of art is in itself complete. There is another side of the question to which justice must be done before we can have this theory of poetic pleasure well balanced. What the Spanish critics want in this respect, the French critics supply. The French, like other schools of criticism, had their own special

CHAPTER V.

views, but for the most part they held firmly to pleasure as in one form or another the end of art. Those who made any doubt about it, as Father Rapin, did so chiefly on the score of religion, which in their eyes made light of all earthly pleasure. Rapin allows delight to be the end of poetry, but he will not hear of it as the chief end, because by that phrase he understands—the public weal which all human arts ought to look to as their highest work. It is scarcely needful to say that here is but a mistake of terms. Father Rapin is thinking of ultimate ends, whereas those who dwell on pleasure as the chief end of art, have no thought but of its immediate object. The strongest statement of what that object is, I have already given from one of Molière's plays. If French critics did not commonly advance the doctrine of pleasure with like fearlessness of logic, still they accepted it freely. In the tempest of discussion which rose on the publication of Corneille's drama of the *Cid*, one of his defenders who professed to be but a simple burgess of Paris and churchwarden of his parish took his stand on this simple principle: "I have never read Aristotle, and I know not the rules of the theatre, but I weigh the merit of the pieces according to the pleasure which they give me." La Motte said, without mincing, that poetry has no other end than to please, and La Harpe taking note of this, declares, "If he had said that to please is its

Accepts the universal doctrine.

CHAPTER V.

chief end, I should have been entirely of his mind." There is no limit to the quotations from French criticism which might be made in the same sense. It may be enough to summon Marmontel, who puts the case as follows: "L'intention immédiate du poëte est de plaire et d'interesser en imitant." All the critics have their little varieties of statement that go to limit the sort of pleasure which art seeks. One says that it is a pleasure excited by imitation, another that it is a pleasure which leads to profit; but one and all seize on the idea of pleasure as the purpose of art.

The peculiarity of French criticism.

What is most peculiar to French criticism received its impulse from the revolution wrought in French literature at the beginning of the seventeenth century. It is a revolution, the converse of that which overthrew French society towards the close of the eighteenth: and for that very reason, indeed, the two revolutions are intimately related. That which gave a new turn to French literature in the days of the earlier Bourbons, was led by the most brilliant bevy of bluestockings that ever lived, whose ways and works, whose very names are almost unknown in this country. How many Englishmen know who was Salmis, or Sarraïde or Sophie; who was the brilliant Arthenice; who the gracious Sophronie; who the charming Féliciane; who was Nidalie, or Stratonice, or Célie, or the rare Virginie; who can tell where was the

Began to show itself in the early days of the Bourbons.

palace of Rozelinde, and the bower of Zyrphée? Arthenice was the poetical name of Madame de Rambouillet,* whose residence, known as the palace of Rozelinde, with a certain famous hall in it, known as the blue room, and another as the bower of Zyrphée, was the chief haunt of those bright ladies, whom we should call blue-stockings, and who under an Italian princess, Marie de Medici, and a Spanish one, Anne of Austria, introduced refinement into France.

Picture of France on the death Henry IV.

When, in 1610, Henry IV. died, and the child Louis XIII. began to reign, there was no want of greatness in the country. There was a superabundance of force in the French nation that showed itself in great soldiers, great statesmen, great thinkers. But taste was wholly wanting. Manners needed refinement and literature the regulation of taste. Of the grossness of French manners in those days it is difficult to give in few words an adequate idea. The most simple method of conveying an impression of it to English readers is to refer them to the earlier portion of the preceding century, of which they have some inkling through the not unknown

The utter want of refinement.

* The names of the others run as follows: Salmis was Mademoiselle de Sully; Sarraïde and Sophie were Madame and Mademoiselle Scudery; Sophronie was Madame de Sevigné; Féliciane was Madame de la Fayette; Nidalie was Ninon de Lenclos; Stratonice was Madame Scarron; Célie was Madame de Choisy; and Virginie was Madame de Vilaine. Generally the names were so chosen that the initial of the fictitious should correspond with that of the real name.

CHAPTER V.

Illustrated by reference to the preceding century.

writings of Rabelais and of Margaret of Angoulême; the one rector of Meudon, the other Queen of Navarre, and sister of Francis I. Priest and Queen wallowed in filth, and strange to say, they did not seem to know it. The more indecent writers of the English school are thoroughly conscious of their trespasses, and take good care to show that they regard superfluity of naughtiness as a sign of spirit. But the Queen of Navarre and the priest of Meudon indulged in their coarseness with such an air of simpleness, that the most outrageous disclosures, and the most hideous obscenity, seemed to come as a matter of course, and to be all perfectly right. Priest as he was, Rabelais had no self-reproach, and gets the credit of being a great moral thinker, at heart earnest and eager for reforms. As for the Queen of Navarre, she passed for a Lutheran, she delighted in the Bible, she loved to compose spiritual songs. Brantôme says that her heart was very much turned to God; and in token thereof she chose for her device a marigold, that ever turns to the sun. If those who, like Rabelais, were great moral thinkers, and those who, like the Queen of Navarre, mayhap, turned their hearts to heavenly things, and certainly represented the highest society, were unutterably gross, and indeed bestial, in their plainspeaking, what are we to imagine of the lightheaded and the bad? It is enough to say, that when Henry IV. died, the French were, while abounding in all brilliance and force, the most vicious and worst behaved nation in Europe. Their language showed none of that rare taste for which it has since become renowned; it was loose in every sense—loose for the lack of grammar, loose for the lack of modesty.

At Henry's death the worst behaved nation in Europe.

But the nation, sound at heart, and rejoicing in its strength, was ripe for a reform, and reform came from Italy. To the Italians belong the credit of inspiring the French with taste in cookery, in manners, and in criticism. When Henry died, his widow, of the Florentine house of Medici, was left regent of the kingdom. It was under, though not through her, that the reform began. Strictly speaking, it can never be right to describe a social revolution as the work of one mind, but it may be safe to say that the reform of which we speak made its first appearance and had its head-quarters in the Hôtel, or as it was then written, the Hostel of Catherine de Vivonne, Marchioness of Rambouillet.

But sound at heart, and ripe for reform.

Reform came from Italy.

This lady, whose baptismal name was transformed by her admirers into Arthenice, by which she is best known in French literature, was the daughter of Jean de Vivonne, Marquis of Pisani, who held great place at the court of the Tuileries, and who, at the age of three-score and three, had married a Roman lady of illustrious birth, Giulia Savelli. Three years after

Catherine de Vivonne.

CHAPTER V.

Her education.

their marriage, a daughter, Arthenice, that is, Catherine, was born at Rome, and there, for some time, brought up. When in her eighth year she came with her Italian mother to France, the Marquis of Pisani was tutor to a little boy of her own age, the son of the Prince of Condé. Catherine de Vivonne, carefully trained by her mother, took part in the games of this little prince, who was carefully trained by her father. So much strictness was observed in the education of these young people, that when the Prince, at the age of eight, ventured to kiss Mademoiselle de Vivonne, of the same age, the Marquis thrashed him for it soundly. When in her twelfth year the little lady espoused the Marquis of Rambouillet, she soon found that the manners and customs of the French court were too gross to be endured, and she chose to withdraw from it as much as possible. But she knew how to entertain brilliantly, and by degrees she drew her friends about her to the Hôtel Rambouillet. In a celebrated blue chamber there she held assemblies, into which princes and princesses of the blood were glad to be admitted, and which outshone in brilliancy of wit and refinement of manner, if not in wealth and in numbers, the great gatherings of the court.* To the blue

And how she became mistress of the Hôtel Rambouillet.

* Les premiers visiteurs lettrés de l'hôtel de Rambouillet furent: Malherbe, Gombaud, Racan, dès l'origine; peu après Balzac, Chapelain, et Voiture, qui avoit assez de fortune pour figurer parmi la noblesse, et trop d'esprit, disoit M. de Chaudebonne, pour

chamber of the Marchioness flocked a dainty troop of bluestockings, aiming at refinement—refinement of manner, refinement of taste, refinement of speech. The gold of society had to be cleared of its dross, and their society was to present in its pureness all that was precious in the metal. These purists accordingly came to be called Precious, and the refinements which they favoured Preciosity.

CHAPTER V.

Origin of the Précieuses.

On mistakes committed about them.

Very few Englishmen, and not many Frenchmen, ever think of the sayings and doings of those who haunted the blue chamber and the lodge of Zyrphée, in the Hôtel Rambouillet, as worthy of admiration. To talk of a Précieuse is to kindle their mirth. It is because they have in their minds the witty play in which Molière made his first great hit, and in which he exposed the follies, not of the Précieuses, but of

rester dans la bourgeoisie. Présenté à la Marquise, "réengendré par elle et M. de Chaudebonne," Voiture devint *l'âme du rond.* Il y trouva Vaugelas, puis le jeune évêque de Luçon, qui se plaisoit, dans les loisirs de son épiscopat, à y soutenir des thèses d'amour. Là encore brilloient la princesse de Condé, Mlle. de Scudéry, la marquise de Sablé; plus tard, la duchesse de Longueville, Mme. d' Adington, depuis comtesse de la Suze; la femme de Scudéry; Costar, si dévoué à Voiture, qui se moquoit de lui; Sarasin, Conrart, Mairet, Patru, Godeau, Pierre Corneille, Rotrou, Benserade, Saint-Evremont, Charleval, Ménage, La Rochefoucauld, Bossuet, Fléchier, et enfin, le galant marquis de la Salle, chansonnier accompli, improvisateur fécond, dont on a tant assombri l'image pour en faire l'austère duc de Montausier, et dont nous ne voyons plus les traits, à tout âge, que sous le masque du Misanthrope.—From M. Livet's Preface to the *Dictionnaire des Précieuses* of Somaize.

CHAPTER V.

Molière and his real object with regard to them.

the *Précieuses Ridicules*, who at the third, fourth, fifth hand, attempted an imitation, and achieved a burlesque of the true blues. The true Précieuses were of the best blood, the highestb reeding in France; the ridiculous ones whom Molière shot at were the city dames and the country hoydens, who aped the manners of the great, and who made themselves ridiculous, both by pretending to habits which were above their reach, and by a caricature of the habits which really existed in the upper ranks. It must be remembered that Molière came forth with his banter when Madame de Rambouillet was over seventy years of age, and when amid the sorrows and infirmities of her approaching end she was no longer able to hold her court in the blue chamber. She had done her work; noble ladies of the lesser houses followed in her wake, tried to imitate her, and passed on the desire of imitation to lower and lower ranks in the social scale, till burgesses and upstarts caught the infection, and limped in the footsteps of the great original.

The false Précieuses whom Molière ridiculed.

When Molière laughed at this limping gait, none more heartily applauded him than the fine old lady whose heart was with the dead; and all that bright society which used to gather to her call joined in singing his praises. His satire, however, was so pungent, so amusing, so directly levelled against a weakness of French taste, that whereas it professed only to strike at the absurdities of the upstarts, in the end it glanced off, and hit the true blues, so that whatever they failed in lives a jest, and all the silliness of low-bred imitation and mock-purity cleaves to their memory. What they actually achieved is little known, because it has passed into French literature, and become part and parcel of it. They made the French taste—that taste which still inherits the weakness derided by Molière. It is because that weakness is an essential part of the French taste that the satire which the comedian brought to bear on it is to this day relished as much as ever, and as special criticism never is relished two hundred years after the occasion which called it forth has passed away. The bluestockings of the Hôtel Rambouillet made the French taste, I repeat, so that thenceforward, until the Deluge of '89 introduced a new order of things, the leading characteristic of French art and literature, and all things French, was Preciosity. The two greatest thinkers whom France has produced, Descartes and Pascal, were formed before the Precious had reached the height of their power; but one can trace in the refinement of their style some of the Precious influences that were, so to speak, in the air; and as for later writers, even when like Boileau, they made a show of resistance to the over-delicacies of the new school; or when, like Molière, they get the credit of entirely exploding it; or when, like Bossuet, they soar above mere tastefulness into grandeur; in one

The real Précieuses made the French taste.

And live to this day.

CHAPTER V.

and all we can detect a certain purism, a touch as of the precisian which marks them as essentially Precious.

The clue to French art and criticism.

The moment we feel at home in the blue room of the Hôtel Rambouillet we get the clue to French art and criticism. It was here that the theory of the fit and few—the caviare theory of art—first grew into importance, and became a power in criticism. Anyone who has but a smattering of French history will know of how small account up to the time of the great revolution were the people and all popular belongings. The people were nought; the aristocracy all in all; and it was but a matter of course that the new movement should go to establish an aristocracy of taste as distinct from, and infinitely superior to, popularity of taste. The more extreme of the French purists were aghast to find Boileau, notwithstanding his purism, speak of the belly of a pitcher; and they were amazed that, without loss of dignity, Racine, himself a visitant of the blue room, could, in referring to Jezebel, make mention of the dogs that licked her blood. What would they say to Homer with his lowly similes about peas and beans, and his homely picture of Achilles roasting a steak upon the fire? La Harpe and other critics of his school made it their chief accusation against Shakespeare that he sacrificed to the rabble. Certainly the French poets could not be charged with this fault. They showed so little regard

French purism, its origin

for popular taste, that Madame de Stael passed this just judgment on them: "La poésie Française étant la plus classique de toutes les poésies modernes, elle est la seule qui ne soit pas répandue parmi le peuple." It stands alone in this respect. It has nothing that can stand a comparison with the ballads of Spain, with those of England and Scotland, with the polished strains that are familiar to every Italian beggar, with the folksongs of Germany. It would be amusing to hear what a French critic, with all the blue and gold of Versailles in the chambers of his heart, would say to the master singers of Nuremberg and other chief towns of Almayne in the middle ages; to the honest cobblers that, like Hans Sachs, were powerful in honied words as well as in waxed threads; to the masons that built the lofty rhyme; to tailors that sang like swans while they plied the goose; to smiths that filed verses not less than iron tools; to barbers that carolled cheerily while as yet the music of Figaro slept far from its rise in the unborn brain of Mozart, and while as yet, indeed, music, in the modern sense of the word, had not even glimmered in the firmament of human thought. It is in a state of savage revolt against the ancient priggishness of French criticism that Victor Hugo now proclaims himself the admirer of genius, even when it stoops to folly and meanness. For me, he says, I admire all, be it beauty or blur, like a very brute, and it seems to

And singularity.

Hugo's revolt against it.

CHAPTER V.

me that our age—he ought to have added our nation—needed such an example of barbaric enthusiasm and utter childishness.

La Mesnardière.

Jules de la Mesnardière, physician, poet, and critic, was one of the most remarkable of the men of letters who danced attendance in the saloons of the Marchioness of Rambouillet. He published the earliest work of systematic criticism of the new school, a book called *La Poétique*, which is very scarce, and which, from a phrase of Bayle's, it would se m that even in his time it was difficult to get.* But La Mesnardière was a great man with the Précieuses, and what he has to say of the dominion of pleasure in art has the perfect tint of azure. I might quote others of that brilliant coterie who are better known; as Georges de Scudéry, whose sister's name has become proverbial for romances of the bluest blue, and who himself had among the assemblies of the elect no mean name as a poet and a critical authority. Scudery's statement of the precious doctrine of pleasure will be found in the preface to that grand epic bug—his poem of Alaric. But La Mesnardière was before him, and stated the case in the more formal manner of a systematic treatise. It has been already intimated that La Mesnardière is one of those who insist very much on the uses of art, and

A great man with the Précieuses.

* It is not to be found in the British Museum, it is not mentioned in the first edition of Brunet, and I believe that only one copy exists in England besides my own.

CHAPTER V.

never like to speak of its pleasure apart from profit. But beyond this, he maintains, what now more nearly touches our argument, that the pleasure which art aims at is never that of the many. He runs foul of Castelvetro for suggesting the contrary, and heaps terms of contempt on the rude, the low, the ignorant, the stupid mob—a many-headed monster, whom it is a farce to think of pleasing with the delicacies of art. No, he says, it is kings, and lords, and fine ladies, and philosophers, and men of learning that the artist is to please. Who but princes can get a lesson from the story of kings? who but ministers of state from the fall of rulers? What is Clytemnestra to the vulgar herd? Tragedy is of no good but to great souls—great by birth, by office, or by education. Art in a word is only for the Precious few,—for fine ladies and gentlemen, for those who, whether literally or metaphorically, may be said to wear the blue riband.

His criticism.

If the views of the Precious school as represented by La Mesnardière seem to be expressed with rare absurdity, they nevertheless open some questions which are worth attending to, and which are not easily answered. After we have reached the point of critical analysis which the Spanish dramatists came to when they propounded a doctrine in art, the equivalent of that in politics which Bentham made so much of —the necessity of studying the greatest pleasure

Absurd, but not to be despised.

CHAPTER V.

of the greatest number, we are quickly thrown back upon an inevitable tendency of human nature to define and square the standard of pleasure. If pleasure is an enviable thing, it is also very envious—envious even of itself, and lives by comparison. Pleasure varies—it differs in different men, and in the same men at different times. Notwithstanding this diversity, which is well known, men are ever bent on finding something that will act as a sort of thermometer or joy-measure; and so the Spartan ruler decreed that no harp should have more than seven strings, the French critics cried aloud for a proper observance of the three unities, and purists in architecture stood out for the five orders. What is to be said in presence of such a fact as Tasso encountered in his critical analysis—that the romances of Ariosto gave more pleasure to his countrymen than the epics of Homer and Virgil? Is Ariosto, therefore, the greater artist? Tasso very quickly settled that question for himself: it did not trouble him. But this was precisely the sort of question that troubled the French critics most, and which lay at the root of La Mesnardière's objection to consulting the pleasure of the commonalty. Your highly educated persons—your true blues—might be able to appreciate the classics, to get the full quantity of pleasure from them—a pleasure which need not shun comparison or competition with the pleasure

On varieties of taste.

And critical questions thence arising.

afforded by the lower art of the moderns. But put the same comparison before the uneducated, and inevitably antique art will be sent to the right-about. They do not understand the ancients; they do understand the moderns. The former kindle no pleasure at all, or but a few faint sparks; the latter give a great blaze of pleasure. And it therefore appears that if art is to be measured by the amount of enjoyment thus evolved in rude minds, all our most approved critical judgments would be upset. So La Mesnardière held lustily to his point, that if pleasure be the aim of poetry and art, it must be the pleasure of those who wear the blue riband and are free of the blue chamber. He was easily able to satisfy himself, but had he pushed his inquiries further he would have found the same difficulty confronting him in another shape. In that shape the difficulty has so staggered another Frenchman, M. Victor Cousin, that he refuses to acknowledge in pleasure the immediate end of art. He argues that if pleasure be the end of art, then the more or less of pleasure which an art affords should be the standard of its value, and that in such a case music with its ravishing strains should, in spite of its vagueness, stand at the head of the arts. But this, according to Cousin, lands us in an absurdity that reflects upon the soundness of the principle from which we set out.

How La Mesnardière urged these questions.

And in the present day M. Cousin.

Although we may not be able to adopt the

CHAPTER V.

These objections legitimate.

conclusions either of La Mesnardière or of Cousin, still their objections are taken from a legitimate point of view, and ought to throw some additional light upon the quality of art pleasure. Now the chief thing to be noted here is that the standard of pleasure is within us, and that therefore it varies, to some extent, with the circumstances of each individual. We can never measure it exactly as we can heat with a thermometer. Sometimes a man feels cold when the thermometer tells him it is a warm day, and sometimes a man derives little pleasure from a work of art which throws all his friends into rapture. There is no escaping from these variations of critical judgment, whatever standard of comparison we apply to art. It is impossible to measure art by the foot-rule, to weigh it in a balance with the pound troy, or to deal it forth in gallons. But though the results of art are not reducible to number, and there is no known method of judgment by which we can arrive at perfect accuracy and unanimity, still there is a sort of rough judgment formed, which is as trustworthy as our common judgments on the temperature of the air. Nor is there any need of greater accuracy. We should gain nothing by being able to say that this artist is so many inches taller than that, or that one art gives so many more gallons of pleasure than another.

Statement of the question.

But granting that perfect accuracy is out of the question, La Mesnardière comes in here with his suggestion: Is your standard accurate enough to show that Homer, who gives less pleasure than Ariosto, is a greater artist? and M. Cousin chimes in with the question: Is your standard capable of showing that music, which gives the most exquisite thrills of enjoyment, is yet on account of its vagueness a lower form of art than the drama, which is more articulate? These two questions are identical in substance, though there may be some difficulty in granting to M. Cousin the facts upon which his form of query proceeds. Those who are best able to judge of such compositions as the ninth symphony of Beethoven, or the C minor, will not grant that as works of art they are to be placed below any human performance. Mr. J. W. Davison, than whom no one is better able to make the comparison, assures me that, judge he never so calmly, he cannot accord to Beethoven a rank in art below that of Shakespeare; and one of our ablest thinkers, Mr. Herbert Spencer, declares, at the end of an elaborate essay devoted to prove it, that music must take rank as the highest of the fine arts—as the one which, more than any other, ministers to human welfare. After these testimonies, there may be some difficulty, I say, in granting to M. Cousin his facts. For the sake of argument, however, let it be granted that music, as the least expressive, is the lowest form of art. How are we to reconcile this supposition with the fact that it gives

But an objection to be urged to M. Cousin's form of it.

CHAPTER V.

a keener pleasure than any art? or, to return to La Mesnardière, how are we to reconcile the greatness of the ancients with the superiority of the pleasure which our more familiar modern poets yield?

Answer to M. Cousin.

Drawn from his own opinion regarding science.

One might reply to the argument of M. Cousin by a parallel argument, which would be good as against him, at least. Thus, if the end of art is pleasure, the end of science is knowledge. That, then, is the king of the sciences, it may be argued, which gives us the most knowledge and the clearest. But metaphysics has always hitherto held the place of honour among the sciences; it certainly holds that place in M. Cousin's regard, and considering the grandeur of its ambition, many thoughtful men will be inclined to concede its claim to the honour. Undoubtedly, therefore, it must be the clearest, the best, and the most certain of the sciences. Is it so? Is it not well-nigh the direct opposite of this? In that sense, is there no absurdity in speaking of knowledge as the end of science, when the grandest of all the sciences gives us the least certain knowledge? Pursuing the line of argument of which M. Cousin has set the example, I might urge that science must have some other more dominant end than knowledge, such, perhaps, as that which Lessing indicated when, in reply to Goeze, he said that it is not truth, but the striving after truth, which is the glory of man; that if God in his right hand held every truth, and in his left but this one thing, the thirst for truth, albeit mixed up with the chances of continual error; and that if he bade the child of earth take his choice, he, Lessing, would humbly reach to the left hand, saying, "O Father, give me that, pure truth is for thee alone." If metaphysics be entitled to the crown of the sciences, it is not because of the amplitude of the knowledge which it conveys, but because of its dignity. And so if we are to make comparisons between art and art (a thing in itself as useless as it would be to run comparisons between science and science), we have it in our power to say that the intensity of the pleasure produced by an art is not always the standard of its value. The prolongation of intense enjoyment is sometimes a positive pain, and to procure a lasting pleasure, we must descend to a lower level. To use the language of geometry, pleasure has two dimensions, length as well as height. Increase the height, you cut short the length; increase the length, you lessen the height. The sum of enjoyment is not to be measured by the height alone of its transports. It is impossible to adjust exactly the comparison which M. Cousin suggests between pleasure and pleasure; but there is no reason to suppose that, fairly balanced, the pleasure produced by the most expressive art, which is the drama, is one whit inferior, is not rather superior to the pleasure awakened by the least expressive, which is music. Sir Joshua Reynolds, for one, was quite

CHAPTER V.

willing to accept the standard of merit which M. Cousin objects to. He commences his fourth discourse with these very words:—"The value and rank of every art is in proportion to the mental labour employed on it, or the mental pleasure produced by it."

The objection, however, deserves a more direct reply.

That is a sufficient answer to M. Cousin personally, but further consideration of his argument must be included in what I have now to say of La Mesnardière and other critics. Hitherto I have made the case turn on the comparison suggested by Tasso, between the pleasure which Homer or Virgil awakens, and that which Ariosto stirs in the breast of an Italian. But as that comparison is complicated by the fact of Homer writing in a language foreign to the Italian, let us change the illustration. Let us take Milton, who has been said to equal both Homer and Virgil combined. There is a celebrated sentence of Johnson's, that much as we admire the *Paradise Lost*, when we lay it down we forget to take it up again. We prefer the pleasure of a novel. Is the novel, therefore, a more successful work of art? Or take the question as put by La Mesnardière. The great mass of the people like nothing so well as buffooneries. What can they know of the true pleasure of art who stoop to the lower pleasures of farce and frivolity?

Here it must be observed that our feeling and choice of delight is perfectly distinct from

CHAPTER V.

Our sense of delight is distinct from our estimate of it.

our opinion of it. In the pleasure of the palate there is a good example. A friend tells me that he never enjoyed any food so much as a barley bannock and some milk, which once, when he lost himself in childhood among the Ross-shire hills, and became faint with hunger, he got from some quarrymen who were eating their simple dinner, and kindly offered him a share. Does he therefore say that a barley bannock and milk is the most enjoyable food? It gave him, famished as he was, the utmost enjoyment, and he remembers that meal with the poor quarry-men, and their great sandy fingers, as it were a banquet of the gods; but to enjoy it equally again, he must be again in the same plight, with the simple tastes of childhood. We learn thus instinctively to separate our estimate of what is pleasurable from the choice which the accidents of time, place, or health impose upon us. The man who, stretched upon a knoll with his gun by his side, calls for a draught of bitter beer from the pannier that carries the luncheon, knows right well that though this be the beverage which for the moment he prefers, there are liquids beyond it in taste. There is nothing to puzzle one in this, and neither is there any real puzzle in the case of a man who takes up a novel in preference to a great epic. The deliberate selection of the lower form of pleasure does not interfere with our estimate of the higher.

An example drawn from the sense of taste.

CHAPTER V.

Another from the pleasure of sadness.

Or take another example from the state of mind which is clearly described in the following quatrain:—

> Go, you may call it madness, folly,
> You shall not chase my gloom away;
> There's such a charm in melancholy,
> I would not if I could be gay.

The man is happy in his way, and clings to his melancholy mood—

> That sweet mood when pleasant thoughts
> Bring sad thoughts to the mind,

while he recognises the existence of a livelier joy which is not for him.

Application of these examples to the argument.

The bearing of these facts must be obvious. The critic is apt to denounce a partiality for the lower forms of art, either as on the one hand betokening depravity of taste, or on the other hand rendering null the standard of pleasure. The case is precisely parallel to that of the man who, in the midst of his shooting, asks for bitter beer when he might be drinking, if he chose, the finest Château Margaux. It cannot be said that his taste is depraved, neither can it be said that the superiority of rare claret over beer is not meted, even in his mind who quaffs the beer, by a standard of pleasure.

The ideal of pleasure as distinct from the reality.

The fact is that we all cherish an ideal of pleasure which is not always the real joy of the moment. It is a commonplace of moralists that man never is, but always to be blest. He has an ideal bliss before him, of which sometimes even his highest actual joys seem to fall short.

The mind thus forms an estimate of pleasures of which it does not partake. And we now, therefore, arrive at this further conclusion, that the standard of pleasure in art is not always actual, it is ideal. The Greeks teach us that the pleasure is based on truth; the Italians that it must tend to good; the Spaniards that it belongs to the masses, and is not peculiar to a few; and the French that it is an ideal joy which may not always be present as a reality.

The German school of criticism.

V. And what say the Germans? If any school of criticism is likely to disown the doctrine of pleasure as the end of art, it is the German; but they have all along allowed it.

The earliest luminaries of German criticism, Lessing and Winckelmann, most distinctly accept the doctrine. The confession of Lessing's faith will be found in his treatise on the Laocoon. There he describes pleasure as the aim of art, though he adds that beauty is its highest aim. Winckelmann, in like manner, in the forefront of his work, places on record the statement that art, like poetry, may be regarded as a daughter of pleasure. Kant, at a later period, promulgated the self-same doctrine, and Schiller developed it into his theory of the Spieltrieb or play-impulse. Art compared with labour, said Kant, may be considered as a play. In every condition of man, said Schiller, it is play, and only play, that makes him complete.

CHAPTER V.

Man is only serious with the agreeable, the good, the perfect; but with beauty he only plays, and he plays only with beauty. In case this may appear somewhat shadowy, I refer for a more distinct view to Schiller's essay on tragic art, where he says, that an object which, in the system of life, may be subordinate, art may separate from its connection and pursue as a main design. "Enjoyment may be only a subordinate object for life; for art it is the highest."

What is peculiar to its view of art.

It is not easy to compress into a single phrase what is peculiar to the German definition of art. The schools of thought in Germany are widely sundered; each views art from its own stand point, and has its own term for the work of art. Putting aside minor differences, however, one can detect something like a common thought running through all German speculation on this subject. Hitherto, we have seen that in the various schools of criticism, art came to be defined as something done (perhaps imitated, perhaps created) for pleasure. The German schools advanced upon this notion so far as to make out that art not only goes to pleasure, but also comes of it. According to them, it is the free play or pleasure of the mind embodied for the sake of pleasure. How embodied, whether in imitation, or in a creation, or in a mimic creation, is a different question, that no doubt, as in the system of Schelling, from which our own Coleridge borrowed largely, occupies a most impor-

That art comes of pleasure as well as goes to it.

tant place. But whatever is of essential value in that speculation really works into the definition of art which I have attempted, a sentence or two back, to draw for the Germans as a whole. Thus it is a great point with Schelling that art is a human imitation of the creative energy of nature—of the world soul—of God. But this is only another mode of saying that it is the exercise of a godlike power, therefore of a free power, which cannot be conceived as under compulsion, and subsists only as play or pleasure. Art, I repeat, is, in the German view, the free play or pleasure of the mind, embodied for pleasure.

But the German thinkers confine the pleasure of art to the beautiful.

Most of the German thinkers, however, when speaking of the pleasure of art, are disposed to confine it to the pleasure of the beautiful. They derived this tendency from one of the fathers of their philosophy, Wolf, and from his disciple Baumgarten, who first attempted to establish a science of Æsthetic. Wolf went to work in a right summary fashion. Philosophy, high and dry, had not then thought much of the human heart, and rather despised the fine arts. Baumgarten wrote an apology for deeming them worthy of his notice. So when Wolf came to look into the mystery of pleasure and pain, he made short work of it. He said that pleasure is simply the perception of the beautiful, and pain the sense of ugliness. On the other hand, beauty is the power which anything possesses of yield-

How this bias was given to German philosophy by Wolf.

CHAPTER V.

ing us pleasure, ugliness its power of giving pain. He indeed went much further, and, if I understand him rightly, spoke of the beautiful, the good, and the perfect as synonyms, and of each as correlative to pleasure. Thus it came to pass that when his disciple Baumgarten, overcoming the coyness of philosophy, ventured to think that the pleasure of art might be worthy of examination, and saw in his mind's eye the outlines of a science to which he gave the hitherto unknown, and still incomprehensible name of Æsthetic, instead of drawing the obvious inference that since art aims at pleasure, a science of criticism must be the science of pleasure—he argued that since art aims at pleasure, and since pleasure comes only from the beautiful, the science of criticism must be the science of the beautiful. The mistake which was thus committed at the outset by the man who first came forward to rear a science of the fine arts, was never afterwards corrected in Germany, and gave to all subsequent speculation a fixed bias in favour of beauty as the one theme of art. Even when further analysis showed that beauty was but one of the sources of pleasure, the critics continued to speak of it as the one idea of art. There was a reason and a defence of the mistake so long as with Wolf and Baumgarten the pleasurable and the beautiful were co-ordinate terms—that is to say, when everything pleasing was to be defined as beautiful, and everything beautiful as pleasing. It was

And by his disciple Baumgarten;

And how their conclusion remained in force long after the premiss from which they started was rejected.

unreasonable and indefensible when the origin of the theory was forgotten, and it was recognised that beauty is but a part of pleasure.

How the Germans are bewitched with the notion of beauty.

When, however, the doctrine of beauty as the essence of art came to be placed distinctly before the minds of Germans, it exerted over them such a fascination that whenever their critics approached the idea of the beautiful they seemed incapable of containing themselves, burst into raptures, and, instead of their usually patient analysis, went off in swoons of ecstacy, shrieks, interjections, vocatives, and notes of admiration. Nothing is more curious than to see how, in Schiller especially, the rapturous, interjectional sort of criticism is mixed up with good sense, hard facts, and stiff logic. After every sober bit of argument, he breaks into inarticulate rhapsody, which we can only interpret as the fol-de-diddle-dido, fol-de-diddle-dol at the end of a song. But other Germans also are more or less so bewitched, and some of them so besotted with beauty, that with scarcely an exception they fall down and worship it as the be-all and end-all of art. Baumgarten, Lessing, Winckelmann, Kant, Schiller, Schelling, Hegel, and the Schlegels, all treat of art as the empire of the beautiful, and of the beautiful as the one article of Æsthetic. It was reserved for Richter to rebuke them, and call them back to reason. That man of true genius was a loose, vague thinker, and an extravagant writer, but he could poise pretty

(Margin notes: Their raptures. — They are called back to reason by Richter.)

CHAPTER V. well as a critic, and he saw clearly the weakness of those who insisted upon beauty as the one thought of art. Long ago Horace laid down the principle that it is not enough for a work of art to be beautiful; it must have other sources of interest. And now in his fashion Richter pointed out that art has to manifest ideas of the sublime, of the pathetic, of the comical, as well as of the beautiful. His criticism was quite successful, as against his countrymen who magnified the province of beauty and made it a king where it is only a peer; but if those whom he criticised had turned upon him and asked him to state precisely what is the definition of art which he proposed to substitute for theirs, he could have given them only the impotent answer that the thing to be defined is indefinable.

Richter's own deficiency.

On the German notion of beauty—what it is.

Though Wolf, at the fountain-head, led the German school of criticism into error by identifying all pleasure, and therefore the pleasure which art seeks with the sense of beauty, the consideration which was thus given to the nature of the beautiful led directly to what I have described as the German contribution to the doctrine that pleasure is the end of art. What is beauty? Now, here again, the German answer to that question trails back to Wolf. Beauty, said the philosopher, arguing out the case after the manner of mathematicians in a regular sequence of propositions and demonstrations, with attendant corollaries and scholia,—

Here again they own their bias to Wolf.

beauty is perfection, and perfection is beauty. Everything is beautiful which is perfect of its kind. A perfect toad is beautiful; a perfect monster. You cannot define beauty further, because you cannot define perfection; but you can vary the terms of your definition. Accordingly upon the terms of the definition all manner of changes were rung. The essence of beauty, said Schelling and a whole set of thinkers, is in character—in being—in life—in individuality. Where you have a man or thing of perfect being or character—there is beauty. No, said Goethe, it is not in the character itself, but in the expression or form of it that the beauty lies—the perfect expression even of imperfect character. Ah, said Hegel, we must unite the two views of perfect expression and perfect character, and then we shall arrive at the conclusion that the beautiful is the perfect expression of the perfect idea—my grand idea of the absolute, in which contraries are at one, and the all is nothing. So, in turn, other philosophers saw in art the manifestation of the beautiful, and in the beautiful the perfect expression of their pet ideas.

How succeeding thinkers rung the changes upon Wolf.

Gradually it crept into sight that art may or may not be the expression of an idea about which the philosophers could wrangle as much as they pleased, but that it certainly is the expression of the artist's character. In this connection one might take up the view of Novalis, that the poet is a miniature of the world, a view which would

What view came gradually into sight.

CHAPTER V.

satisfy the philosophers who look to find in art the expression of their highest generalisations. If poetry expresses the poet, and the poet is a miniature of the world, why then art is the expression of their world-ideas. Happily, however, we need not trouble ourselves to throw sops to the philosophers. It is enough to state what is Goethe's final view of the beautiful in art. Art, in his view, is an embodiment of beauty, and the beautiful is a perfect expression of nature, but chiefly the poet's or artist's nature—either of his whole mind, or of a passing mood. But between the lines of this definition we are to see the handwriting of Schiller interposing his remark on the grandeur of the play-impulse in man—that man is only perfect when his mind is in free play, moving of itself, and its movement is a play or pleasure. All that has been put forth by me, said Goethe, consists of fragments of a great confession. But art, said Winckelmann, is the daughter of pleasure. Art, said Kant, is play. Art, re-echoed Schiller, is the expression or product of the impulse to play. I put both views together, and arrive at the conclusion that, according to the Germans, art is the play or pleasure of the mind, embodied for the sake of pleasure. With which doctrine compare and see how little they vary the words of Shelley, that poetry is the record of the best and happiest moments of the best and happiest minds; and those of Mr. Ruskin, that art is the

Goethe's final view of the beautiful in art,

And summary of the German doctrine of pleasure.

expression of man's delight in the works of God.

CHAPTER V.

The German doctrine needs to be balanced by a counter statement of the sorrows of art.

The statement so far, however, is incomplete, and needs for its proper balance a counterstatement of the sorrows of art. In the heaven which is promised to the saints there is no sorrow, and the tears are wiped from every eye; but the paradise of art is peculiar in this respect, that sorrow and pain enter into it. Through the sense of pain art has reached some of its highest triumphs, and Christian art has in it so deep a moaning as to make Augustus Schlegel say, that whereas the poetry of the ancients was the poetry of enjoyment, that of the moderns is the expression of desire. It is quite clear that there is more of pain in modern than in ancient poetry, just as there is more of a penitential spirit in the Christian than in the Olympian faith. But will the Christian, with all his sadness, admit that he has no enjoyment? Does he not luxuriate in his melancholy? Will he not smile through his tears, and say that he has attained a higher happiness than the Greek, with all his lightheartedness, could even conceive? In these things we are apt to play with words. We say that our religion is the religion of sorrow; but what do we mean? Do we mean that the Greeks had pleasure in their religion, and that we have none in ours? Not so; the Christian maintains that his is the higher joy, and that it is not the less joy because

CHAPTER V.

The modern sense of enjoyment as compared with the ancient.

Is it less enjoyment?

it has been consecrated by suffering. So in art; the modern sense of enjoyment as there displayed is no doubt different from that of the Greeks, with stranger contrasts of light and shade; but it would be quite false to say that theirs was the poetry of enjoyment, and that ours is the poetry not of enjoyment but of desire. Some have gone so far as to say that the pleasure coming from sorrow is the greatest of all; as Shelley, that it is "sweeter far than the pleasure of pleasure itself;" or as Schiller, that "the pleasure caused by the communication of mournful emotion must surpass the pleasure in joyful emotion, according as our moral is elevated above our sensuous nature." In the same sense, Bishop Butler, in his sermon on compassion, says that we sympathize oftener and more readily with sorrow than with joy; and Adam Smith maintains that our sympathy with grief is generally a more lively sensation than our sympathy with joy. It is possible that these statements are not altogether accurate; for it is characteristic of pleasure that we do not think of it, while on the other side we do think of our pains; we count every minute of woe, while years of happiness are unaware gliding over our heads; and we are thus prone to make a false reckoning of the intensity and relative values of our pleasurable and painful feelings and fellow-feelings.

But the existence of delicious pain is a great

The existence of delicious sorrow a great fact.

fact, and in modern art a prominent one, which hasty thinkers of the Schlegel type are sure to misinterpret. There is a crowd of facts which go to justify the statement of Shelley, that poets

> Are cradled into poetry by wrong,
> And learn in suffering what they teach in song.

But the suffering of the artist is not inconsistent with the fact that his art emerges from pleasure.

And people do not all at once see how to reconcile such a statement with that other of Shelley's, already quoted, that poetry is the record of the best and happiest moments of the best and happiest minds. So when the Chancellor von Müller, the close friend of Goethe, says that most of Goethe's writings sprang from a necessity which he felt to get rid of some inward discordance, some impression with which he was laden to distress; and when, on the other hand, Mr. Lewes, in one of the finest biographies in our language—in his life of Goethe—say that "he sang whatever at the moment filled him with delight," we are struck with what seems to be a contradiction. In reality, there is none. The artist, like other men, must get his experience of life through suffering, and sometimes he suffers much and long; but the power of expressing himself in art implies, if not perfect relief, a certain recovery—implies that he has so far got the better of his trouble as to be curious about it, and able to dandle it. Those who cherish the luxury of woe, of course will not admit this. It is a pleasure

The power of expression implies recovery.

CHAPTER V.

to them to think that they are utterly miserable; the idea of solace is distasteful to them; and when, to convict them of their error, we ask, "Why, then, are ye so tuneful?" the question seems as heartless as that of the rustic in the fable, who said to the roasting shell-fish: "Oh, ye Cockles! near to death, wherefore do ye sing?" Notwithstanding our self-deception, the fact remains, as Euripides has expressed it in verses which appear in every modern edition of the *Suppliants*, but are probably an interpolation from some other play—that if the poet is to give pleasure, he must compose in pleasure; and this is as true of Christian as of classical art. If the art of the Greeks be more distinctly joyous than that of any other people, it is to the Germans we owe the more distinct elucidation of the fact that the sense of joy underlies all art.

The English school of criticism beginning with Bacon,

VI. At last we come to English writers, and among them is no name greater than that of Bacon. Everyone has by heart the definition of poetry which is contained in the most eloquent work of criticism ever penned. "To the king" —it is addressed, and as we read it we are kings In this definition, and in the context, as well as in many other passages scattered throughout his works, Bacon plainly presents poetry as an art which studies above all things the desires and pleasures of the mind. The criticism of the

And the Elizabethans.

Elizabethan period is not of much importance, and perhaps it is enough if I further quote from Webbe's treatise on English poetry. There the author tells us that "the very sum or chiefest essence of poetry did always for the most part consist in delighting the readers or hearers with pleasure;" and when, in another passage, he asserts, after the Italians, that the right use of poetry "is to mingle profit with pleasure, and so to delight the reader with pleasantness of art as in the meantime his mind may be well instructed with knowledge and wisdom," it will be observed that he still regards pleasure as the immediate end. All our best criticism, however, dates from the time of Dryden, and in his school nothing was more clearly recognised than the subservience of art to pleasure. Dryden himself says that delight is the chief, if not the only end of poetry, and that instruction can be admitted only in the second place. In the same strain wrote Johnson: "What is good only because it pleases, cannot be pronounced good until it has been found to please." Dugald Stewart follows in the beaten path: "In all the other departments of literature," he says, "to please is only a secondary object. It is the primary one in poetry."

But our best criticism dates from Dryden.

Towards the end of last century English criticism began to breathe a new spirit. But did the critics then newly inspired discover that the end of poetry is different from what it

A new spirit breathed into criticism at the end of last century.

CHAPTER V.

was supposed to be? On the contrary, they saw more clearly, and declared more stoutly than ever, that the end of art is pleasure. "The end of poetry," says Wordsworth, "is to produce excitement in coexistence with an overbalance of pleasure." In the same mood, Coleridge maintains that "the proper and immediate object of poetry is the communication of immediate pleasure;" and again, though, as I have tried to show, less accurately, that "a poem is that species of composition which is opposed to works of science by professing for its first immediate object pleasure, not truth." I have already quoted Shelley in the same sense, and I reserve to the last a writer who belongs not to the present, but to the past century. I thus refer to him out of his proper place, because he is the only critic known to me who draws the inference upon which I have insisted, that if poetry be the art, criticism must be the science of pleasure, though he cannot be said to have fully understood, or to have carried out his own doctrine. "The fine arts," said Lord Kames, "are intended to entertain us by making pleasant impressions, and by that circumstance are distinguished from the useful arts; but in order to make pleasant impressions, we ought to know what objects are naturally agreeable, and what naturally disagreeable." He draws the inference rather faintly, but still he draws it, and therefore he is worthy to be singled out from his

But ever the same doctrine as to the end of art is taught.

And Lord Kames even draws in a faint way the inference that criticism must be the science of pleasure.

fellows. It is not with his inference, however, that we are now concerned, but with the grand fact which stands out to view, that in all the critical systems poetry is regarded as meant for pleasure, as founded on it, and as in a manner the embodiment of all our happiness—past, present, and to come.

CHAPTER V.

What is peculiar in the English view of art?

But now it will be asked, is there anything peculiar in the English mode of rendering the definition of art? The point about art which the English school of thinkers has most consistently and strenuously put forward is, that it it is the offspring of imagination. Not that other schools have ignored this doctrine. All along, while speaking of the peculiarities of the different schools of thought, I have been anxious to show that the lesson taught most prominently in each has not been wholly overlooked by the others; and of a surety the French and German schools of criticism have not been backward to acknowledge the influence of imagination in the work of art. In English criticism, however, imagination is the Open Sesame—the name to conjure with. It is the chief weapon, the everlasting watchword, the universal solvent, the all in all. When we come to ask what it really means, we are amazed at the woful deficiency of the information which we can obtain about this all-sufficient power; but be the information much or little, the importance of the power—its necessity, is so thoroughly established in

It dwells chiefly on the power of the imagination in art.

CHAPTER V.

England, that (though after all it comes to the same thing) it is more fully recognised among us that art is the creature of imagination than that it is created for pleasure.

Bacon it was that first taught us to treat of art as the creature of imagination.

Bacon it was who forced English criticism into this furrow, assisted by a word of Shakespeare's. Our great philosopher arranged all literature in three main divisions, corresponding to three chief faculties of the human mind. History, science, and poetry were severally the products of memory, reason, and imagination. There was something very neat in this arrangement, which D'Alembert afterwards adopted, when, in the preface to the celebrated French Encyclopædia, he attempted to make a complete map of liberal study. Plato, who thought of the Muses as daughters, not of imagination, but of memory, would have been not a little startled by the division; and D'Alembert, in following Bacon, had yet to show that imagination was as essential to, and as dominant in Archimedes, the man of science, as in Homer, the man of art. Bacon himself, too, had some little doubt as to the perfect wisdom of his arrangement.* Still

* This doubtfulness appears in a passage in the *Advancement of Learning*, where he speaks of imagination, and seems to find a difficulty in fixing upon its specialty. "The knowledge," he says, "which respecteth the faculties of the mind of man is of two kinds; the one respecting his understanding and reason, and the other his will, appetite, and affection; whereof the former produceth position or decree, the latter action or execution. It is

CHAPTER V.

for general purposes he deemed it sufficient, and he defined poesy, "the pleasure or play of imagination." We had Shakespeare's word for it, too, that the poet is of imagination all compact; and both authorities combined to form in the English mind the conception of art as the product mainly of imagination. After that we know how imagination came to be the grand engine of our criticism. Addison wrote essays on the pleasures of it; Akenside wrote a long poem on it; Johnson described poetry as the art

A word of Shakespeare's assisted.

And since then it has been the favourite dogma of English criticism.

true that the imagination is an agent or nuncius, in both provinces, both the judicial and the ministerial. For sense sendeth over to imagination before reason have judged: and reason sendeth over to imagination before the decree can be ac. d: for imagination ever precedeth voluntary motion. Saving that this Janus of imagination hath differing faces: for the face towards reason hath the print of truth, but the face towards action hath the print of good; which nevertheless are faces,

'Quales decet esse sororum.'

Neither is the imagination simply and only a messenger; but is invested with or at leastwise usurpeth no small authority in itself, besides the duty of the message. For it was well said by Aristotle, 'That the mind hath over the body that commandment, which the lord hath over a bondman; but that reason hath over the imagination that commandment which a magistrate hath over a free citizen;' who may come also to rule in his turn. For we see that, in matters of faith and religion, we raise our imagination above our reason; which is the cause why religion sought ever access to the mind by similitudes, types, parables, visions, dreams. And again, in all persuasions that are wrought by eloquence, and other impressions of like nature, which do paint and disguise the true appearance of things, the chief recommendation unto reason is from the imagination. Nevertheless, because I find not any science that doth properly or fitly pertain to the imagination, I see no cause to alter the former division. For as for poesy, it is rather a pleasure or play of imagination, than a work or duty thereof."

of uniting pleasure with truth, by calling imagination to the help of reason. Then, at a later date, Shelley, not altering his meaning, which I have already given, but altering his phrases, said that "poetry may, in a general sense, be defined to be the expression of the imagination;" and Mr. Ruskin came to the conclusion that "poetry is the suggestion by the imagination of noble grounds for the noble emotions." It thus became the first commandment of English criticism that in poetry there are no gods but one—imagination. To imagination belongs the creative fiat of art. It furnishes the key to all critical difficulties—it possesses the wondrous stone that works all the marvels of poetical transmutation. It was one of Coleridge's dreams to write a great work on poetry and poetical alchymy, the basis of which should be a complete exposition of what he called the Productive Logos—in plain English, the imagination.

Criticism cannot advance a step without first understanding what imagination is.

This power of imagination is so vast and thaumaturgic that it is impossible to lift a hand or move a step in criticism without coming to terms with it, and understanding distinctly what it is and what it does. On the threshold of every inquiry, it starts up, a strange and unaccountable presence, that frights thought from its propriety, and upsets all reason. I propose, therefore, to devote the next few chapters to a fresh and thorough-going analysis of it, which ought to yield some good results. In the meantime, it

CHAPTER V.

will be enough for the purposes of this chapter to point out, as far as it can be done at the present stage of our inquiry, what imagination has to do with pleasure.

The relation of imagination to pleasure.

All English criticism admits, and indeed insists, that art is the work, or, as Bacon more strictly puts it, "the pleasure of imagination." Even if, however, we reject the word pleasure, and speak of art simply as the product of imagination, this, it will be found, is but an implicit statement of what is stated more explicitly in German criticism, that art is the mind's play. In accepting imagination as the fountain of art, we accept art also as essentially a joy, for imagination is the great faculty of human joyance.

Imagination to be largely identified with the source of pleasure.

It is the food of our desires even more than the things themselves which we desire. Of course we cannot live upon dreams. Bolingbroke was quite right when he cried:

> Oh! who can hold a fire in his hand,
> By thinking of the frosty Caucasus?
> Or clog the hungry edge of appetite
> By bare imagination of a feast?
> Or wallow naked in December's snow,
> By thinking on fantastic summer's heat?

But when he adds that, "the apprehension of the good gives but the greater feeling to the worse," his experience is not that of a man gifted with strong imagination. The power of dreaming is proverbial as a magic that brings far things near—that transports us whither we will, and that turns all things to pleasure. Call it

CHAPTER V. glamour—call it lunes—call it leasing; we need not now dispute about the name, if we can only agree as to the fact that imagination is often as good to us as the reality, and sometimes better. Is any feast so good as that which we imagine? Is any landscape so glorious as that which we see in the mind's eye? Is any music so lovely as that which floats in dreams? Is the pleasure which Alnaschar could derive from the possession of unbounded wealth to be compared with that which he feels when in the fancied possession of wealth he kicks over his basket of wares? Not only is the bare imagination of pleasure thus often beyond the pleasure itself—that of real pain is in many cases a source of enjoyment. It is not seldom a pleasure to remember past suffering.

Limits, however, to that view of it.

There is, no doubt, another side to the picture, in the known facts that the terror of ill is worse to bear than the ill itself, and that the sympathetic pain which the good Samaritan feels in seeing a wound is frequently more acute than the pain felt by the wounded man himself. That there are nightmares, however, and aches of imagination, does not obliterate the general fact that imagination is the house of pleasure, and that dreamland is essentially a land of bliss. Wordsworth speaks of imagination as that inward eye which is the bliss of solitude; Shakespeare gives to it a name which bespeaks at once its elevation and its delightfulness—the heaven of invention; and my argument is, that if in this heaven is the birthplace of art, and if from this heaven it comes, its home is heavenly, its ways are heavenly, to a heaven it returns, for a heaven it lives.

Re-statement of the English contribution to criticism, and its deficiency.

This, then, may be described as the English gift to the definition of art—that it comes of imagination, and that it creates a pleasure coloured by the same faculty. All pleasure, obviously, is not poetical: it becomes poetical when the imagination touches it with fire. It must be repeated, however, that when we ask for distinct information as to what this means, it is not easy, it is indeed impossible, to get it; and I make bold to claim for the next few chapters this praise at least, that they are the first and only attempt which has been made to give an exhaustive analysis of imagination—to give an account of it that shall at once comprise and explain all the known facts. Those writers who give us a rounded theory of imagination ignore half the facts; those who recognise nearly all the facts are driven, either like Mr. Ruskin, to confess that they are a mystery inscrutable, or like Coleridge, to throw down their pens with a sigh, not because the mystery is inscrutable, but because their explanations would be unintelligible to a stiff-necked and thick-headed generation of beef-eating, shop-keeping Britons.

Although imagination

The result of this backward state of criticism

CHAPTER V.

is magnified and everywhere asserted, it is, however, nowhere explained.

is, that when we come to ask the first of all questions, what is art? we discover to our chagrin that we are answered by statements that keep on running in a vicious circle. Thus, if poetry is defined by reference to imagination; on the other hand, imagination is defined by reference to poetry. If we are told that poetry must be imaginative, we are also told that imagination must be poetical—for there is an imagination which is not poetical. Thus, when we inquire into the nature of poetry, we are first pushed forward to search for it in imagination, and then when we examine into the imagination, we are thrown back on the original question—what is poetical? Few things, however, are more remarkable in the world than the faculty which the human mind has of seizing, enforcing, and brooding over ideas which it but dimly comprehends; and although in English criticism, indeed in all criticism that makes much of it, imagination is, as it were x, an unknown incalculable quantity, still the constant recognition of that something unknown is a preserving salt which gives a flavour to writings that would often taste flat from the want of precision and clear outcome. Rightly understood, also, there is no critical doctrine to be compared for importance with that of the sovereignty of imagination in art, and in art pleasure, which the English school of critics has ever maintained. Let me add, though at the present stage of the discussion I

Imagination an unknown quantity.

But the continual recognition of that unknown something of immense importance.

cannot make it clear that the leading doctrine of English criticism is in effect but an anticipation of the prime doctrine of the Germans. The English and the Germans, nearly allied in race, are so far also allied in their thinking, that the views of art upon which they mainly insist are virtually the same. The German expression of these views is the more precise. On the other hand, the English expression of them is, in point of time, the earlier, and in point of meaning will be to most minds the more suggestive.

Summary of this chapter.

If the foregoing statement be rather lengthy, and have inevitably been loaded with the repetitions of a multitude of authorities, the upshot of all may be stated very shortly. All the schools of criticism, without exception, describe art as the minister of pleasure, while the more advanced schools go further, and describe it also as the offspring of pleasure. Each may have a different way of regarding this pleasure. The Greek dwells on the truth of it; the Italian on its profit. The Spaniard says it is pleasure of the many; the Frenchman says it is of the few. The German says that it comes of play; the Englishman that it comes of imagination. But all with one voice declare for pleasure as the end of art. The inference is obvious—the inference is the truism which is not yet even recognised as a truth; that criticism, if it is

CHAPTER V. ever to be a science, must be the science of pleasure. What wonder that it shows no sign of science, when the object of the science is not yet acknowledged?

ON IMAGINATION.

CHAPTER VI.

ON IMAGINATION.

IMAGINATION is the Proteus of the mind, and the despair of metaphysics. When the philosopher seizes it, he finds something quite unexpected in his grasp, a faculty that takes many shapes and eludes him in all. First it appears as mere memory, and perhaps the inquirer lets it escape in that disguise as an old friend that need not be interrogated. If, however, he retain his hold of it, ere long it becomes other than memory; suddenly it is the mind's eye; sudden again, a second sight; anon it is known as intuition; then it is apprehension; quickly it passes into a dream; as quickly it resolves itself into sympathy and imitation; in one moment it turns to invention and begins to create; in the next moment it adopts reason and begins to generalize; at length it flies in a passion, and is

A general description of imagination and its manifestations.

CHAPTER VI.

lost in love. It takes the likeness, or apes the style by turns of every faculty, every mood, every motion of thought. What is this Proteus of the mind that so defies our search? and has it like him of the sea, a form and character of its own, which after all the changes of running water and volant flame, rock, flower, and strange beast have been outdone, we may be able to fix and to define? Is there such a thing as imagination different from the other faculties of the mind? and if so, what is it?

Has imagination a character of its own?

What most strikes one when we approach the inquiry into the nature of this power—the acknowledged potency of imagination.

Any one attempting to grapple with this question, will at once be struck with a remarkable fact. Everybody knows that imagination sways and overshadows us, enters into all our studies and elaborates all our schemes. If we swerve from the right path, it is fancy, we are told, that has led us astray; if we pant after splendid achievement, forsooth, it is the spirit of romance that leads us on. Imagination, say the philosophers and divines, the Humes and Bishop Butlers, is the author of all error, and the most dangerous foe to reason; it is the delight of life, say the poets, the spur of noble ambition, the vision and the faculty divine. For good or ill, it gives breath and colour to all our actions; even the hardest and driest of men are housed in dreams; it may be dreams of tallow or treacle or turnips, or tare and tret; but in dreams they move. By all accounts, the imagination is thus prevalent in human life, and the language of all men, learned and simple, bears witness to its puissance.

But notwithstanding its potency, the philosophers do not tell us what it is.

Nevertheless, imagination, thus rife, thus potent, whose dominion, even if it be that of a tyrant against whom it is wisdom to rebel, we all acknowledge, whose yoke, will or nill, we all wear—is as the unknown god. First-born of the intellectual gifts, it is the last studied and the least understood. Of all the strange things that belong to it, the strangest is that much as the philosophers make of it, much as they bow to it, they tell us nothing about it or next to nothing. This is no hyperbole, but a plain fact. Any one, who, fired by the magnitude and variety of the effects attributed to imagination, inquires into the nature of their causes, will be amazed at the poverty of all that has been written on the subject, and the utter inadequacy of the causes assigned. Most philosophers, though they defer to popular usage in speaking of imagination, yet when they examine it closely, allow it no place whatever among the powers of the human mind. In the account of our faculties given by Locke, and almost every other English psychologist, down to Herbert Spencer, the imagination is put out of doors and treated as nought. The chief source of illusion, it is itself an illusion; it is an impostor; it is nothing; it is some other faculty. I repeat that here I am using no figure of speech, but speaking literally. Whereas in common

And indeed assure us that it is nought.

CHAPTER VI. parlance and in popular opinion imagination is always referred to as a great power, the authorities in philosophy resolve it away. It is some other faculty, or a compound of other faculties. It is reason out for a holiday; it is perception in a hurry; it is memory gone wild; it is the dalliance of desire; it is any or all of these together.

The current opinions I have summarised in the parable of Proteus.

The sum of the information about it which I have been able to glean I have endeavoured to convey in the parable of Proteus. One man says this, and another man says that. Each one gives a little of the truth, but none the whole truth. Nor indeed is the whole truth conveyed in the parable of Proteus. All that is attempted in that similitude is to bring together the scattered fragments of opinion and to mould them into something like a consistent whole. The current opinions of imagination are all fragmentary: there is no wholeness about them. They may be summed up under four heads—those which identify imagination with memory; those which melt it into passion; those which make it out to be reason; and lastly those which represent it as a faculty by itself, different from the other powers of the mind. Let us take a hasty glance at each of these sets of opinions.

These current opinions may be examined under four heads.

Most commonly imagination is described as a department of memory. So it appeared to the Greeks, in whose idea the muses were daughters, not as we should say of God and imagination, but of Zeus and Mnemosyne. Even those who, like Aristotle, distinguished between fantasy and reminiscence, failed to establish any clear difference between them, save such as may exist between whole and part. Aristotle, indeed, says distinctly that memory pertains to the same region of the mind as fantasy; that it is busied with the self same objects; and that such objects of memory as are without fantasy are objects accidentally. So in modern times, we find Wolf, who is the father, even more directly than Leibnitz, of German philosophy, giving in his *Rational Psychology* a long chapter to the imagination. It is the same chapter in which he treats of memory. In his *Empirical Psychology*, he gives a separate chapter to each of the two faculties; in his *Rational Psychology*, he is fain to treat of both together as but phases of the same power.

CHAPTER VI.

Imagination is sometimes identified with memory.

From Aristotle to Hume we may say roundly, that those who—whether in form or in substance—identified imagination with memory, defined imagination as a loose memory of the objects of sense. I say loose memory rather than bad, because among the philosophers I refer to there is some difference of opinion as to the relative force of the two names—imagination and memory. Thus Hobbes, while he tells us that these are two names for one and the same thing, seems to indicate that the imagination is a

Generally in this way it is regarded as a loose memory.

CHAPTER VI.

lively memory. It is in the same sense that Locke defines fancy as a quick memory. Hume, on the other hand, who often refers to the workings of imagination, who tells us that it is the greatest enemy of reason, and who has a famous passage in which he compares it to the wings of cherubim hiding their faces and preventing them from seeing, sets out with the assertion that it is nothing but a dim memory. Whichever of these views be correct, it is a pity that the philosophers do not stick to one or other, and instead of pouring their anathemas on such a nonentity as imagination, attack the real sinner—a loose memory. It is because they never know whether to describe imagination as a department of memory or memory as a department of imagination. Some, like Locke, make imagination a part of memory; some, like Malebranche, make memory a part of imagination; some, like Hobbes, regard the one as identical with the other. The philosophers have a vague idea that imagination and memory are in a manner involved one with the other; but when they cast blame on one of the confederates and acquit the other, when they vilify imagination and glorify memory, they betray a suspicion that in the former there are elements which are not to be found in the latter. What are these elements?

Yet from their manner of treating it, many of those who identify imagination with memory show that they really regard it as more than memory.

Descartes is among those who virtually defined imagination in terms of memory. This he did in his *Méditations* on the more abstract

Imagination is sometimes identified with passion.

questions of philosophy; but when he came to write on the passions of the soul, he saw that he had to account for certain arbitrary compounds, such as gorgons and hydras and chimeras dire, which are created by imagination and are not furnished by memory. He then defined imagination as a passion partly of the soul and partly of the body—a passion directed in its combinations partly by the will, partly by the chance movements of the bodily spirits. But before Descartes, we were, in this country, accustomed to insist in even a stronger sense than he would allow, on the passionate element of imagination. There was a strong tendency in our language to identify imagination with desire. Shakespeare constantly uses fancy as a synonym for love, and this sense of the word still survives. To love a thing is to have a fancy for it. In the same spirit Bacon writes. After ascribing poetry to the imagination (as history to memory, and philosophy to reason), he indicates what imagination is, by saying that poetry is a submission or adaptation of the shows of things to the *desires* of the mind. I believe that Dr. Thomas Brown is the latest of our philosophers who has seen in desire the presiding element of imagination. In his view imagination is only desire operating upon the suggestions of memory. In the same vein, Shelley among the later poets sees in imagination the attitudes of love and of sympathy. It

CHAPTER VI.

is the faculty by which we forget ourselves and love our neighbours, putting ourselves in their place.*

Imagination identified with reason.

A not less important band of thinkers make out reason to be the characteristic feature of imagination. It is Wordsworth's view that imagination is but reason in her most exalted mood. One can trace the germ of this opinion back to the early days of logic, when the Stoics divided that science into invention and judgment. In course of time the heap of irrelevancies which were elaborated under the name of invention and which were supposed to help out the discovery of middle terms was rejected from the science. But although formally rejected from logic as a thing which could be taught, it was always understood that invention is a part of reasoning. It was very much, though not entirely in this sense, that dragons and hippogriffs, which

* Shelley's words are worth quoting. "Poetry," he says, "lifts the veil from the hidden beauty of the world, and makes familiar objects be as if they were not familiar. It reproduces all that it represents; and the impersonations clothed in its Elysian light stand thenceforward in the minds of those who have once contemplated them as memorials of that gentle and exalted content which extends itself over all thoughts and actions with which it coexists. The great secret of morals is love, or a going out of our own nature, and an identification of ourselves with the beautiful which exists in thought, action, or person, not our own. A man, to be greatly good, must imagine intensely and comprehensively; he must put himself in the place of another, and of many others: the pains and pleasures of his species must become his own. The great instrument of moral good is imagination; and poetry administers to the effect by acting upon the cause." — *Essays and Letters*, vol. i. p. 16.

CHAPTER VI.

From the days of the Schoolmen downwards.

we should now deem the offspring of sheer imagination, were, in the language of the Schoolmen, described as beings of reason—*entia rationis*. It was natural that those who took invention for the prime element in imagination should in one form or another identify that faculty with reason. Gassendi, the great opponent of Descartes, would have it that there is no real difference between imagination and what he calls intellection. In Sir John Davies' pithy account of fantasy it is described as forming comparisons, holding the balance and exercising all the faculties of judgment. Henry More, the Platonist, regarded reason and imagination as so involved together that when, after having said his say about imagination, he came to speak of reason, he merely observed—" we need say nothing of it apart by itself." Dugald Stewart is perhaps the firmest recent upholder of this view; for he treats the imagination as a composite faculty, made out of the elements of reason—such as apprehension, abstraction, judgment and taste. Dr. Carpenter, another good authority, has probably Stewart's analysis in his mind, when he says that the imagination " involves an exercise of the same powers as those concerned in acts of reasoning." He is at fault in his further assertion that the chief difference between imagination and reason is that the one has to do with fictitious, the other with real objects; and I summon him here only to bear witness that apart from the objects

To Dugald Stewart and others.

CHAPTER VI.

with which they are engaged, the two faculties are almost indentical.

Even those who treat of imagination as a power by itself are struck by its rationality.

Even some of those who do not go so far, but allot to imagination a walk of its own, are puzzled with a certain rationality which it displays, and which the separation of it from reason seems to render unaccountable. Thus D'Alembert maintained, contrary to the general opinion, that imagination is as essential to the mathematician as to the poet, and boldly declared that he who in all antiquity deserved to be placed next to Homer for strength of imagination is Archimedes. Herein however he is but following up a hint of Descartes' to which Dugald Stewart gives a flat contradiction, that the study of mathematics tends to develop the imagination, and that this is the reason why mathematicians seldom succeed in metaphysics. No, said Stewart—" of all the departments of human knowledge, mathematics is that in which imagination is least concerned;" and he left it to be inferred (I fancy he said it explicitly, but I cannot recall the passage) that in the metaphysician imagination exists in full force. Sir William Hamilton at least adopted this view, and said that it may reasonably be doubted whether Aristotle or Homer were possessed of the more powerful imagination; only Sir William is more consistent in maintaining this of Aristotle than D'Alembert was in maintaining it of Archimedes, for his analysis of the fantasy

CHAPTER VI.

And at last work up to the conclusion that there is an imagination for every faculty of the mind.

or creative imagination had given him the result, that it is a compound of reason and memory or at least of what is commonly so called. But as if even this were an account of imagination not quite satisfactory to him, Sir William Hamilton adopts in modified terms the statement of Ancillon, that there are as many different kinds of imagination as there are different kinds of intellectual activity.* There is the imagination of abstraction, that of wit, that of judgment, that of reason, that of feeling, that of volition, that of the passions—and an addition to all, imagination proper. In point of fact, however, it is not

* The statement of Ancillon is very remarkable, and as we may have to refer to it in the sequel, it may be well to quote it here. The curious thing is that it occurs in his chapter on Memory. Both memory and imagination are treated in the same chapter (*Essais Philosophiques*, tome ii. page 139), and yet into this chapter on memory he introduces the following:

"On peut même dire qu'il y a autant de genres différens d'imagination, qu'il y a de facultés de l'âme, à qui l'imagination fournit les élémens nécessaires à leur travail. Il y a l'imagination de l'abstraction, qui nous présente certains faces de l'objet sans nous présenter les autres, et en même temps le signe qui rèunit les premières; l'imagination de l'esprit, qui reproduit les disparates, les antithèses, les contrastes, entre lesquels on saisit ensuite des rapports ou des ressemblances; l'imagination du jugement, que à l'occasion d'un objet reproduit toutes les qualités de cet objet, et les lie principalement sous le rapport de substance, d'attributs, et de modes; l'imagination de la raison, qui à l'occasion d'un principe reproduit les conséquences, à l'occasion des conséquences le principe; l'imagination du sentiment, qui reproduit toutes les idées et toutes les images accessoires, qui ont de l'affinité avec un certain sentiment, et qui lui donnent par-là même plus d'étendue, de profondeur et de force; l'imagination de la volonté, qui dans un moment donné reproduit toutes les idées, qui peuvent imprimer à la volonté une direction fixe,

CHAPTER VI.

possible to separate between a mental act or state and the imagination of it. To imagine feeling is to feel; to imagine judgment is to judge; and to say that there is an imagination of every faculty in the mind is simply to say that imagination takes the form of every faculty.

All these views of imagination are compatible.

Any one who will gather together these different views of imagination may see that though on the surface they conflict one with another (as when one set of philosophers make imagination an exalted mood of reason, while another set denounce it for the worst enemy of reason) yet essentially they are compatible and their variances are but the variances of partial statement. The North says, "I am the North and there is no South." The East wind whistles, "I am of the East and I have never found the West."

And we arrive at the view of imagination as the Proteus of the mind with which we started.

So then at length we return to our starting-point, and out of many theories which are all more or less true, form the idea of a Protean power. Imagination remembers, feels, desires, wills, dreams, invents, judges, reasons. It is a name which we give for a change to every

---

ou bien l'ébranler et la rendre vacillante; l'imagination des passions, qui selon la nature et l'objet de la passion, reproduit toutes les représentations qui lui sont homogènes ou analogues; enfin l'imagination proprement dite, l'imagination pure, si je puis m'exprimer ainsi, qui ne travaille que pour elle-même, et qui produit les images de la nature sensible, celles des sentimens, et celles des idées, uniquement pour enfanter des combinaisons nouvelles; c'est l'imagination du poète."

CHAPTER VI.

But the question still recurs Has imagination no character of its own?

faculty in the mind, and to almost any combination of these faculties. But is imagination which bulks so large in popular theories, and in common language, nothing of itself? Is the power of which we hear so much, and which now looks like reason, now like memory, and now like passion, blessed with no character, n standing of its own? Is it nothing but a name to conjure with—an empty sound, a philosophical expletive, a popular delusion? Here we come upon the fourth set of partial opinions to which I proposed to call attention. According to every intelligible analysis of imagination that I have seen, it is a name, and nothing more. On the other hand, there are a few writers who regard it as a king in its own right, with a territory of its own; but they give us no intelligible account of it. Thus Jean Paul Richter, after saying that fantasy can do duty for the other faculties, and is their elemental spirit, but that the other faculties cannot take the form and do the work of fantasy, proceeds to tell us what this fantasy or creative imagination is. What is it? Die Phantasie ist die Weltseele der Seele, und der Elementargeist der übrigen Kräfte. Wenn der Witz das spielende anagramm der Natur ist; so ist die Phantasie das Hieroglyphen-Alphabet derselben, wovon sie mit wenigen Bildern ausgesprochen wird. I fear that I cannot make this clearer in English. Fantasy is the world-soul of the soul—

Those who declare that imagination has a character of its own either fail to explain what it is,

CHAPTER VI.

and the elemental spirit of the other faculties. As wit is the playful anagram of nature, fantasy is its hieroglyphic alphabet. What all this comes to, it is not easy to say; only it looks big. Nothing, however, looks half so big as Coleridge's definition. "The imagination I consider either as primary or secondary. The primary imagination I hold to be the living power and prime agent of all human perception, and as a repetition in the finite mind of the eternal act of creation in the infinite I AM. The secondary I consider as an echo of the former." Oh gentle shepherds! what does this mean? Is it something very great or very little? It reminds me of a splendid definition of art which I once heard. When the infinite I AM beheld his work of creation, he said Thou ART, and ART was. The philosopher of Highgate never explained himself. He was a great believer in the independence of imagination, but when he had written a few sentences of his chapter on what he called with a fine flourish the esemplastic power—the Productive Logos, he suddenly stopped short and got a friend to write him a letter, or perhaps he himself wrote the letter which he published, begging him not to put forth his theory, for it would be unintelligible to the addle-pated public, and he should reserve it for another and a better world. Mr. Ruskin follows in the same track, but more honestly, with all the frankness of a transparent and clear-seeing

Or, like Mr. Ruskin, they say frankly that it is inscrutable.

mind. He has written several magnificent chapters on the work of imagination. The words come from his mouth like emperors from the purple, and describe with commanding power the effects of imagination. But for the faculty itself all that Mr. Ruskin has to say of it is that it is utterly inexplicable. It is not to be dissected or analysed by any acuteness of discernment.*

CHAPTER VI.

Imagination therefore demands a new analysis, and we must define it for ourselves.

Thus nobody tells us what imagination really is, and how it happens that being, as some say, nothing at all, it plays an all-powerful part in human life. Driven to our own resources, we must see if we cannot give a clearer account of this wonder-working energy, and above all, cannot reconcile the philosophical analysis which reduces imagination to a shadow with the popular belief which gives it the empire of the mind. I propose this theory, that the

* In this history of opinions, James Mill's theory of imagination ought not to be forgotten. "Imagination," he says, "is not a name of any one idea. I am not said to imagine unless I combine ideas successively in a less or greater number. An imagination, therefore, is the name of a *train*. I am said to have an imagination when I have a train of ideas; and when I am said to imagine I have the same thing; nor is there any train of ideas to which the term imagination may not be applied. In this comprehensive meaning of the word Imagination there is no man who has not imagination, and no man who has it not in an equal degree with any other. Every man imagines; nay, is constantly and unavoidably imagining. He cannot help imagining. He can no more stop the current of his ideas than he can stop the current of his blood."—James Mill's *Analysis of the Human Mind*, chap. vii.

CHAPTER VI.

It is not a special faculty, but a special function.

The Hidden Soul.

imagination or fantasy is not a special faculty but that it is a special function. It is a name given to the automatic action of the mind or any of its faculties—to what may not unfitly be called the Hidden Soul. This is a short sentence. Perhaps to some it may appear a trifling one, with which to docket and explain the grand mystery of imagination. At least those who have not well considered the subject will scarcely see its pregnancy of meaning. It involves an immense deal, however; and to the next three chapters is assigned the task of showing what it involves. It seems possible to get out of it a more suggestive definition of the nature of art than any which has yet been propounded. That definition will be furnished in the ninth chapter of the present volume to which the whole argument leads up. But I must ask the reader, if he should be curious about the definition, and should glance forward to see what it looks like, not to decide upon it off-hand, but to come back and read the argument which is now to be opened out. The result to which the argument tends may have the air of paradox to those who have not formed previously an acquaintance with the vast array of facts upon which it proceeds, and their peculiar significance. The facts which have to be unfolded are among the most curious in human nature; but they are also among the most neglected, and I must beg for them a careful attention.

They are, in very truth, by far the most important with which any science of human nature can have to deal; and they provide us with a key to more than one problem that hitherto has been deemed insoluble. Whether the conclusion as to art which may here be drawn from them be correct or not, they are otherwise valuable, and deserve some systematic arrangement. And as the facts are important, so also I think I may count upon the reader's interest in the strange history which I now undertake to relate.

Importance of the facts which we have now to study.

Only before buckling to that task let me point out distinctly what it is that I am going to show the working of. I have said that imagination is but another name for the automatic action of the mind or any of its faculties. Now for the most part this automatic action takes place unawares; and when we come to analyse the movements of thought we find that to be quite sure of our steps we are obliged very much to identify what is involuntary with what is unconscious. We are seldom quite sure that our wills have had nought to do in producing certain actions, unless these actions have come about without our knowledge. Therefore although involuntary does not in strictness coincide with unconscious action, yet for practical purposes, and, above all, for the sake of clearness, it may be well to put out of sight altogether such involuntary action as may consist with full consciousness, and to treat of

Statement of the problem to be solved.

the automatic exercise of the mind as either quite unconscious or but half conscious. And if on this understanding we may substitute the one phrase for the other as very nearly coinciding, then the task before me is to show that imagination is but a name for the unknown, unconscious action of the mind—the whole mind or any of its faculties—for the Hidden Soul. If this can be made good—evidently it will meet the first condition of the problem to be solved. It will reconcile philosophical analysis with popular belief. It will grant to the satisfaction of philosophers that imagination is nothing of itself; and it will prove to the satisfaction of the multitude that it is the entire mind in its secret working.

THE HIDDEN SOUL.

CHAPTER VII.

THE HIDDEN SOUL.

THE object of this chapter is not so much to identify imagination with what may be called the hidden soul, as to show that there is a mental existence within us which may be so called — a secret flow of thought which is not less energetic than the conscious flow, an absent mind which haunts us like a ghost or a dream and is an essential part of our lives. Incidentally, there will be no escaping the observation that this unconscious life of the mind—this hidden soul bears a wonderful resemblance to the supposed features of imagination. That, however, is but the ultimate conclusion to which we are driving. My more immediate aim is to show that we have within us a hidden life, how vast is its extent, how potent and how constant is its influence, how strange are its effects.

CHAPTER VII.

—

The object of this chapter is to show that there is a hidden soul, and what it means.

CHAPTER VII.

This unconscious part of the mind is so dark, and yet so full of activity; so like the conscious intelligence and yet so divided from it by the veil of mystery, that it is not much of a hyperbole to speak of the human soul as double; or at least as leading a double life. One of these lives—the veiled life, now awaits the rudeness of our scrutiny.

The character of the facts to be studied.

Many of the facts which in this exposition it will be requisite to mention must be known to some readers, and nearly all of them indeed should be recognized as more or less belonging to common experience. But notwithstanding their familiarity we must needs go the whole round of the facts that bear witness to the reality of a hidden life within us, for it is only from a pretty full muster of the evidence—the familiar with the unfamiliar—that we can see the magnitude of our hidden life, the intimacy of its relations with our conscious every-day thinking, the constancy and variety of its working in all the nooks and crannies of the mind. Though some of these facts are familiar, they are also interesting enough to be worth repeating. To lay bare the automatic or unconscious action of the mind is indeed to unfold a tale which outvies the romances of giants and ginns, wizards in their palaces and captives in the Domdaniel roots of the sea. As I am about to show how the mind and all its powers work for us in secret and lead us unawares to results so

The interest of the subject.

much above our wont and so strange that we attribute them to the inspiration of heaven or to the whispers of an inborn genius, I seem to tread enchanted ground. The hidden efficacy of our thoughts, their prodigious power of working in the dark and helping us underhand, can be compared only to the stories of our folk-lore, and chiefly to that of the lubber-fiend who toils for us when we are asleep or when we are not looking. There is a stack of corn to be thrashed, or a house to be built, or a canal to be dug, or a mountain to be levelled, and we are affrighted at the task before us. Our backs are turned and it is done in a trice, or we awake in the morning and find that it has been wrought in the night. The lubber-fiend or some other shy creature comes to our aid. He will not lift a finger that we can see; but let us shut our eyes, or turn our heads, or put out the light, and there is nothing which the good fairy will not do for us. We have such a fairy in our thoughts, a willing but unknown and tricksy worker which commonly bears the name of Imagination, and which may be named—as I think more clearly —The Hidden Soul.

The romance of the mind.

It is but recently that the existence of hidden or unconscious thought has been accepted as a fact in any system of philosophy which is not mystical. It used to be a commonplace of philosophy, that we *are* only in so far as we know that we are. In the Cartesian system, the

The existence of hidden thought only recently acknowledged.

CHAPTER VII.

The Cartesian doctrine opposed to it.

essence of mind is thought; the mind is nothing unless it thinks, and to think is to be conscious. To Descartes and his vast school of followers, a thought which transcends consciousness is a nullity. The Cartesian system is perfectly ruthless in its assertion of the rights of consciousness, and the tendency of the Cartesians has been to maintain not only that without consciousness there can be no mind, but also that without consciousness there can be no matter. Nothing exists, they inclined to say, except it exists as thought (in technical phrase, *esse* is *percipi*), and nothing is thought except we are conscious of it. In our own times, the most thorough-going statement of the Cartesian doctrine has come from Professor Ferrier, in one of the most gracefully written works on metaphysics that has ever appeared. "We are," says Ferrier, "only in so far as we know; and we know only in so far as we know that we know." Being and knowledge are thus not only relative, but also identical.

Leibnitz first suggested the modern doctrine.

To Leibnitz is due the first suggestion of thought possibly existing out of consciousness. He stated the doctrine clumsily and vaguely, but yet with decision enough to make it take root in the German system of thought. There it has grown and fructified and run to seed; there, also, it has expanded into all the absurdities and extravagancies of the transcendental philosophy. But though much of that philosophy is mere folly, and though to most of us it is nearly all unintelligible, we must take heed not to scout it as a baseless fabric. It has a foundation of fact, and that foundation of fact is recognised now by our most sober thinkers, who—be they right or wrong—at least never quit the ground of common sense. It is recognised by Sir William Hamilton; it is recognised by his opponent, Mr. Mill; it is recognised by another great authority, Mr. Herbert Spencer. How they recognise it, whether or not they are consistent in what they say of it, and what use they make of the fact they have learned to acknowledge, are questions which we need only glance at. For me, the great point is that they admit the principle.

Which is also allowed in our time by Hamilton, Mill, and Spencer.

Sir William Hamilton is not consistent in his assertions with regard to consciousness. Everybody who is acquainted with his writings must know how forcibly he has described the existence within us of what he calls a latent activity. He shows as clearly as possible how the mind works in secret without knowing it. His proof of the existence of hidden thought is one of the most striking points in his philosophy. Yet it shows the effect of his training that again and again he lapses into the old Cartesian way of speaking, and in many little passages which I might quote says that mind is co-extensive with consciousness—that thought exists only in so far as we know it exists.

Sir William Hamilton's view.

CHAPTER VII.

Mill's view.

Then again for Mr. Mill, I do not know that he is inconsistent in his views with regard to the reality of hidden thought; but some of us may object to the conclusions which he draws from that reality. He has attacked in the person of Sir William Hamilton the established philosophy of Europe. He challenges the whole of that system of philosophy which now reigns, and has reigned for the last century, having begun in a recoil from Hume. He has a rival system to propound — a reassertion of Hume; and the grand weapons by which he proposes to beat down the current philosophy and to establish his own are what he calls the law of inseparable association and its attendant law of obliviscence. I must not vex my readers with the object of the discussion, which is rather dry, and indeed of little interest save to professed metaphysicians; and it is enough to state the bare fact that the argument—whatever it be and whithersoever it tend—turns entirely on the fact of hidden thought—the mind acting in a certain way and without knowing it.

Statement of Herbert Spencer.

As for Mr. Herbert Spencer, he has stated the case very pithily in his defence of the current philosophy against Mr. Mill's attack. He comes upon a strange contradiction, which no one who will fully and fairly relate the facts of his consciousness can escape. Mr. Spencer puts the contradiction in its most suicidal attitude, and assures us that we cannot avoid it. "Mysterious as seems the consciousness of something which is yet out of consciousness," we are "obliged to think it." Here then is admitted the fundamental fact out of which all the fogs of the transcendental philosophy have arisen—the fact that the mind may be engaged in a sphere that transcends consciousness. I do not at present ask the reader to accept any of these views or any of these statements. The views may be faulty, and the statements may be obscure. But I ask him to understand that I am not about to preach to him an utterly new doctrine, or a doctrine which none but transcendental philosophers have allowed.

But in one form or another the view has been of old standing.

In point of fact it is an old doctrine. Although Leibnitz was the first to indicate plainly and soundly the existence of thought working for us in our minds occult and unknown, it is not to be supposed that this phenomenon had wholly escaped previous observers. On the contrary, the fact of vast tracts of unconscious, but still active, mind existing within us, lies at the base of all the theories of the mystics. And I know not that in Shakespeare there is a more profound saying than one which is uttered by a nameless lord. Parolles, soliloquizing, as he thinks in secret, expresses a fear that the hollowness of his character has been discovered, and that all his bombast and drumming and trumpeting are understood at length to be but sound and fury, signifying nothing: "They begin to smoke me,

It is the foundation of mysticism.

And it is often suggested by the poets.

CHAPTER VII. and disgraces have of late knocked too often at my door. I find my tongue is too fool-hardy; but my heart hath the fear of Mars before it, and of his creatures, not daring the reports of my tongue. Tongue, I must put you into a butter-woman's mouth, and buy myself another of Bajazet's mule." The anonymous lord who overhears this extraordinary soliloquy, then asks, "Is it possible he should *know* that he is, and *be* that he is?" It is a question which goes down to the very centre of life—how far knowledge is compatible with being, existence with the consciousness of existence. Here it is the crucial test of an irrecoverable ass. Look at Dogberry anxious to be written down an ass, and proving his donkeyhood by utter unconsciousness of it. Look at Falstaff, on the other hand, laughing at himself and stopping the laughter of others when he says, "I do begin to perceive that I am made an ass." And it is not only the final test of donkeyhood, but goes down to the deeps of life. Shakespeare is very fond of such phrases as these: "The fool doth think he is wise, but the wise man knows himself to be a fool." "The worst is not as long as we can say, This is the worst." "I am not very sick, since I can reason of it." Shakespeare—could Shakespeare himself have *known* what he was, and yet have *been* that he was?

General description of the

Not so; we are far more than we know; and, paradoxical though it may appear, yet

Facts with which we have now to deal.

our life is full of paradoxes, and it is true that the mere circumstance of our knowing that we are, is often a valid proof to the contrary. I hope to avoid the nonsense and the jargon of those who have discoursed most on the sphere of the transcendental—that is, the sphere of our mental existence which transcends or spreads beyond our consciousness; but that consciousness is not our entire world, that the mind stretches in full play far beyond the bourne of consciousness, there will be little difficulty in proving. Outside consciousness there rolls a vast tide of life, which is, perhaps, even more important to us than the little isle of our thoughts which lies within our ken. Comparisons, however, between the two are vain, because each is necessary to the other. The thing to be firmly seized is, that we live in two concentric worlds of thought,—an inner ring, of which we are conscious, and which may be described as illuminated; an outer one, of which we are unconscious, and which may be described as in the dark. Between the outer and the inner ring, between our unconscious and our conscious existence, there is a free and a constant but unobserved traffic for ever carried on. Trains of thought are continually passing to and fro, from the light into the dark, and back from the dark into the light. When the current of thought flows from within our ken to beyond our ken, it is gone, we forget it, we know not what has become of it. After a time it comes back to us changed and grown, as if it were a new thought, and we know not whence it comes. So the fish, that leaves our rivers a smolt, goes forth into the sea to recruit its energy, and in due season returns a salmon, so unlike its former self that anglers and naturalists long refused to believe in its identity. What passes in the outside world of thought, without will and for the most part beyond ken, is just that which we commonly understand as the inscrutable work of imagination; is just that which we should understand as the action of the hidden soul, and which, after these generalities, it is necessary now to follow in some detail.

These facts are to be divided into three groups.

The facts with which we have to deal fall naturally into three groups, corresponding to the first three groups of opinion, as to the nature of imagination enumerated in the last chapter. There it was stated that imagination has been identified by philosophers with memory, with reason, or else with passion; and that there is a fourth group of thinkers who, not satisfied with any of these views, declare that in imagination there is something special, though they cannot tell what it is. The argument here is that each of the first three sets of thinkers are quite right. Imagination is memory; imagination is reason; imagination is passion. But the argument goes further, and will have it that the fourth set of thinkers are also right, and that imagination has

And statement of the argument to be followed.

a specialty. It is memory—but it is memory automatic and unconscious. It is reason—but it is reason of the hidden soul. It is passion and all that we connect with passion, of instinct, feeling, and sympathy—but it is passion that works out of sight. It is, in a word, the whole power or any power of the mind—but it is that power energising in secret and of its own free will. Now, for the present, let us put by the question whether it be right or wrong to say that this is a sufficient account of what we understand by the imagination. Hold that question in abeyance until we have completed a survey of the hidden soul. At present, what we are to keep in view is this, that as the conscious soul may be roughly divided into faculties of memory, of reason, and of feeling, so the unconscious or hidden soul may be divided in the same manner, and may be considered as memory, as reason, and as feeling. Let us examine it in these three aspects.

On memory and its hidden work.

I. In memory we encounter the oftest-noted marvel of hidden thought. It is a power that belongs even more to the unconscious than to the conscious mind. How and where we hide our knowledge so that it seems dead and buried; and how in a moment we can bring it to life again, finding it in the dark where it lies unheeded amid our innumerable hoards, is a mystery over which every one capable of think-

CHAPTER VII.

A constant marvel.

Contradictions of memory.

The clue to it in the hidden life.

ing has puzzled. The miracle here is most evident and most interesting when memory halts a little. Then we become aware that we are seeking for something which we know not; and there arises the strange contradiction of a faculty knowing what it searches for, and yet making the search because it does not know. Moreover, nothing is commoner than, when a man tries to recollect somewhat and fails, to hear him say, "Never mind, let us talk of something else, I shall remember it presently," and then in the midst of his foreign talk, he remembers. So that the condition of his remembrance depends on this odd contradiction that he shall not only forget what he wants, but even forget that he wanted to remember it. When Daniel surpassed all the magicians, the astrologers, and the soothsayers of Babylon, by discovering to Nebuchadnezzar the dream which he had forgotten, he did not perform a more wonderful feat than the king himself would have accomplished had he been able by an effort of his own memory to recover the lost vision. In the plenitude of his powers, Newton could not remember how he arrived at the binomial theorem, and had to fall back upon his old papers to enable him to discover the process.

The clue, but only a clue, to this perpetual magic of reminiscence lies in the theory of our hidden life. I do not attempt to follow out the explanation, since at best it only throws the

CHAPTER VII.

riddle but a step or two backwards, and for the present inquiry it is enough that I should barely state the facts which indicate the reality and the intensity of our covert life. Strictly speaking the mind never forgets: what it once seizes, it holds to the death, and cannot let go. We may not know it, but we are greater than we know, and the mind, faithful to its trust, keeps a secret watch on whatever we give to it. Thus beams upon us the strange phenomenon of knowledge, possessed, enjoyed, and used by us, of which nevertheless we are ignorant—ignorant not only at times, but also in some cases during our whole lives.

Story of the Countess of Laval and others.

First of all, for an illustration, take the well-known story of the Countess of Laval, who always in her sleep spoke a language which those about her could not understand and took for gibberish. On the occasion of her lying-in, however, she had a nurse from Brittany who at once understood her. The lady spoke Breton when asleep, although when awake she did not know a word of it, and could attach no meaning to her own phrases which were reported to her. The fact is that she had been born in Brittany, and had been nursed in a family where only the old Celtic dialect of that province was spoken. This she must have learned to prattle in her infancy. Returning to her father's home, where French only was spoken, and Breton not at all, she soon forgot her early speech—lost all traces of it in

CHAPTER VII.

Captain Marryat.

her conscious memory. Beyond the pale of consciousness memory held the language firm as ever, and the Countess prattled in her dreams the syllables of her babyhood. Captain Marryat gives an account of what happened to himself, not so striking perhaps, but equally pertinent. A man belonging to his ship fell overboard, and he jumped into the sea to save him. As he rose to the surface he discovered that he was in the midst of blood. In an instant the horror of his situation flashed on him. He knew that the sharks were around him, and that his life was to be measured by seconds. Swifter than pen can write it, his whole life went into the twinkling of an eye. Burst upon his view all that he had ever done, or said, or thought. Scenes and events in the far past which had been long blotted from his remembrance came back upon him as lightning. The end of the story is that he escaped, the sharks having followed the ship, while he, left behind, was picked up by a boat; but the point of it for us lies in the fealty of memory to its trust, and in the perfectness of the art by which it held all the past of the man's life to the veriest trifle of gossip in safe keeping.

De Quincey.

De Quincey, in the dreams of his opium-eating days, felt the same power in himself. Things which, if he had been told of them when waking he could not have acknowledged as parts of his former experience, were in his dreams so placed before him with all the chance colour and feelings of the original moment, that at once he knew them and owned their memorial identity. As he thus noted the indelibility of his memory, he leaped to the conjecture which divines before him had reached, that in the dread day of reckoning the book which shall be opened before the Judge is but the everlasting roll of remembrance.

Two things to be chiefly noticed in memory.

In this unfailing record two things particularly call for attention; the first, that understanding is not essential to memory; the second, that the memory of things not understood may be vital within us. A word or two on each of these great facts.

The first, that understanding is not essential to it.

That understanding is not essential to memory we see in children who learn by heart what has no meaning to them. The meaning comes long years afterwards. But it would seem as if the process which we have all observed on such a small scale goes on continually on a much larger scale. Absolute as a photograph, the mind refuses nought. An impression once made upon the sense, even unwittingly, abides for evermore. There has long been current in Germany a story about a maid in Saxony who spoke Greek. Henry More refers to the fact as a sort of miracle and an antidote against atheism. Coleridge tells a similar story of later date and with explanatory details. In a Roman Catholic town in Germany, a young woman, who could neither read nor write, was seized with a fever, and was

Story of the maid of Saxony.

said by the priests to be possessed of a devil, because she was heard talking Latin, Greek and Hebrew. Whole sheets of her ravings were written out, and were found to consist of sentences intelligible in themselves but having slight connection with each other. Of her Hebrew sayings, only a few could be traced to the Bible, and most seemed to be in the Rabbinical dialect. All trick was out of the question; the woman was a simple creature; there was no doubt as to the fever. It was long before any explanation save that of demoniacal possession could be obtained. At last the mystery was unveiled by a physician who determined to trace back the girl's history, and who, after much trouble, discovered that at the age of nine she had been charitably taken by an old Protestant pastor, a great Hebrew scholar, in whose house she lived until his death. On further inquiry it appeared to have been the old man's custom for years to walk up and down a passage of his house into which the kitchen door opened, and to read to himself with a loud voice out of his books. The books were ransacked, and among them were found several of the Greek and Latin Fathers, together with a collection of Rabbinical writings. In these works so many of the passages taken down at the young woman's bedside were identified, that there could be no reasonable doubt as to their source. A succession of unintelligible sounds had been so caught

CHAPTER VII.

by the ear that years afterwards the girl could in her delirium repeat them. And so we may say generally, that, whether we know it or not, the senses register with a photographic accuracy whatever passes before them, and that the register, though it may be lost, is always imperishable.

Memory absolute as a photograph.

As it is only by a variety of illustrations that this great fact can be thoroughly impressed upon the mind, I may be allowed to detain the reader with yet another anecdote pointing to the same conclusion. It is told by Abercrombie; indeed, he has several like it. Thus, he makes mention of one of his patients who had in health no kind of turn for music, but sang Gaelic songs in his delirium. The most remarkable case, however, which he describes is that of a dull awkward country girl—who was considered uncommonly weak of intellect, who in particular showed not the faintest sense of music, and who was fit only to tend the cattle. It happened that while thus engaged with cattle, she had to sleep next a room in which a tramping fiddler of great skill sometimes lodged. Often he would play there at night, and the girl took notice of his finest strains only as a disagreeable noise. By and by, however, she fell ill, and had fits of sleep-waking in which she would imitate the sweetest tones of a small violin. She would suddenly stop in her performance to make the sound of tuning her instrument, and then after a light prelude would

Other illustrations given by Abercrombie.

CHAPTER VII.

dash off into elaborate pieces of music, most delicately modulated. I have forgotten to mention that in the meantime a benevolent lady had taken a liking to her, and received her into her family as an under-servant. This accounts for the fact of her afterwards imitating the notes of an old piano which she was accustomed to hear in the house. Also, she spoke French, conjugated Latin verbs, and astonished everybody who approached her in her sleep-waking state, with much curious mimicry, and much fluent and sometimes clever talk on every kind of subject—including politics and religion. Here the Highland lass is but exhibiting in another form the same sort of phenomenon as Coleridge described in the German girl. In both of these anecdotes the fact stands out clear, that the memory grips and appropriates what it does not understand—appropriates it mechanically, like a magpie stealing a silver spoon, without knowing what it is, or what to do with it. The memory cannot help itself. It is a kleptomaniac and lets nothing go by.

Conclusion, that the memory lets nothing go by.

Nor must we have mean ideas as to the nature of the existence in the mind of things preserved beyond our knowledge and without our understanding. This is the second point aforesaid which calls for attention. When we think of something preserved in the mind, but lost and wellnigh irrecoverable, we are apt to imagine it as dormant; when we know that it

The second point to be noticed, that the memory of things not understood may be vital within us.

was unintelligible we are apt to imagine it as dead. On the contrary, the mind is an organic whole and lives in every part, even though we know it not. Aldebaran was once the grandest star in the firmament, and Sirius had a companion star once the brightest in heaven, and now one of the feeblest. Because they are now dim to us, are we to conclude that they are going out and becoming nought? The stars are overhead, though in the blaze of day they are unseen; they are not only overhead, but also all their influences are unchanged. So there is knowledge active within us of which we see nothing, know nothing, think nothing. Thus, in the sequence of thought, the mind, busied with the first link in a chain of ideas, may dart to the third or fourth, the intermediate link or links being utterly unknown to it. They may be irrecoverable, they may even be unintelligible, but they are there, and they are there in force.

Knowledge active within us of which we know nothing.

As it is sometimes difficult to follow a general statement like this without the help of example, I will suppose a case in point, suggested by the story of the girl who in her waking state had no ear for music, but yet in her sleep-waking could imitate the music of the violin with wondrous accuracy and sweetness. Take the case of a man who has no ear for music, who cannot keep time in a simple dance, who can neither remember nor recognise a tune, and to whom melody is but an unmeaning succession of sweet

Examples in illustration.

CHAPTER VII.

noises. That man may, nevertheless, through associations the most fine and indefinable of any, but also the most sure and irresistible—through an association of unknown musical ideas—connect two objects of thought which are otherwise far apart. The hearing a Methodist hymn sung, for example, may put him in mind of a snow storm. Say that the hymn is sung to the air of *Scots wha hae wi' Wallace bled.* He may not know this; neither may he know that *The Land o' the Leal* which he once heard has the same air transposed to the minor key; but forthwith on hearing the hymn, his mind reverts to the idea of the snow-drift which is mentioned in the first verse of the Scotch song. The knowledge of the strain, once heard, is in the mind, quick and quickening, although he knows it not nor understands it. So, in the days of our feebleness we have witnessed scenes and events for which we seemed to have no eyes and no ears, and a long time thereafter we describe as from imagination what is really a surrender of the memory. Looks and tones come back upon us with strange vividness from the far past; and we can picture to the life transactions of which it is supposed that we have never had any experience. Shelley was filled with terror when he thought of these things. In a walk near Oxford, he once came upon a part of the landscape for the first time (as he deemed) which nevertheless his memory told him that he

Showing how what we attribute to imagination is but a surrender of hidden memory.

had seen before. When long afterwards, in Italy, he attempted to describe upon paper the state of his mind in half feeling that he had seen this landscape before in a dream, he became so terror-stricken in contemplation of his thought that he had to throw down his pen and fly to his wife to quell in her society the agitation of his nerves.

Plato maintained in view of these facts the theory of pre-existence.

No wonder that Plato when he saw the vast resources of the mind—when there came to him a dim feeling that much of what he seemed to create he was only drawing from remembrance, and when he could trace back to no period in the present life the origin of impressions which had been self-registered, and ideas which had been self-grown in the dark of his mind, straightway started the hypothesis of a previous life passed in a previous world, before we found our way hither to be clogged by clay. Many a time since then men have caught at the same idea.* One of our least known poets, but a true one, Matthew Green, has it in the following terms:—

As prisoners into life we've come;
Dying may be but going home;
Transported here by bitter fate,
The convicts of a prior state.

* A query has been raised as to the meaning of the question which we find in the Gospel of St. John: "Master, who did sin, this man or his parents, that he was born blind?" How could the man have sinned before he was born, except on the supposition of pre-existence?

CHAPTER VII.

The same view suggested by Wordsworth.

But he who has in modern times most emphatically expressed it is Wordsworth. In the finest of his poems he says:

Our birth is but a sleep and a forgetting;
The soul that rises with us, our life's star,
Hath had elsewhere its setting,
And cometh from afar;
Not in entire forgetfulness,
And not in utter nakedness,
But trailing clouds of glory, do we come
From God, who is our home.

Summary of the facts relating to memory.

So much then for memory, in so far as it represents the immense involuntary life which we lead out of consciousness. If the facts I have brought together do not account for all, certainly they account for much of what we understand by the word imagination. They account for much even of what is most mysterious in the processes called imaginative. In the mechanical accuracy with which memory all unknown to us registers the flitting impressions of our daily life, and in the faithfulness with which at times and in ways of its own choosing, it surrenders to consciousness these impressions, we have a glimpse of what is meant by the creativeness of imagination. It is true, that the theory of unconscious memory does not explain all the creative work of fantasy. There is in the mind, as I shall afterwards have to show, a genuine creative process, over and above the seeming creativeness of unconscious memory. Still, it is difficult to exaggerate the importance of mere memory—involuntary and secret—as a worker of miracles, as a discoverer of things unknown, and as contributing to invest all objects of thought with a halo of mystery, which is but the faint reflection of forgotten knowledge. The Platonic theory of pre-existence is but the exaggeration of a truth. Our powers of memory are prodigious; our powers of invention are very limited. The same fables, the same comparisons, the same jests are produced and reproduced like the tunes of a barrel-organ in successive ages and in different countries.

Anecdote of Sir Walter Scott.

When Sir Walter Scott was engaged on the composition of *Rokeby*, he was observed to take notes of the little wild flowers that grew not far from the cave which he was going to allot to Guy Denzil. He describes how Bertram laid him down:

> Where purple heath, profusely strewn,
> And throat-wort, with its azure bell,
> And moss and thyme his cushion swell.

To one who expressed surprise that for such details he did not trust to imagination, meaning the faculty of invention, he replied that this faculty is circumscribed in its range, is soon exhausted and goes on repeating itself, whereas nature is boundless in its variety, and not to be surpassed by any efforts of art. Thus it is not so much to a trained invention as to a trained memory that the poet who seeks for variety must

CHAPTER VII.

chiefly trust; and it will be found that all great poets, all great artists, all great inventors are men of great memory—their unconscious memory being even greater than that of which they are conscious. These unconscious memories stirring we know not what within us, fill some men with a sense of the mystery of life, and shed on all things visible the hues of poetry,—that light, which, according to Wordsworth, never was on sea or land. Other men they enrich with visions of what they fancy they have never seen. In a moment at a single jet the picture is in the mind's eye complete to a pin's head with all the perfectness of imaginative work. One blow, one flash, is all we are conscious of; no fumbling, no patching, no touching up. We are unconscious of the automatic energy within us until its work is achieved and the effect of it is not to be resisted. We see the finished result; of the process we know nothing. We enjoy the one and we stand in awe of the other. We endow these extraordinary memories with divine honours. Ye are as gods, we say to the poets. And thus far at least one can see a deeper wisdom in the doctrine of the Greeks that the muses were all daughters of Mnemosyne.

On the hidden life of reason.

II. Let us now look for the exercise of reason in the hidden soul, by reason understanding not merely what the logicians mean, but all that is

CHAPTER VII.

included in the popular sense of the term—as judgment, invention, comparison, calculation, selection, and the like movements of thought, forethought and afterthought.

The complexity of thought.

When we come to look into the complex movement of our thoughts, we discover that in almost every mental operation there are several distinct wheels going, though we may be conscious of only one. No better illustrations need we seek for, than the favourite ones of playing on the piano-forte and of reading a book. The beginner on the piano-forte strikes the notes far between like minute guns. For every key that he touches a distinct enterprise of thought is required. After a time he fingers the scale more deftly, and can grasp whole handfuls of notes in quick succession with greater ease than at first he could hit upon a single key. See how many things he can do at once. With both hands he strikes fourfold chords—eight separate notes; he does this in perfect time; he lifts his foot from the pedal so as to give the sound with greater fulness; meanwhile his eye, fixed on the music-book, is reading one or two bars in advance of his hand; and to crown all, he is talking to a companion at his side. This enumeration of the various courses which the mind pursues at one and the same moment, is far from complete; but it is enough to show that many lines of action which when first attempted require to be

We do a great number of things at once, but are not conscious of all.

CHAPTER VII.

carried on by distinct efforts of volition become through practice mechanical, involuntary movements of which we are wholly unaware. In the act of reading we find the mind similarly at work for us, with a mechanical ease that is independent of our care. There are indeed well attested cases of readers overtaken with sleep and continuing to read aloud, although thus overpowered. Children at the factories have fallen asleep over the machines which their fingers kept plying. Postmen have gone upon their daily rounds dead asleep, without oversight of consciousness or intervention of will. In these cases the mind spontaneously went forward in certain accustomed grooves.

Further examples, showing how the mind pursues several distinct actions at once.

More particular examples are at hand. Houdin could not only keep four balls tossing in the air, but also while these were flying about could read a book placed before him. Canning dictated despatches to three secretaries at once, and we may rest assured that in the complicated operations of thought required for such a performance, he very much depended on certain self-acting processes which he had taught his mind to follow. Sir Walter Scott sometimes dictated his narratives, and the penman whom he employed on one occasion very soon discovered that he was carrying on two distinct trains of thought, one of which was already arranged and in the act of being spoken, while the other was further advanced, putting together what was afterwards to be said. It was a proof of this double movement, that sometimes Scott would let slip a word which was wholly out of place, and was even superfluous (as *entertained* for *denied* or in addition to it), but which clearly belonged to the following sentence, and there fell into its proper place. It became thus evident that he was composing the one sentence while he was dictating the other, and that a word occasionally dropped from the sentence which was in his mind into that which was on his tongue. The act of composition had in his mind become so automatic that when he was released from the irksomeness of penmanship, and could rely upon another hand to drive the quill, he would forget what he had done — every incident, character, and conversation of his book. It was thus that during an illness, the *Bride of Lammermoor* was composed amid groans of suffering which seemed far more than the story to engross his mind. The sentences of this, one of his finest tales, flowed on freely in spite of the cries with which they were mingled; but when the work was finished, Scott had no memory of it; to no one did the tale appear a greater novelty than to himself; and he read the proofs in a fever of fright lest he should come upon some huge blunder.

Several of these distinct actions

The self-working of his mind was however still more evident in another habit. When

CHAPTER VII.

become quite unconscious.

in the conduct of his plot he became entangled in a knot which he could not quickly unravel, or when he was stopped by any considerable difficulty, it was his custom to put aside his papers for the day, and to forget his embarrassment in other occupations. When he awoke on the morrow the problem was solved, and he got rid of the difficulty with ease. Some may account for the clearance of the stumbling-block, by the increased vigour of the mind after it had been freshened with sleep.

The mind in secret broods over its work.

The true explanation is that the mind, though it seemed to be otherwise engaged, was really brooding in secret over its work, and mechanically revolving the problem, so that it was all ready for solution at peep of dawn. There are few thinking minds that have not had experiences which bear out this view. They too have had to face perplexity, have been baffled in the first encounter, and have withdrawn for a time from the fray. Perhaps they resolve, as the saying is, to sleep upon it. What then? Not always does light come in the morning; it comes at other times when the mind has had no chance of rest. It may flash upon us unexpectedly when we are lost in other cares, in the deeps of sorrow, or in the roar of business, or in the whirl of pleasure. Many of us can remember that in our college days when some hard mathematical problem had fairly mastered us, and we were driven in despair to throw it aside, suddenly the solution shot into the mind when we were bent on different thoughts in the hunting-field, or at a wine party, or in the house of prayer. Archimedes was in the bath when he jumped to the shout of Eureka; and the angel of the Lord appeared unto Gideon as he threshed wheat by the wine-press in Ophrah, to hide it from the Midianites. I believe it was Goethe who pointed out that Saul the son of Kish found a kingdom while his only thought was to find his father's asses.

That the mind calculates, invents, judges, digests for us without our knowing it.

The gist of these anecdotes is, I hope, clear. By a flood of examples I am trying to make manifest the reality of certain mental ongoings of which, from their very nature, scarcely anything is known. Out of them all emerges the fact that the mind keeps watch and ward for us when we slumber; that it spins long threads, weaves whole webs of thought for us when we reck not. In its inner chamber, whither no eye can pierce, it will remember, brood, search, poise, calculate, invent, digest, do any kind of stiff work for us unbidden, and always do the very thing we want. Although we cannot lift the veil and see the mind working, yet the facts crowd upon us which show that it does work underhand. They are of all sorts, from the most simple to the most complex. For a very simple illustration of the law, we may note what is called absence of mind. We are all more or less absent, and having thoughts

CHAPTER VII.

here and far away, in sight and out of sight, may be described as double minded. But some men attend more habitually than others to the under-currents of thought, and are thus remarkable for their absence. From such simple illustrations of undersong and involuntary concealed action in the mind, we rise to higher examples.

The story of Avicenna

There is the case of Avicenna. Avicenna was a very hard student who went regularly to the mosque to pray that Allah would help him in his studies, and get him middle terms for the syllogisms he required. The story goes that Allah heard his prayers and found him the middle terms while he slept; at least they came to him in dreams. Without supposing that Allah was so deeply interested in his syllogisms as to work a miracle in his behalf, we can still believe in the efficacy of the philosopher's prayer.

There are many things which we cannot do if we are conscious, but can do easily if we become unconscious.

Kneeling was the highest expression of his anxiety, and this anxiety so urged his mind that what it could not reach under the disturbing gaze of consciousness, it seized in sleep easily when its movements were allowed to become spontaneous. So it happens often. There are things which we fail to do if we are watched, and which we do easily if no one is by; which we cannot do at all if we think about it, and which we do readily if we do not think. "His memory was great," says Sir Philip Warwick of Lord Strafford, "and he made it greater by confiding in it." I have already referred to the saying of Mozart: "If you think how you are to write, you will never write anything worth hearing. I write because I cannot help it." What we try to do, we cannot do; when we cease trying, we do it. Is this because trying is useless, and when we are sore pressed for middle terms, we must ring down the Almighty with a church bell? On the contrary, it is trying that succeeds, and Heaven helps with inspiration only those who help themselves. In one of the English versions of the Psalms there is a fine expression: "Oh tarry thou the Lord's leisure;" but the most luminous gloss upon this text is to be found in the saying of Father Malebranche, that attention is the prayer of the intellect; only here we must limit ourselves to attention that is passive. Think you, says Wordsworth,

CHAPTER VII.

> Think you, 'mid all this mighty sum
> Of things for ever speaking,
> That nothing of itself will come,
> But we must still be seeking?
> * * *
> Nor less, I deem that there are powers
> Which of themselves our minds impress,
> And we can feed this mind of ours
> In a wise passiveness.

Action of the mind in sleep.

That story of Avicenna reminds us that in sleep we have the boldest evidence of the mind's latent activity. Like those heavenly bodies which are seen only in the darkness of night, the realities of our hidden life are best seen in the darkness of slumber. We have observed that in the gloaming of the mind, memory displays a rich-

CHAPTER VII.

ness which it is fain to conceal in the full glare of consciousness. It has languages, it has music at command of which when wide awake it has no knowledge. Time would fail us to recount the instances in which through dreams it helps us to facts—as where a stray will is to be found, or how the payment of a certain sum of money can be proved—which in broad day we have given up for lost. Nor is there any end to the cases which might be cited of actions begun in consciousness and continued in sleep—soldiers thus marching, coachmen driving, pianists playing, weavers throwing the shuttle, saddlers making harness, seamstresses plying the needle, swimmers floating, sailors mounting the shrouds or heaving the log. Probably our first impulse when we hear of these things is to make merry with the sleeping palace where for a hundred years a somnolent king sits on the throne, surrounded by drooping counsellors, while not far off the butler dozes with a flask between his knees, the steward reposes amid his wrinkles, the page in a dream is intent on a slumbering maid of honour, the sentinel hybernates in his box, the winds are all snoring, the trees are all nodding, the fowls are all roosting, the fires are all dormant, the dogs are all heavy with the selfsame spell that sent the beautiful Princess to drowse for an age upon a golden bed. Especially may we be inclined to smile at such a picture of life, since in the philosopher's rendering of it the sleepers would

There is no act of waking life which we cannot carry on in our sleep.

not as in the poet's fable be arrested in their actions, but would go on acting without let or hindrance.

Similar facts perceived in drunkenness.

One is not more inclined to treat the matter gravely, when one remembers how closely and how ludicrously these experiences of actions continued in sleep are connected with the phenomena of narcotics. We laugh to hear of the drunken Irish porter who forgot when sober what he had done when drunk, and who had to get drunk again in order to remember any circumstances which it was necessary for him to recall, so that having once in a state of intoxication lost a valuable parcel, he could give no account of it, but readily found it again in his next drinking bout. We laugh as we remember the story of the ancient Persians who would undertake no important business unless they had first considered it drunk as well as sober. We laugh to think that in this England of ours, and in a time of terrible storm, the helm of the state was held by a prime minister, the Duke of Portland, who almost lived on opiates, was always in a state of stupor, and would fall dead asleep over his work. We have our jokes about the sleep-bound cabinet that from the brow of Richmond Hill sent an order to Lord Raglan to go and take Sebastopol. We have our memories of Laputa, in which the philosophers were so wise, so absent-minded and so given to sleep that they had to hire flappers who with bladders at the end of strings would

CHAPTER VII.

flap them on the head and rouse them to their senses.

Though many of these facts have a ludicrous side, they are deserving of the most serious attention.

Laugh as we may, we return to the mystery of sleep with ever-increasing wonderment. What is most wonderful in it is the ease with which the mind works and overtakes results that waking it would either fail to approach, or would approach with faltering painful steps. Heaps of examples are at hand. None is better known than that of Coleridge, who in a sleep composed the beautiful fragment of Kublah Khan. Notwithstanding their sibilation, nothing can be more musical than such lines as these.

Account of some of the actions performed in sleep.

> A damsel with a dulcimer,
> In a vision once I saw:
> It was an Abyssinian maid,
> And on a dulcimer she played,
> Singing of Mount Abora.

Coleridge's sleep was produced by opium; but the Queen of Navarre, Augustus la Fontaine, Voltaire and others, in their natural sleep made verses which they remembered on waking. Thomas Campbell woke up in the night with the line, "Coming events cast their shadows before," which he had been beating his brains for during a whole week. In like manner, Tartini composed the Devil's Sonata, in a dream in which the enemy of mankind seemed to challenge him to a match on the fiddle. In sleep Benjamin Franklin forecast events with a precision which in the daytime he could never attain, and which by contrast seemed the result rather of a second-sight than of his ordinary work-a-day faculties. In sleep, Father Maignan used to pursue his mathemetical studies, and when he worked out a theorem in his dreams, he would awake in the flush and pleasure of his discovery. In sleep, Condillac would mentally finish chapters of his work which, going to bed, he had left unfinished. Abercrombie tells of an advocate who had to pronounce a legal opinion in a very complicated case which gave him much concern. His wife saw him rise in the night, write at his desk, and return to bed. In the morning he informed her that he had a most interesting dream, in which he had unravelled the difficulties of the case and had been able to pronounce a most luminous judgment, but unfortunately it had escaped his memory and he would give anything to recover it. She had but to refer him to his desk and there the judgment was found clear as light.*

* I place in a foot-note a remarkable story which appeared in *Notes and Queries*, 14th January, 1860. The story is told on the authority of the Rev. J. de Liefde. A brother clergyman, whom he perfectly trusted, told him as follows:—"I was a student at the Mennonite Seminary at Amsterdam, and frequented the mathematical lectures of Professor Van Swinden. Now, it happened that once a banking-house had given the professor a question to resolve which required a difficult and prolix calculation; and often already had the mathematician tried to find out the problem, but as to effect this some sheets of paper had to be covered with ciphers, the learned man at each trial had made a mistake. Thus, not to overfatigue himself, he communicated the puzzle to ten of his students—me amongst the number—and begged us to attempt its unravelling at home.

CHAPTER VII.

Somnambulism and its wonders.

This last example, however, is not ordinary dreaming, but comes under the head of sleep-walking or waking, a peculiar class of phenomena, so well and so long recognised that when, in the year 1686, a brother of Lord Culpepper was indicted at the Old Bailey for shooting one of the guards and his horse, he was acquitted on the plea of somnambulism. In this state as in that of

My ambition did not allow me any delay. I set to work the same evening, but without success. Another evening was sacrificed to my undertaking, but fruitlessly. At last I bent myself over my ciphers, a third evening. It was winter, and I calculated to half-past one in the morning—all to no purpose! The product was erroneous. Low at heart, I threw down my pencil, which already that time had beciphered three slates. I hesitated whether I would toil the night through, and begin my calculation anew, as I knew that the professor wanted an answer the very same morning. But lo! my candle was already burning in the socket, and, alas! the persons with whom I lived had long ago gone to rest. Then I also went to bed, my head filled with ciphers, and tired of mind I fell asleep. In the morning I awoke just early enough to dress and prepare myself to go to the lecture. I was vexed at heart not to have been able to solve the question, and at having to disappoint my teacher. But, O wonder! as I approach my writing table, I find on it a paper, with ciphers of my own hand, and think of my astonishment, the whole problem on it solved quite aright, and without a single blunder. I wanted to ask my *hospita* whether any one had been in my room, but was stopped by my own writing. Afterwards I told her what had occurred, and she herself wondered at the event, for she assured me no one had entered my apartment. Thus I must have calculated the problem in my sleep and in the dark to boot, and what is most remarkable, the computation was so succinct, that what I saw now before me on a single folio sheet, had required three slatefuls closely beciphered at both sides, during my waking state. Professor Von Swinden was quite amazed at the event, and declared to me that whilst calculating the problem himself, he never once had thought of a solution so simple and concise."

ordinary dreaming the precision and the facility of the work we can do are very remarkable. The sleep-walker seldom makes a false step, or sings a wrong note. She rivals the tones of the Swedish nightingale, warbling in her presence; and high on some giddy edge she foots it with the skill of a rope-dancer. Especially is it curious to see how the waking and the sleep-waking states are severed from each other as by a wall. Just as the Irish porter, already mentioned, had no remembrance in his sober state of what he had done in his fits of intoxication, and had to get drunk in order to discover it, the sleep-waker leads in vision a life which has no discernible point of contact with his daily life. His day life is a connected whole in keeping with itself; his night life is the same; but the two are as distinct as parallel lines that have no chance of meeting. By day the man has not the faintest recollection of what goes on at night; and by night he has in his memory no trace of what passes in the day. The physiologists attempt to account for this by regarding the brain as a double organ, one-half of which may be active while the other is in repose. But these physical explanations are not satisfactory. Even in full consciousness, when it may be supposed that both sides of the brain are active, we sometimes know of a double life being prosecuted something like that which sleep-waking shows. Sir James Mackintosh

The double life of the somnambulist seen in a fainter degree in our waking states.

was a man who mixed much in the world and took a forward part in public affairs; but from his youth upwards, he led another life of curious reverie. He was the Emperor of Constantinople, his friends were his ministers and generals. In endless day-dreams he saw transacted the history of his empire; he watched the intrigues of his palace; he gave rewards to his faithful servants; and formed alliances with neighbouring powers. To the last the habit clung to him. Among his friends he was the gentle clansman of the north country, born to belie the rhyme,

> Of all the Highland clans,
> The Macnab is the most ferocious,
> Except the Macintyres,
> The Macraws and the Mackintoshes.

In long-drawn dreams he soared far above the Clan Chattan, he stood imperial upon the Golden Horn, he made war upon his enemies, and without remorse he chopped off the heads of rebellious subjects. He thus led two lives which were quite distinct from each other, and which resembled the double life of sleep-wakers in all but this, that in the one state he did not lose his consciousness of the other.

The hidden life of passion and instinct.

III. If memory has its hiding places in the mind, and if there too is to be found a hidden reason; so also, nearly all that we understand by passion, feeling, sympathy, instinct, intuition is an energy of the hidden soul. It is so entirely a hidden work that in popular regard it is readily accepted as of kin to imagination. Instinct, intuition, passion, sympathy—these are forces which we at once recognise as of themselves poetical, as for the most part indistinguishable from imagination, and as involved in the recesses of the mind. They are processes which never fairly enter into consciousness, which we know at best only in a semi-consciousness, and less in themselves than in their results. The instinctive action of the mind so clearly belongs to the hidden soul—to that part of the human intelligence which is automatic and out of sight, that we need not dwell upon it so minutely as on those actions of the mind of which secrecy is not the rule. The operations of reason, for example, are chiefly known to us in their conscious exercise; and it was necessary at some length, to show that there is a prodigious empery of reason which is not conscious. Secrecy, on the other hand, is the normal condition of passionate and instinctive movements. The mere existence of such forces as instinct and passion is a vulgar fact which to those who read it aright will at once tell a tale of the hidden soul.

Passion notoriously a blind force.

Passion, whether we view it as feeling or as fellow-feeling, is notoriously a blind unconscious force. Love is a blind god, and Shakespeare says that it has no conscience—a word

CHAPTER VII.

which in his time had the sense of consciousness besides that which it now bears:

> Love is too young to know what conscience is;
> Yet who knows not, conscience is born of love.

It is thus the type of all passion. It matters not which of the passions we select for cross-examination: they are all, in this respect, alike. But love is the emotion which, in literature, has received the most thorough scrutiny. It is the central fire of modern poetry and romance. And if all poetry and all romance, bear witness to the greatness of its power, they are also full to overflowing of the proofs of its mystery, its waywardness, its unreason. It is a mighty potentate that springs from a chance look, that feeds on itself, and that is not to be outdone. The preference of the lover is accorded to one knows not what, for often it flies in the face of all reason—even the reason of the lover himself. It catches him like a fever, and rides him like destiny. It is a spell that works within him, he knows not how, and drives him he cares not whither. Under its sway he is no longer himself; perhaps he is greater than himself; at least, he is another being. He is caught in a dream, and his known self becomes the sport and creature of a hidden self which neither he nor his friends can always recognise as verily his. He rejoices in the accession of a new life, because then, for the first time, he becomes aware of his hidden soul—of dim Elysian fields

The mystery of love.

CHAPTER VII.

of thought, far stretching beyond the bounds of his daylight consciousness; and he blesses the angel, or the fairy, or the goddess—call her anything but a woman—through whom this witching sense of endowment comes to him. Nor is a passion, because it is blind, to be branded as untrustworthy. It is quite capable of error; it makes huge mistakes; but I know not that it makes more mistakes than the more conscious forces of the mind, and I do know that very often, far more often than we think, the greatest of all mistakes is not to be in a passion—not to feel. There is a well-known remark of a French actor (Baron, I think), who, however, had only his own business in his eye, that passion knows more than art—blind feeling more than all science. It is a saying which applies to passion generally, and to that hidden soul of which it is a part.

And passion because blind is not therefore trustworthy

Passion reminds us of sympathy, and we may take sympathy as next door neighbour to instinct. It is a strange power which the mind possesses of taking a colour from whatever besets it, like the chameleon that takes the colour of the place it passes. We imitate without knowing that we imitate; and this is sympathy. One man smiles, and another without knowing it repeats the action. So we have a fellow-feeling with the joy and sorrow and every motion of each other's minds. Remember Grétry's trick. He had a clever method of slackening or quick-

Sympathy and its unconscious action.

CHAPTER VII.

ening the pace of any companion in his walks. When he did not like to tell his friend that the pace was too fast or too slow, he sung softly an air to the time of their march, and then by degrees either quickened or slackened it according to his wishes. It is strange too to note how little will suffice to set a strong sympathy in action. St. Bernard preached the crusade in Latin to the German peasants, and we know how they were roused by sermons of which they did not understand a word. As he pondered over this marvel of unconscious imitation, Bacon could not see a way to the understanding of it, but by supposing a transmission of spirits from one to another. "It would make a man think (though this which we shall say may seem exceeding strange) that there is some transmission of spirits," and he promises to treat of this transmission more at large when he comes to speak of imagination. His suggestion is but one more form of a conjecture that continually recurs to all who have much noted the hidden action of the mind. It is inspiration, we say; it is genius; it is magic; it is the transmission of spirits; it is anything but the natural mind—the mind of which we are conscious. Here again, therefore, in sympathy, and in Bacon's account of it, we have additional evidence of the hidden soul.

And how Bacon accounted for it.

Instinct, and Cuvier's definition of

Then for instinct, Cuvier pitching about for a definition of instinct as it appears in the lower animals, felt that he could compare it to nothing so fitly as to the action of the human mind in somnambulism. It is the clearest and most pregnant definition of this mysterious power which has yet been suggested. The mind of beasts, void of self-knowledge and the reason which looks before and after, may well be compared to the belated mind of the sleep-walker; and on the other hand, the processes which we can trace in sleep-walking remind us for their easy precision of nothing so much as instinct. The bee never fails in his honeycomb; the swallow is unerring in her calendar; and the sleep-walker is equally precise. And as when you wake the somnambulist to reason you render him incapable; so when you teach the savage that lives by instinct to think, you make him stupid. For men as well as beasts have their instincts, and in each of them, the power is to be defined in the same terms. It is said of the wolf that when he was in his hornbook, he spelt every word, l, a, m, b. This is a perfect description of the instinctive process, however various its forms.

It as akin to somnambulism.

The more we examine into these instinctive mental actions, the more are we surprised at their variety and their number. You do not know, for example, how many steps there are in the staircase of your house, but your foot knows. You can ascend and descend in the dark, and when you reach the landing, your foot makes of

The immense variety of instinctive actions.

CHAPTER VII. its own accord the appropriate action. This is but one of a great class of mental actions going on ever unknown to us. It resembles reason, as all instinct does; and without any breach of propriety, it might be called an effort of the hidden reason, because this hidden knowledge and calculation comes of experience. But it is scarcely possible to resolve into any exercise of reason or into the lesson of experience, certain other actions of the unconscious muscles. The artist can trust to his hand, to his throat, to his eye, to render with unfailing accuracy subtle distinctions of tone and shades of meaning with which reason seems to have nothing to do—with which no effort of reason can keep pace. It is told of Madame Mara that she was able to sound 100 different intervals between each note of music. The compass of her voice was at least three octaves, so that the total number of intervals at her command was 1500. This immense variety of sound is produced by the less or greater tension of certain muscles of the throat. The difference between the least and the greatest tension of these muscles in a woman's throat is the eighth of an inch. Therefore, all the 1500 varieties of musical sounds which Madame Mara could produce came from degrees in the tension of her muscles which are to be represented by dividing the eighth part of an inch into 1500 subdivisions. Which of us by taking thought can follow such arithmetic? No singer

The instinctive action of our muscles.

Madame Mara and her singing.

can consciously divide the tension of her vocal chords into 12,000 parts of an inch, and select one of these; nevertheless she may hit with infallible accuracy the precise note which depends upon this minute subdivision of muscular energy. It would be easy to multiply examples of the same sort. Mr. Ruskin has shown with great felicity how infinitely the hand of a painter goes beyond the power of seeing in the delicacy and subtlety of its work—the gradations of light and form which it can detail being expressible only in fabulous arithmetical formulas with no end of ciphers in them.* The eye itself too is an arithmetician that beats us hollow in its calculations. Mr. Nunneley tells us that when we behold red colour the retina pulsates at the rate of 480 billions of times between every two ticks of a clock. This is what the most advanced science of our time teaches us, and as in practice we are quite unconscious of it, we can only stand in awe of that instinctive power wherewith we are endowed—a power that with the greatest ease reaches spontaneously to results beyond reckoning, beyond understanding.

What Mr. Ruskin says of the subtle instinct of the hand.

It seems to be the same sort of power as that which the brain exerts in secret over the whole body. The brain keeps guard over the various processes of the body—as the beating of the heart and the breathing of the lungs;

The secret power which the brain exerts over the whole body.

* Mr. Ruskin's statement is too long for a foot-note, but it will be found at the end of this chapter.

sets them a rhythm and keeps them to it. Grief in one night will silver the hair, fear fills the bladder, rage dries the mouth, shame reddens the cheek, the mere thought of her child fills the mother's breast with milk. In numerous facts like these there is evidence of a hidden life of thought working with a constant energy in our behalf in the economy of the bodily frame. Curiously enough too for my argument one great division of this mental energy goes expressly by the name of imagination. It is an old notion, though whether it be true or false has yet to be determined, that the mind of the mother has a marked influence on the outward appearance of her child. It is not merely that she imparts her own character to her child—but that some chance event, some passing thought, some momentary vision, may so impress itself in her mind during the period of her pregnancy, as to leave upon her babe an indelible and recognisable sign. This is said to be the effect of imagination, and many books have been written on it. I shall not soon forget the surprise with which—when some years ago I wanted to master this subject of imagination, and read everything about it I could lay my hands on—I chanced on a number of books in Latin, in Italian, and in French, as, for example, Fienus *De Viribus Imaginationis*, or Muratori *Della Forza della Fantasia*, and found that they were all about the freaks of the mind in preg-

On the effect of imagination in pregnancy.

nancy. But why should this particular class of hidden mental influences be called Imagination? If such mental action exists, there can be no objection to our calling it imagination; for the theory of this chapter is that imagination is but a popular name given to the unconscious automatic action of the hidden soul. But I fail to see why in popular phraseology this class of the hidden actions of the mind upon the body should be selected and set apart and honoured with the name of imagination. There is a hidden energy of the brain working day and night in every province of the body—controlling every motion of every limb, and directing like any musical conductor the movement of the vital forces. It is but a part of a vast and manifold energy which the mind exerts in secret, and which because of its separation from our conscious life, I have ventured to name the Hidden Soul.

But why call this particular class of hidden mental actions imagination?

Parallel to these movements of hidden thought in the bodily functions—movements which may be roughly classed under the general name of instincts—there is another class of the same order, though belonging to the more spiritual part of our nature, which are known by the name of intuitions, and which give the mystics a foundation to build upon. Mysticism is the oldest and widest spread system of philosophy, and gives a tinge to many schemes of thought which, like that of Plato, cannot strictly be called mys-

On those hidden movements which we call intuition.

What is true in mysticism.

tical. Whether we find it in the bud, as in Plato, in Malebranche, in Berkeley and in some of the Germans, or in full bloom as among the Brahmins, among the schools of Alexandria, in the religious system of Bernard and many another saint, in fantastic dreams of Rosicrucians, in the illuminations of Behmen, and in the inspirations of George Fox, the mystical theory has a deep root in human nature, and could not be so rife but that it springs from fact. The great fact out of which it springs is the felt existence within us of an abounding inner life that transcends consciousness. We feel certain powers moving within us, we know not what, we know not why —instincts of our lower nature, intuitions of the higher, dreams and suggestions, dim guesses, and faint, far cries of the whole mind. There is a vast and manifold energy, spontaneously working in a manner which at once reminds us of Cuvier's definition of instinct as akin to somnambulism. The mystic is keenly alive to the reality and the magnitude of this hidden life which is known to us mainly in its effects, and not being able to analyse it or to trace its footsteps, he starts the theory now of a special faculty of spiritual insight bestowed on man, and now of special enlightenment and inspiration from on high. Socrates had his demon; Numa his Egeria; Paracelsus had a little devil in the pummel of his sword; and Henry More was befriended by a spirit with the look of a Roman-nosed matron.

And how powerfully the creed of the Mystic bears on the existence of hidden soul.

The theory of mysticism is a great subject—none more suggestive. It is impossible to do justice to it here, and my business with it now is merely this, to show that the theory of an instinctive, automatic action of the mind, the theory of a hidden mental life which is only now beginning to be understood, has, although misunderstood, been always fully recognised in philosophy as one of the great facts of our moral nature, and as such has been the fertile seed of many a strange, many a potent system of thought. Nor only in philosophy is this great fact recognised. It is understood in practical life that there are many things which we must believe before we can know them to be true. So sings the poet in reference to love :

> You must love her ere to you
> She will seem worthy of your love.

It is on precisely the same principle that we are sometimes told to accept the Christian doctrine before we see it to be true, and as the first step to a recognition of its truth; and it is in this vein of thought that Prior gave utterance to the fine couplet :

> Your music's power your music must disclose,
> For what light is, 'tis only light that shows.

On the hidden life of the believer.

I will only add in this connection that the reality of a hidden life is a cardinal doctrine of our faith. The believer is said to have a life hid with Christ in God. When the Apostle

CHAPTER VII.

describes the existence within him of a spiritual life, he says, "I live, yet not I, but Christ liveth in me." This is one of the favourite texts of Platonic and Puritanic divines, who are keenly alive to the existence of a life within them other than that which comes within the scope of ordinary consciousness. "The wind bloweth where it listeth, and thou hearest the sound thereof, but canst not tell whence it cometh, and whither it goeth: so is every one that is born of the Spirit." That is another of their favourite texts.

Especially recognised by Platonist and Puritan divines.

It is a great charm in the writings of these divines—Platonists and Puritans—that they are haunted with the sense of another life within them which is not the known and surface life of thought. They mistake however in supposing that it is only the saint who has a hidden life, as no doubt many persons also err who, discovering that they possess a hidden life, leap to the conclusion that it can be nothing else than the indwelling of the Holy Ghost. It is to this inner life that Wordsworth refers when in one of his prettiest little poems he addresses a child as follows:

> Dear child! dear girl, that walkest with me here,
> If thou appear untouched by solemn thought,
> Thy nature is not therefore less divine.
> Thou liest in Abraham's bosom all the year,
> And worship'st at the Temple's inner shrine,
> God being with thee when we know it not.

It must be remembered that we are

"Inner shrine." I find that I have reversed this image and have been speaking of the un-

CHAPTER VII.

speaking in metaphors chiefly when we have to describe the hidden life.

conscious tracts of the mind as an outer ring, a great chase as it were spreading far beyond the cultivated park of our thoughts. It matters not which metaphor we take so long as we recognise that it is but a metaphor, and that from metaphor we cannot escape. Whether we speak of our unconscious activities and our stores of memory, as belonging to an inner place, as it were an ark within the veil, or to an outlying territory beyond the stretch of observation, the meaning is still the same. The meaning is that a part of the mind and sometimes the best part of it, is covered with darkness and hidden from sight. When one is most struck with the grandeur of the tides and currents of thought that belong to each of us, and yet roll beyond our consciousness, only on occasions breaking into view, one is apt to conceive of it as a vast outer sea or space that belts our conscious existence something like the Oceanos of Homer. When like Wordsworth one is most struck with the preciousness of what passes in our mind unconsciously, when one feels that we are most conscious of the mere surface of the mind, and that we are little conscious of what passes in its depths, then one turns to other metaphors and speaks of the inner shrine and secrets of the deep.

> Thou liest in Abraham's bosom all the year,
> And worship'st at the Temple's inner shrine,
> God being with thee when we know it not.

I have now at some length, though after all we

CHAPTER VII.

Summary of the evidence of a hidden life or soul within us.

have but skimmed along the ground, gone over nearly all the heads of evidence that betoken the existence of a large mental activity—a vast world of thought, out of consciousness. I have tried to show with all clearness the fact of its existence, the magnitude of its area and the potency of its effects. In the dark recesses of memory, in unbidden suggestions, in trains of thought unwittingly pursued, in multiplied waves and currents all at once flashing and rushing, in dreams that cannot be laid, in the nightly rising of the somnambulist, in the clairvoyance of passion, in the force of instinct, in the obscure, but certain, intuitions of the spiritual life, we have glimpses of a great tide of life ebbing and flowing, rippling and rolling and beating about where we cannot see it; and we come to a view of humanity not very different from that which Prospero, though in melancholy mood, propounded when he said:

Stated in the words of Prospero.

> We are such stuff
> As dreams are made of; and our little life
> Is rounded with a sleep.

We are all more or less familiar with this doctrine as it is put forward by divines. "The truth is," says Henry More, "man's soul in this drunken, drowsy condition she is in, has fallen asleep in the body, and, like one in a dream, talks to the bed-posts, embraces her pillow instead of her friend, falls down before statues instead of adoring the eternal and invisible God, prays to stocks and stones instead of speaking to Him that by his word created all things." Such expressions as these however have about them the looseness of parable; and one can accept Prospero's lines almost literally. For what is it? Our little life is rounded with a sleep; our conscious existence is a little spot of light, rounded or begirt with a haze of slumber—not a dead but a living slumber, dimly-lighted and like a visible darkness, but full of dreams and irrepressible activity, an unknown and indefinable, but real and enjoyable mode of life—a Hidden Soul.

Position of the argument thus far.

See, then, the point at which we have now arrived, and let us look about us before we go further. It has been shown that our minds lead a double life—one life in consciousness, another and a vaster life beyond it. Never mind for the present how much I have failed in the attempt to map with accuracy the geography of that region of the mind which stretches out of consciousness, if the existence of such a tract be recognised. We have a conscious and voluntary life; we have at the same time, of not less potency, an unconscious and involuntary life; and my argument is that the unknown, automatic power which in common parlance we call imagination is but another name for one of these lives—the unknown and automatic life of the mind with all its powers. Our conscious

CHAPTER VII. life we know so well that we have been able to divide it into parts, calling this part memory, that reason, and that other, feeling; but of the unconscious life we know so little that we lump it under the one name of imagination, and suppose imagination to be a division of the mind co-ordinate with memory, reason, or feeling. I should hope that by the mere description of the hidden life I may have, to some extent, succeeded in making this thesis good—or may at least have established a presumption in its favour. The completion of the proof however will rest upon the next chapter, in which it ought to be shown that the free play of thought, the spontaneous action of the mind, generates whatever we understand as the creation of fantasy. This chapter has been all analysis; the next should be synthetic. Hitherto we have regarded the existence of the hidden soul only as a fact: now it has to be shown that imagination is nothing else. I could not help giving, in the course of this chapter, a few indications of the proof. Now the proof may be demanded in all due form.

NOTE.

Mr. Ruskin makes the following statement, to which reference has been made at page 243, with regard to the subtlety of Turner's handiwork. "I have asserted," he says, "that, in a given drawing (named as one of the chief in the series), Turner's pencil did not move over the thousandth of an inch without meaning; and you charge this expression with extravagant hyperbole. On the contrary, it is much within the truth, being merely a mathematically accurate description of fairly good execution in either drawing or engraving. It is only necessary to measure a piece of any ordinarily good work to ascertain this. Take, for instance, Finden's engraving at the 180th page of Rogers' poems; in which the face of the figure, from the chin to the top of the brow, occupies just a quarter of inch, and the space between the upper lip and chin as nearly as possible one-seventeenth of an inch. The whole mouth occupies one-third of this space, say one-fiftieth of an inch, and within that space both the lips and the much more difficult inner corner of the mouth are perfectly drawn and rounded, with quite successful and sufficiently subtle expression. Any artist will assure you that in order to draw a mouth as well as this, there must be more than twenty gradations of shade in the touches; that is to say, in this case, gradations changing, with meaning, within less than the thousandth of an inch.

"But this is mere child's play compared to the refinement of any first-rate mechanical work—much more of brush or pencil drawing by a master's hand. In order at once to furnish you with authoritative evidence on this point, I wrote to Mr. Kingsley, tutor of Sidney-Sussex College, a friend to whom I always have recourse when I want to be precisely right in any matter; for his great knowledge both of mathematics and of natural science is joined, not only with singular powers of delicate experimental manipulation, but with a keen sensitiveness to beauty in art. His answer, in its final statement respecting Turner's work, is amazing even to me, and will, I should think, be more so to your readers. Observe the successions of measured and tested refinement: here is No. 1:

"'The finest mechanical work that I know, which is not optical, is that done by Nobert in the way of ruling lines. I have a series ruled by him on glass, giving actual scales from ·000024 and ·000016 of an inch, perfectly correct to these places of decimals, and he has executed others as fine as ·000012, though I do not know how far he could repeat these last with accuracy.'

"This is No. 1, of precision. Mr. Kingsley proceeds to No. 2:

"'But this is rude work compared to the accuracy necessary for the construction of the object-glass of a microscope such as Rosse turns out.'

"I am sorry to omit the explanation which follows of the ten lenses composing such a glass, 'each of which must be exact in radius and in surface, and all have their axes coincident;' but it would not be intelligible without the figure by which it is illustrated; so I pass to Mr. Kingsley's No. 3:

"'I am tolerably familiar,' he proceeds, 'with the actual grinding and polishing of lenses and specula, and have produced by my own hand some by no means bad optical work, and I have copied no small amount of Turner's work, and *I still look with awe at the combined delicacy and precision of his hand;* IT BEATS OPTICAL WORK OUT OF SIGHT. In optical work, as in refined drawing, the hand goes beyond the eye, and one has to depend upon the feel; and when one has once learned what a delicate affair touch is, one gets a horror of all coarse work, and is ready to forgive any amount of feebleness, sooner than that boldness which is akin to impudence. In optics the distinction is easily seen when the work is put to trial; but here too, as in drawing, it requires an educated eye to tell the difference when the work is only moderately bad; but with "bold" work, nothing can be seen but distortion and fog; and I heartily wish the same result would follow the same kind of handling in drawing; but here, the boldness cheats the unlearned by looking like the precision of the true man. It is very strange how much better our ears are than our eyes in this country: if an ignorant man were to be "bold" with a violin he would not get many admirers, though his boldness was far below that of ninety-nine out of a hundred drawings one sees.'

"The words which I have put in italics in the above extract are those which were surprising to me. I knew that Turner's was as refined as any optical work, but had no idea of its going beyond it. Mr. Kingsley's word 'awe' occurring just before, is, however, as I have often felt, precisely the right one. When once we begin at all to understand the handling of any truly great executor, such as that of any of the three great Venetians, of Correggio, or Turner, the awe of it is something greater than can be felt from the most stupendous natural scenery. For the creation of such a system as a high human intelligence, endowed with its ineffably perfect instruments of eye and hand, is a far more appalling manifestation of Infinite Power, than the making either of seas or mountains. — *The Two Paths.* — pp. 263-265.

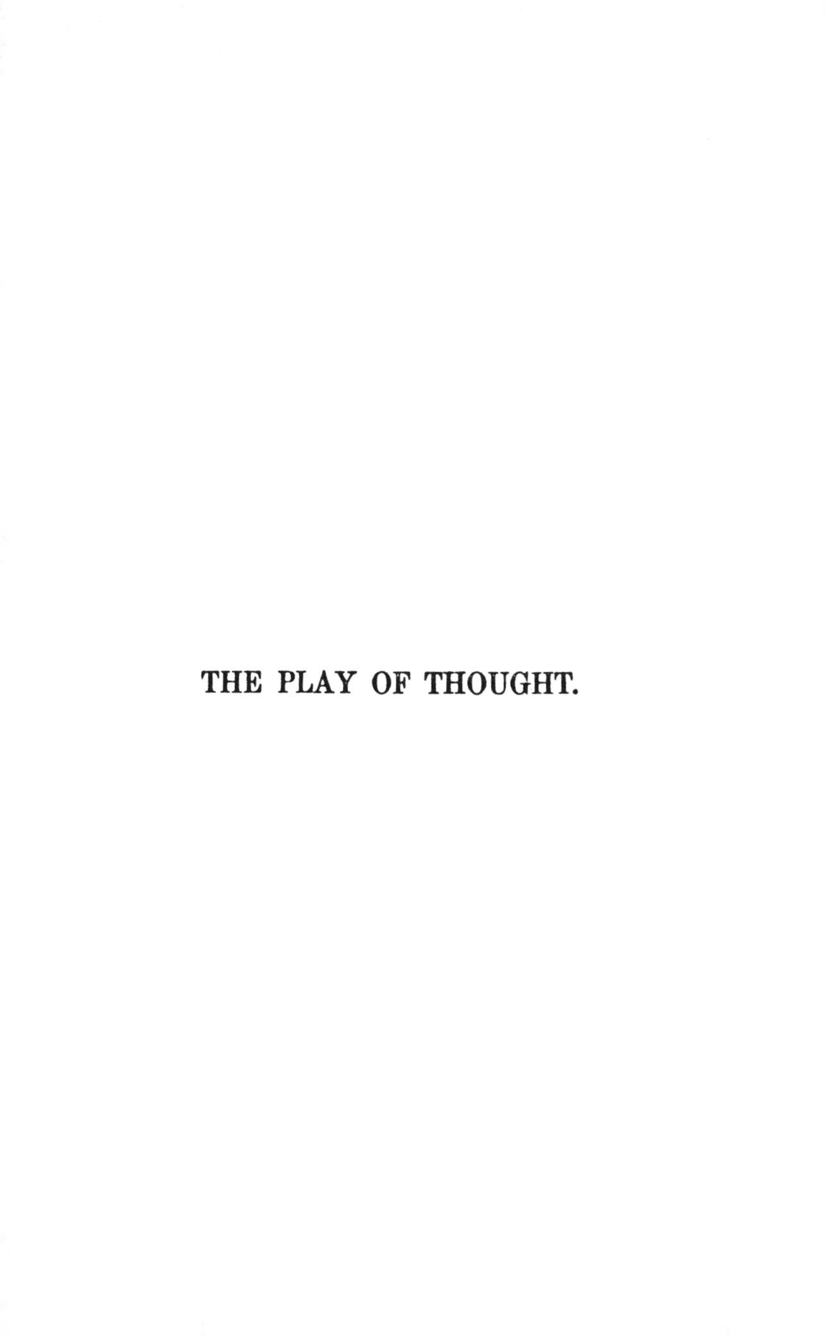

THE PLAY OF THOUGHT.

CHAPTER VIII.

THE PLAY OF THOUGHT.

IF IMAGINATION is to be identified with the automatic action of the mind, with the free play of thought, all its characters ought to be there involved. As in imagination we find *a* play of thought, so in *the* play of thought we should find the whole business of imagination. What magic resides in the one, ought also to reside in the other—and more. Like Aaron's wand• that became a serpent, and swallowed the serpent-wands of the magicians of Egypt, the automatic action of the mind, the free play of thought, should not only simulate, but grasp and contain within itself all the sorceries of imagination.

CHAPTER VIII.

That the action of hidden thought accounts for all the facts of imagination.

But is not this an acknowledged fact? Has there ever been any doubt that imagination, whatever be its nature, is at least spontaneous? It is nothing if it does not belong to the auto-

The spontaneousness of imagination an acknowledged fact.

CHAPTER VIII.

matic actions of the mind. If any doubt upon this point is ever expressed, it comes from those who, like Malebranche, discover in imagination some other faculty—say memory—and then call to mind that memory is voluntary as well as involuntary. But a compulsory imagination, a forced fancy, is a contradiction. The attempt to beget such a state of mind is unnatural, and ends ever in falsehood. The type of imaginative activity is dreaming, with which fantasy has always been identified. Indeed, Charles Lamb lays it down that the strength of imagination may be measured by the dream power in any man. He says, that the mind's activity in sleep might furnish no whimsical criterion of the quantum of poetical faculty resident in the same mind waking. But dream by night and reverie by day are not to be raised, nor yet are they to be laid, by efforts of the will. We may coax and cozen imagination; we cannot command it. We must bide its time. The poet is born—not made; he lies in wait for the dawn, and cannot poetise at will. Bacon says truly of poetry, "that it is rather a pleasure or play of imagination, than a work or duty thereof;" but he might have said the like of all imaginative activity: it is spontaneous—it is play. In the same passage (in the *Advancement of Learning*), from which I have drawn the foregoing remark, he says that "imagination ever precedeth voluntary motion;" and Hobbes repeats the statement,

A compulsory imagination a contradiction.

observing that imagination is "the first internal beginner of voluntary motion." It produces volition, and by volition is not to be produced. What control of imagination lies in our power is rightly compared by Henry More with the sort of control which we can bring to bear upon the essentially involuntary act of breathing. In his *Discourse on Enthusiasm* he speaks of the delusions of mankind, and says that they are due "to the enormous strength and vigour of the imagination; which faculty (though it be in some sort in our power as respiration is), yet it will also work without our leave."

The errors of imagination due to its involuntary and unconscious character.

This sentence of More's is particularly happy in tracing to their proper source the errors of imagination. The imaginations of man's heart are only evil continually, says the Scripture; imagination is the source of all error, says Bishop Butler; it is the most dangerous foe to reason, says Hume. But Hume resolves imagination into mere memory, and other philosophers into mere reason; and is it fair to say that memory is the most dangerous foe to reason, or that reason is the source of all error? It is difficult to find out from the more common theories wherein the vice of imagination consists; and we are all the more at a loss to find it out when we know that sundry thinkers go quite in the opposite direction, and describe imagination as the faculty of clearest insight—reason in her highest mood. If imagination be identified

CHAPTER VIII.

with faculties, exact as memory, and sober as reason—where is the source of illusion? It is to be found, as More points out, in the absence of control, in the vagrancy of spontaneous movement, in the freedom from supervision. Its weakness lies in its stronghold. Because it is automatic and unconscious, it reaches to the grandest results; but also because this is its character, when it falls into error, the error is not easy of correction. It has been adopted in a blind, mechanical act of thought, and it is not to be dispelled by determined efforts of conscious reason. By its very nature, imagination is a wanderer; to it belong the thoughts "that wander through eternity." But the habit of wandering implies that it may sometimes lose itself.

If imagination is nothing but the free play of thought why is it called imagination?

We are not to push the argument however further than it will go. Imagination clearly is automatic, and so far I was justified in comparing the automatic action of the mind with Aaron's rod that, becoming a serpent with a serpent's gift of fascination, swallowed and contained within itself the serpent-rods of the magicians. Still, this leaves unsettled the grand point at issue. Granting that imagination is automatic, and only automatic, may it not in kind be different from other faculties which are only at times spontaneous and unconscious? May it not be different from the hidden memory, or the hidden reason, or the hidden instincts and passions — the three orders of hidden power described in the last chapter? If imagination be not different from the other faculties of the mind—if imagination be but a name for these other faculties in their automatic, and for the most part unconscious, exercise—in a word, for the free play of thought, why is it called imagination?

The clue to the name contained in the definition of the faculty.

The clue to the name is contained in the definition of the faculty. It is to be expected, that in the free play of thought certain habits should be of more frequent recurrence than others. There is a saying, as old at least as Horace, that the mind is most vividly impressed through the eye, and it is but natural that when left to itself it should dwell most on the shows of vision—images—whence arises the name of imagination. According to any and every theory of imagination which has been propounded, the name is of less extent than the faculty, and takes a part for the whole. "Our sight," says Addison, "is the most perfect, and most delightful of all our senses. . . . . It is this sense which furnishes the imagination with its ideas, so that by the pleasures of imagination—I mean such as arise from visible objects, either when we have them actually in view, or when we call up their ideas to our mind, by paintings, statues, descriptions, or any the like occasions. We cannot, indeed, have a single image in the fancy that did not make its first entrance

In the free play of thought we dwell most on images of sight.

through the sight." Addison, and the writers who follow in his wake, are so far true to etymology; but no one now-a-days can suppose that they are true to the nature of imagination. We imagine sounds as well as sights; we imagine any sensation. And if it be granted that imagination contains more than its etymology conveys—is the name of a part extended to the whole, then I may turn round and say, that here is granted the principle on which my definition proceeds. Imagination is but a name for the free play of thought, one of the most important features of which, but still only one, is its attachment and sensibility to the memories of sight.

The definition of imagination as free play explains many opinions with regard to it which are otherwise inexplicable.

It is only by supposing that imagination, although so called, must embrace the action (that is, of course, the spontaneous action) of the whole mind, that we can account for many of the opinions which have been held in regard to it. I have already pointed out the inconsistency of those who tell us of the enormous influence of imagination, and yet, when they come to analyse it, reduce it to a shadow—the mere double of some other faculty; and, I trust, that the view which I have been able to present, while it will satisfy the philosophers in granting that imagination is not a faculty by itself, different in structure from the other faculties of the mind, will also satisfy those who see in it the most imperious power in the mind

CHAPTER VIII.

As the opinion of D'Alembert and Hamilton.

of man. Then there is the curious opinion of two such men as D'Alembert and Sir William Hamilton to be accounted for. Who in all antiquity, after Homer, had the greatest force of imagination? Most of us would be inclined to name, perhaps, Æschylus, or Phidias, or at any-rate, some artist. D'Alembert names Archimedes—a mathematician; Sir William Hamilton selects Aristotle—a philosopher. Those who treat of imagination as but a special form of reason, will have no difficulty in understanding that the greatest reasoners should have the greatest force of imagination. But on the other hand, the poetical mind of Homer, seems to be quite unlike the philosophical mind of Aristotle, or the mathematical mind of Archimedes; and it is not easy to see that they are in any respect comparable, according to any known theory of imaginative activity. Once admit, however, that the specialty of imagination lies not in any specialty of structure, but only in specialty of function—a specialty which belongs to any and every faculty of the mind—the specialty of hidden automatic working, and there need be no difficulty in saying, that Aristotle possessed as much imagination as Homer. There must have been a prodigious automatic action in his mind to enable him to accomplish what he did. The difference between the mind of Homer and the mind of Aristotle—the mind of art, and the mind of science—is not the difference

CHAPTER VIII.

between less and more in the amount of hidden action (though that, no doubt, may make some part of the distinction), but it is the difference between possessing, and being possessed by it—the difference in proportion of energy between the known and the unknown halves of the mind.

On imagery.

The name of imagination, however, suggests not only the power of imaging or figuring to ourselves the shows of sense, but also that of imagery, the power of bringing these shows into comparison, and using them as types. Indeed, when we speak of a poetical image, we mean a comparison, a symbol. It falls, therefore, to be considered whether this apparatus of imagery, in all its varying forms of comparison, similitude, metaphor, personification, symbol, and what not, need for its production some special faculty, which we call imagination, or may not rather be due to the free play of thought in general. Here, as before, it can be shown that imagination is but another name for the automatic action of the mind. Here, moreover, it will be found that we get to the heart of what people commonly understand by imagination; for, although we are speaking only of imagery, and although imagery is rarely treated but as a point of language, it involves much larger issues, and cannot properly be handled unless we understand it in the broadest sense, as including the whole work of imagination. It is in this broad sense of the word that we have now to face the question, "Son of

Imagery not to be treated as a mere question of language.

man, hast thou seen what the ancients of the house of Israel do in the dark (of unconsciousness); every man in the chamber of his imagery?"

The absurdities of criticism in regard to imagery.

A book might be written on the absurdities of criticism which this one subject of imagery has engendered, only it would be a waste of labour on barren sand. One of the most piteous things in human life is to see an idiot vacantly teasing a handful of straw, and babbling over the blossoms which he picks to pieces. It is not more piteous than the elaborate trifling of criticism over figures of speech and the varieties of imagery, showing how metaphor differs from simile, how this kind of image is due only to an exercise of fancy, how that comes of true imagination, and how fancy is one thing, imagination another. The worst of it is that, as I have said, these questions are nearly always handled as questions of language, questions of detail, without any clear perception of the relation between different forms of imagery and different forms of art. The full discussion of the subject does not fall within the range of the present inquiry. All I have now to do with it is to show in the rough that the production of imagery, whether we use the word in a narrow sense, as referring merely to figures of speech, or, in a wider sense, as referring also to conceptions of life, and thus including the whole work of imagination, needs no special faculty, but belongs to the general action of the mind, in the dusk of unconsciousness. Perhaps,

CHAPTER VIII.

however, the easiest path of entrance into the subject is the beaten one which lies over the assumption, that an image is but a figure of speech.

The most obvious fact about imagery is that it always contains a comparison.

Now, in imagery, in this narrower sense of the word, the most obvious thing to be noted is, that from the simplest form of similitude to the most complex form of metaphor and symbol, it always involves a comparison of some kind. And this raises the question—is the act of comparison a peculiar property of imagination? The truth is, that every effort of thought, from the least to the greatest, any the faintest twitch of consciousness, is an act of comparison. There is no thought in the mind but has two factors, one to be compared with the other. In the common act of recognising a face as a face we have seen, we are but comparing one impression with another. And so on to the most intricate forms of the syllogism, it can be shown that we never get away from comparison. To compare is the first glimmer of intelligence in the mind of an infant: to compare is the utmost splendour of reason in the mind of a sage. No comparison, no thought. Yet by no means does it therefore follow that the comparisons of poetry may not be the outcome of a special faculty. For if memory be but one form of comparison, if reason be another, and if, nevertheless, the comparisons involved in memory and in reason be so diverse that we attribute them to separate faculties, why may

But all thought implies comparison.

not the comparisons of poetry be the work of a faculty which is different from every other?

CHAPTER VIII.

What is the peculiarity of the comparisons attributed to imagination.

What then is the peculiarity of those comparisons which are fathered on imagination? How, for example, are they distinguished from those of ordinary judgment? The best account of the difference between the two is given by Locke; although, after all, he gives but half the truth. Both Bacon and Father Malebranche had, in a vague way, anticipated Locke, and to appreciate the full force of his statement, it must be remembered that in his time the word wit was used as identical with poetry, and as ruling the whole territory of imagination. And what does Locke say? He describes wit as "lying most in the assemblage of ideas, and putting those together with quickness and variety, wherein can be found any resemblance or congruity, thereby to make up pleasant pictures and agreeable visions in the fancy. Judgment, on the contrary, lies quite on the other side, in separating carefully one from another ideas wherein can be formed the least difference, thereby to avoid being misled by similitude and by affinity to take one thing for another."

Locke's answer.

This, I say, is not a full account of the distinction, but so far as it goes it is good. It is quite true that in imagination we think more of resemblances, and that in the exercise of conscious judgment we make more of differences. But do we find here a distinction great enough to

But does Locke's answer give any sanction to the notion that in the comparisons of imagination there is

CHAPTER VIII.

anything special?

prove the existence of two separate faculties? Is it beyond imagination to see a difference? Is it beyond judgment to see resemblance? In all comparison there is implied difference as well as resemblance, and the perception of the one brings with it that of the other. From this point of view, therefore, it is not to be supposed that the production of imagery needs a faculty of imagination different from that of judgment.

The peculiarity of imaginative comparisons as thus far stated to be explained by the fact of imagination being free play.

The difference between the comparisons of imagination and those of reason is explained by the one proposition for which I am contending, that those of the former are automatic, and that those of the latter are the result of conscious effort. It is hardly possible to make this quite clear, while as yet we have reached but a half-truth as to the nature of imagery; yet at least there should be a presumption in favour of the idea that, in its automatic or dreamy state, the mind looks more to resemblances, and that in its waking efforts it inclines more to detect variety. I must be content in the meantime with a bare statement of the fact, which I hope to make good in the sequel.

But Locke's statement is only half the truth.

Half the truth, however, is less easy of comprehension than the whole, and to understand aright the full meaning of what Locke has advanced, we ought to be able to eke it out with that other view of the subject which he has not advanced. The most royal prerogative of imagination is its entireness, its love of wholes, its wonderful power of seeing the whole, of claiming the whole, of making whole, and—shall I add?—of swallowing whole. Now, to any one who is strongly impressed with the wholeness of imaginative working, the utter absence of nibbling in it, the most striking thing about poetical comparisons is not that they assert resemblance, but that they assert the resemblance of wholes to wholes. And here we get to the root of the matter. For the grand distinction between logical and poetical comparisons is this, that in the former we compare nearly always wholes with parts, or parts with parts; but in the latter, almost always wholes with wholes. Take the two assertions that man is an animal, and that man is a flower. In the form of language these phrases are alike; but we all recognize that they are unlike in the form of thought; that the one belongs to the order of logical, the other to that of poetical judgments. In point of fact language is but a clumsy expedient, and our thoughts are ever more precise than our words. Now, if after the manner of logicians, we attempt to express in words the precision of our thoughts, then the two phrases which I have put side by side will, in all their awkward exactitude, stand thus—that the class man is a part of the class animal, and that the whole class man is like or interchangeable with the whole class flower. In other words, the logical comparison here asserts the identity of a

Statement of the other half.

Imaginative comparison asserts the resemblance of wholes to wholes.

CHAPTER VIII.

But these comparisons are not incompetent to reason.

certain whole with a certain part; the imaginative comparison asserts the identity or interchangeableness of a certain whole with a certain whole. But between these modes of comparison is there any radical difference? Is it beyond reason to compare as imagination does? Is there anything to prevent the every-day faculty of conscious judgment from comparing wholes with wholes? The truth lies in a nutshell.

And are called imaginative because they belong chiefly to the spontaneous exercise of thought.

There is no reason why in conscious judgment we should not compare wholes with wholes; but this sort of comparison belongs rather to the automatic and unconscious action of the mind. Left to itself, in the freedom of unconsciousness, the mind acts more as a whole, and takes more to wholes. It is not much given to the splitting of hairs and the partition of qualities. To make the partitive assertions and comparisons of every-day judgment, there is needed a certain amount of abstraction; to abstract needs attention; and attention is but another name for the rays of consciousness gathered into a sheaf or focus.

The whole truth about imagery; and how it is proposed to treat of it.

Here then are the two halves of one doctrine. Imagination looks out for resemblances rather than differences: there is the one half. It looks out for the resemblance of wholes rather than of parts: there is the other. And these two views are almost inseparable. It is because imagination looks out for resemblance rather than difference that it leaps to wholes. It is because imagination keeps to wholes and avoids analysis that it overlooks difference and seizes on resemblance. In nearly all the attempts which have been made to establish a disinction between fancy and imagination, it will be found that the division of labour between the two supposed faculties corresponds very much to the division of doctrine as above explained. To fancy is assigned chiefly the habit of catching at likenesses; to imagination is allotted chiefly the habit of discerning unity and grasping wholes. The distinction is of little importance to any one who has noted with what constancy the perception of resemblance or identical forms goes hand-in-glove with the perception of total form and unity; and I, who maintain that there is no special faculty of fantasy, must, of course, much more contend that there are not two faculties, one going by the name of fancy, the other known by that of imagination.

We shall treat of the two halves of the doctrine separately.

Nevertheless, it is convenient in practice to consider the two great characteristics of imagery apart, and there is no harm in doing so if we remember that in reality they are seldom found apart. I now therefore ask the reader to bear with me for a few pages more while I dwell in succession on the likenesses and on the wholenesses of imagery. And I promise him that we shall no longer be tied to the consideration of figures of speech. By a rude analysis of these figures we have arrived at a general conclusion

CHAPTER VIII.

as to the characteristics of imagery and the elements of imagination; and what imagery and imagination are in the forms of language that they also are in all their ways. They take and make like: they take and make whole.

Nature of the discussion.

Only as the ensuing remarks must be very brief, the aim of the present discussion must be clearly kept in view. It is no business of ours just now to trace in detail all the footsteps of imagination. We are solely concerned with the inquiry—what is imagination? That it is an automatic action no one doubts. It remains to be shown that it is the automatic action or play not of any special faculty, but of any and every faculty: the play of reason, the play of memory, the play of the whole mind with all its powers at once; in one word, the play of thought. To prove this, it is unnecessary that we should go very much into detail. It will be enough if we rake up only so much of detail as may indicate the general characteristics of imagination.

On likenesses, and how we are to examine them.

I. First of all, let us think for a little of the love of likeness and the tendency of the mind both to discover and to invent it. Does this imply a special faculty, or is it not rather a function of all the faculties? The point is not difficult of proof, if I may be allowed to start with an assumption, namely, that all these likenesses which the mind either finds or makes are to be measured by the same line and rule. They are all in the same case, and spring from the same law of the mind. It may be more difficult to analyze some forms of similitude than others, and to trace their lineage; but if it can be shown that the leading modes of resemblance have nothing to do with imagination in the ordinary acceptance of the word, that the attempt to ascribe them to a special faculty of imagination is a hoax like that which gave the paternity of Romulus and Remus and many another wondrous child to some god, then in those cases wherein the parentage is not very clear we shall be at liberty utterly to reject the supposition that this or that image must be the offspring of a god—imagination. Call it the offspring of imagination if you will, but it must be understood that imagination means no more than the automatic action of any and every faculty.

The tendency of the mind to similitude takes three leading forms.

Now, the tendency of the mind to similitude runs into three forms, and no more. Every possible variety of likeness which the mind either finds or generates takes one or other of these forms. They are:

1. I am that or like that.
2. That is I or like me.
3. That is that or like that.

The first of these forms contains the ruling principle of dramatic art, and is best known as sympathy. The second contains the ruling

CHAPTER VIII.

principle of the lyrical art, and is best known as egotism. The third contains the ruling principle of epic or historical art, and is best known as imagination. A word or two upon each of these in succession.

And first of the likenesses produced by sympathy.

There is no form of imaginative activity more wonderful than sympathy, that strange involuntary force which impels me to identify myself with you, and you to identify yourself with me. If I yawn, you yawn; if you yawn, I yawn. We cannot help it. I have described the attitude of the mind in the formula—I am that or like that. I am no longer myself, but you, or the person, or the thing I am interested in. We are transformed by a subtle sympathy into the image of what we look on. We personate each other; nay, more, we personate things. At bowls a man sways his body to this side or to that, following the bias of the ball. He fancies for the moment that he is the rolling sphere. And so Goethe came to say of an artist painting a tree or a sheep, that for the time he enters into and becomes that which he delineates, he becomes in some sort a tree, in some sort a sheep. Remember that fine passage in which Wordsworth speaks of the girl that grew three years in sun and shower:

She shall lean her ear
In many a secret place,
Where rivulets dance their wayward round,
And beauty, born of murmuring sound,
Shall pass into her face.

The essence of the thought is always the same; its manifestations are infinite. It shows itself in thousands of ways both in life and in art. The most potent of the social forces, it is sympathy which gives meaning to fashion, and makes education possible. We are constantly copying each other, echoing each other, aping each other, personating each other, weeping with them that weep, laughing with them that laugh, catching the trick of a manner, the tone of a voice, the bent of an opinion, and growing into the likeness of the company to which we belong. And when this tendency shows itself in art, it is no other and no more than that with which we are familiar in life. In art, too, there is no proper difference in the nature of the tendency or manner of thinking, whether it shows itself in words and be called an image, a figure of speech, or show itself in action and be called an imitation, a personation. When Romeo goes to the supper of the Capulets, he disguises himself as a holy palmer, and means to play the pilgrim. He assumes that attitude of the mind which we know as the act of personation. When he takes Juliet's hand for the first time he speaks of his lips as two blushing pilgrims:

How prevalent this tendency is in life, and manifested in how many ways.

The tendency is essentially the same, whether it shows itself in speech or in action.

> If I profane with my unworthiest hand
>   This holy shrine, the gentle fine is this—
> My lips, two blushing pilgrims, ready stand
>   To smooth that rough touch with a tender kiss.

But the strain of mind which produces that

CHAPTER VIII.

image is not different from the strain of mind which produces the personation. In the act of personation, Romeo says: I am not myself, but a holy palmer. In the figure of speech, he says: my lips are not themselves, but blushing pilgrims. And so throughout all art and life the formula of sympathy is this: I am you, or like you; I am, or am like, or at least I wish to be, or to be like, something which is not myself:

> See how she leans her cheek upon her hand.
> O! that I were a glove upon that hand,
> That I might touch that cheek.

On sympathy, and what importance was at one time given to the study of it.

It is a pity that this grand subject of sympathy is not more systematically studied among us. It used to be of no small account in philosophy, but it led so many wildgoosechases, that at length our thinkers seem to have become afraid of it, and to underrate its importance. In the old systems of physiognomy the likeness of men to animals was the chief guiding principle. This man must be of a swinish disposition, because he has a long narrow face; that other must be like a bull for some equally cogent reason. And so as we trudge through the writings of Baptista Porta, Cardan, Bacon, Kenelm Digby, and Henry More; we hear of sympathetic cures and influences. If you eat bear's brains it will make you bearlike; if you put a wolfskin ("for the wolf is a beast of great audacity and digestion") on the stomach it will cure the colic. "The heart of an ape worn near the heart com-

CHAPTER VIII.

forteth the heart and increaseth audacity," says, Bacon, quoting from the writers on magic. "It is true that the ape is a merry and a bold beast. The same heart likewise of an ape applied to the neck or head, helpeth the wit. The ape also is a witty beast, and hath a dry brain." This track of thought led to the wildest absurdities and the most comical situations that reflected no small amount of discredit on any attempts to analyze and turn to account the force of sympathy in human nature; and I cheat the reader of some amusement in refusing to arrest the course of this argument in order to laugh over many queer stories.

How important it is in the systems of thought of Bacon, of Malebranche, and of Adam Smith.

The most important writer after Bacon, who made much of sympathy as a power in human nature, was Malebranche. Malebranche regarded it as a form of imagination, and saw in it the source of many errors, leading men to follow authority when they ought to be independent and think for themselves. Long after him came Adam Smith, who based his system of moral philosophy on this one principle of sympathy. The standard of morality, he said, is determined entirely by the measure of sympathy which any action can command. But he never identified sympathy with imagination; nor after him did the Scotch metaphysicians ever speak of imagination unless by itself, or of sympathetic imitations except as a separate power of the mind. Since then the subject of sympathy

CHAPTER VIII.

has chiefly been handled by the writers on physiology, who treat of it for the most part as a purely physical characteristic.

What is the point of the argument about sympathy.

But see now where this rapid survey of sympathy has led us, and what is the point of the argument. The argument is, that you may call this assimilating tendency of the mind imagination; but that imagination can signify no more than automatic action—the free play of any faculty of thought. We gain nothing by the supposition of a special faculty having a special dominion over such resemblances as come within the meaning of sympathy; we only create confusion. There are animals that change colour with the places over which they pass. Spiders have been known to turn white on a white wall; salmon in certain situations change their colour to that of the bed they swim over; the story of the chameleon is familiar to all. But to what purpose should we say that these changes are the result of imagination, if by imagination we meant anything more than that they are spontaneous? Every faculty we possess reflects and simulates as a mirror does. If you laugh, I will laugh too; if you pull a long face, I turn grave; if I see you sucking a peach on a hot summer day, I have the sense in my mouth that I am sucking one also: as I am arguing this very point, it may be that your reason is following mechanically, and reflecting the movements of mine. Here is a constant

It is an ultimate insoluble fact, which is not explained in the least by the hypothesis of a special faculty, called imagination.

automatic action leading to numerous resemblances. What do you gain by refusing to accept this automatic process of imitation as an ultimate insoluble fact, and by starting the hypothesis of a special faculty called imagination, the express business of which is to produce it? The mind reflecting like a mirror, how are the reflections of the one rendered more intelligible by the supposition of a faculty of imagination than are the reflections of the other without any such explanatory supposition? The sympathy of our minds is a wonder of the world; but no one who can see that the fine English word, fellow-feeling, contains the most perfect expression of all that is meant by sympathy will ever dream of a special faculty of fellow-feeling differing from the feelings which are in fellowship. Bacon, it was shown in the last chapter, started the hypothesis of a transmission of spirits, to account for the sympathy we have with each other. When one man mechanically repeats the action of another—a yawn, a laugh, a start—it would seem, says Bacon, that there must be a transmission of spirits from one to the other to produce the assimilation. Nobody now dreams of such a hypothesis. We are all so enlightened and scientific that, with a fine consciousness of our superiority, we smile at Bacon's suggestion. But the prevalent supposition of an imaginative faculty, if by that is to be understood any-

The hypothesis of imagination is no more tenable than Bacon's hypothesis as to the transmission of spirits.

CHAPTER VIII.

thing beyond the power of spontaneous movement, is not a whit more tenable than the hypothesis of Bacon.

People are deceived by words.

It is curious to see how people are deceived by words, and fancy they get a new idea when they get a new phrase. Mr. Buckle announced that the leading object of his two great volumes was to show that the spirit of scepticism promotes free inquiry. He seemed to think that scepticism, because, coming from the Greek, it is a different expression, must also be a different thing from free inquiry. So it is supposed that by this additional word imagination we obtain some new light; and yet, on the other hand, there is no difficulty in showing that in ordinary speech we may get rid of the name of imagination altogether, and still be none the worse. There is a story told of Samuel Rogers, showing the "force of imagination." About the time when plate-glass windows first came into fashion, he sat at dinner with his back to one of these single panes of glass, and he laboured under the impression that the window was wide open. It is related on his own authority that he caught a cold in consequence. The story is no doubt a Yankee jest, and I give it here not as a fact, but as an illustration. Some people say it shows the force of imagination; but are they one whit nearer, nay, are they not further from the truth, than those who drop the word imagination altogether, and say the story shows the force

And the word imagination throws no new light on the facts that have to be explained.

of faith? Here it was distinctly his belief that is supposed to have operated on Rogers, and yet there are writers—I do not mean to say correct, but at least entitled to consideration, Dr. Thomas Reid being one, and Mr. Ruskin another—who maintain that in imagination there never is belief. When faith leads a man to do that which without faith he could never achieve, what do we gain by calling his faith imagination? Call it imagination if you will, but let us distinctly understand that by this term you mean nothing more and nothing else than the automatic action of the faith, whatever it be. And so of fellow-feeling, call it imagination if you please, but let us understand that it is no more than one of the many modes of automatic action.

Secondly, of the likenesses produced by egotism.

This view will be not weakened but strengthened if now we pass from the assimilating tendency of sympathy to consider the assimilating tendency of egotism, which is the germ of lyrical art. Here we come to the second formula of resemblance—That is I, or like me. The sort of imagery which this begets is known as anthropomorphism and personification. "Let the sea roar, and the fulness thereof; the world, and they that dwell therein. Let the floods clap their hands: let the hills be joyful together." There is one example. "For ye shall go out with joy, and be led forth with peace: the mountains and the hills shall break forth before you into singing, and all the trees of the field shall clap

Examples of it.

CHAPTER VIII.

On the pathetic fallacy.

their hands." There is another. Mr. Ruskin calls this form of imagery the pathetic fallacy, and says that it is only the second order of poets who much delight in it—seldom the first order. But this is surely a mistake. It by no means denotes the height of art—first-rate, second-rate, or tenth-rate; it denotes the kind of art—it belongs to the lyrical mood. When Prometheus, as he enters on the scene, makes his magnificent appeal to the various powers of nature, and amongst others to the multitudinous laughter of the waves, the whole speech is lyrical at heart, it breaks again and again into lyrical metres, and the play in which it occurs belongs to the most lyrical of the Greek dramatists. And so when the lover of Maud says in the garden:

Further examples.

> The slender acacia could not shake
>   One long milk-bloom on the tree;
> The white lake-blossom fell into the lake,
>   As the pimpernel dozed on the lea;
> But the rose was awake all night for your sake,
>   Knowing your promise to me;
> The lilies and roses were all awake,
>   They sighed for the dawn and thee:—

and again—

> There has fallen a splendid tear
>   From the passion-flower at the gate.
> She is coming, my dove, my dear;
>   She is coming, my life, my fate!
> The red rose cries, "She is near, she is near;"
>   And the white rose weeps, "She is late;"
> The larkspur listens, "I hear, I hear;"
>   And the lily whispers, "I wait:"—

the egotism which leads the lover to suppose

the flowers like himself with his own feelings is in that kind of art perfectly natural; and to attribute egotistic imagery to second-rate poets is but another way of saying that it is chiefly the second-rate poets who have the lyrical inspiration. With that question we have nothing to do. We have but to examine into the nature of that assimilating tendency in our minds, which has been described as follows:

> Man doth usurp all space,
> Stares thee in rock, bush, river in the face.
> Never yet thine eye beheld a tree,
> It is no sea thou seest in the sea:
> 'Tis but a disguised humanity.

What is meant by attributing this egotism to imagination?

Now if this egotism is to be called in any peculiar sense imagination, it must be on the principle of *lucus a non lucendo*. Imagination is here conspicuous for its absence. The egotism which would make me see in a tree the double of myself is but the inability to imagine an existence different from my own. Call this assimilating tendency of egotism by the name of imagination if you will, but let us not be misled by words, let us fully understand that imagination means no more than egotism, the natural play of thought and the automatic action of the mind.

Thirdly, of the likenesses which are purely objective.

There is a third class of comparisons which it may be more difficult to resolve to the satisfaction of certain minds without the intervention of a special faculty; and I will here, there-

CHAPTER VIII.

fore, remind the reader of the assumption which I asked him to allow me at starting, namely: that similitudes are to be judged as a whole, and that if we find large classes of them owing their origin to no special faculty, then it may be presumed that those others of which it is not so easy to trace the parentage, are of analogous origin, and do not need the figment of a god for progenitor. It is not necessary, however, to lean much upon this presumption. In dealing with the third class of resemblances, we can adduce quite enough to show that they are produced in the play of ordinary thought.

That is, in which we do not bring ourselves into the comparison.

The formula of the class of similitudes which we are now to look into, is purely objective: That is that, or like that. We do not bring *ourselves* into the comparison at all. In both the dramatic and the lyrical systems of comparison—in the systems of comparison which take their rise from sympathy on the one hand, or from egotism on the other, one of the factors in the comparison is always I or mine. But in this third kind of imagery, that is—in the class of comparisons which belong to epic or historical art, there is no appearance of me and mine; the things compared are quite independent of me and mine. They are, if I may repeat the formula, that and that.

They are sometimes very complicated and difficult of explanation.

Now, sometimes comparisons of that and that come to be very complicated, and are so curious that if we look at them alone, and think of them merely as figures of speech, we shall find it difficult to explain them fully. Everybody will, for example, remember how Wordsworth speaks of an eye both deaf and silent; how Milton speaks of both sun and moon as silent:

> The sun to me is dark,
> And silent as the moon
> When she deserts the night,
> Hid in her vacant interlunar cave.

There is no end of fine poetical passages in which a man is said to see a noise: Sir Toby Belch speaks of hearing by the nose; Ariel speaks of smelling music. Samuel Butler makes a jest of these images in mentioning the

> Communities of senses
> To chop and change intelligences,
> As Rosicrucian virtuosis
> Can see with ears and hear with noses.

Sometimes the imagery is even more complicated, and confounds the facts of three or four different senses. There is a famous passage in the beginning of *Twelfth Night*, the description of music:

Examples of very complicated imagery.

> That strain again: it had a dying fall;
> O! it came o'er my ear like the sweet sound
> That breathes upon a bank of violets
> Stealing and giving odour.

Here we have such an involution and reduplication of idea, that in order to improve the passage Pope altered the word *sound* to *south*, which is the common reading. Mr. Charles Knight, however, has wisely insisted on the pro-

CHAPTER VIII.

priety of recurring to the original reading of the first folio, which is quite Shakespearian. May I add, that not only is the original reading Shakespearian in the reduplication of the idea conveyed (a sound, coming o'er the ear, breathing, stealing, and giving odour, and so in the delight and delicacy of its magic, ministering not to one sense only but to three), there is also to my mind clear evidence that whether the word *sound* were actually penned by Shakespeare, or were only a printer's error, still upon that word Milton once alighted, that it caught his fancy, that it became vital within him, and that as a consequence he produced in *Comus* a similar involution and reduplication of ideas, though in a somewhat different arrangement?

> At last a soft and solemn-breathing sound,
> Rose like a steam of rich distilled perfumes,
> And stole upon the air, that even silence
> Was took, ere she was ware.

Notwithstanding the freshness and originality of this passage, who does not feel that nearly all the ideas which are thus connected with dulcet sound—sound breathing on the ear, stealing on the air, and giving odour—owe their suggestion to Shakespeare?

The amalgam of metaphors does not defy analysis.

But this amalgam of metaphors, though fused by the passion of the poet into an apparent unity of thought, unlike any other mode of thinking, and therefore seemingly the product of some peculiar faculty, does not defy analysis. We can reduce it to its elements, and when so reduced we find that the sort of likeness it involves has its analogy in other modes of thought which are not commonly supposed to be the product of imagination. Remember the form of thought we are considering :—That is that, is like that, or may stand for that. There are poets who boast, or whose critics boast for them, that they seldom or never, in certain works, condescend to the weakness of metaphor; that they are sparing of what is especially called imagery—namely, images in figures of speech. But it will be found that these very writers fly to similitude of another kind—to similitude on a large scale—in one word, to symmetry. The classicism which eschews the symmetry of details produced by figures of speech, eschews them only to ensure a wholesale symmetry, as in that sort of architecture where the two sides of the edifice are alike, and as in horticulture where

Symmetry a form of similitude, and no one attributes the love of it to imagination.

> Every alley has a brother,
> And half the garden but reflects the other.

This is only the craving for similitude in another form, and the argument I build upon it is—that since we do not think it necessary to refer the love of symmetry to a special faculty of imagination, neither need we refer to such a faculty the tendency of similitude in other forms.

Take, again, our natural delight in reflections.

CHAPTER VIII.

Our delight in reflections another form of the tendency to similitude.

"Why are all reflections lovelier than what we call the reality?" asks Mr. George Macdonald, in a fairy romance of rare subtlety, entitled *Phantastes*. "Fair as is the gliding ship on the shining sea, the wavering, trembling, unresting sail below is fairer still. Yea, the reflecting ocean itself reflected in the mirror has a wondrousness about its waters that somewhat vanishes when I turn towards itself. All mirrors are magic mirrors. The commonest room is a room in a poem when I turn to the glass." This is a form of imagery or simile which the poets delight in, and constantly use.

We paused beside the pools that lie
Under the forest bough;
Each seemed as 'twere a little sky
Gulfed in a world below;
A firmament of purple light,
Which in the dark earth lay,
More boundless than the depth of night,
And purer than the day.

In which the lovely forests grew,
As in the upper air,
More perfect both in shape and hue
Than any spreading there.
There lay the glade and neighbouring lawn,
And through the dark green wood
The white sun twinkling like the dawn
Out of a speckled cloud.

Sweet views, which in our world above
Can never well be seen,
Were imaged by the water's love
Of that fair forest green;
And all was interfused beneath
With an Elysian glow,
An atmosphere without a breath,
A softer day below.

This is one of Shelley's finest passages, and it would be easy to quote many parallel ones from other poets, showing how they love to dwell on mirror-like reflections. Take a single instance:

> The swan on still St. Mary's lake
> Floats double, swan and shadow.

These reflections are the painter's form of metaphor.

But such reflections more strictly belong to painters, and are their favourite mode of simile and metaphor. Truly to represent reflections and shadows, and to give all that is contained in the system of reflected colour, is one of the most refined exercises of the artist's power, and wonderfully enhances the beauty of a picture. The system of reflected colour occupies a very prominent place in modern art, and, I repeat, is to picture what metaphor is to poetry. Metaphor is the transfer to one object of the qualities belonging to another. This is precisely what we understand by reflected colour. A lady in white leans on the arm of a soldier in scarlet. The scarlet of his uniform is transferred by reflection to the white of her dress, and makes it appear no longer what it really is. It becomes transfigured. And so throughout the whole of a picture there is scarcely an object which does not suffer some sort of metamorphosis by the shadows and reflections that are cast upon it from other objects. My argument is that all this metamorphosis, which is but the painter's mode of metaphor, is not to be explained by a transfiguring faculty of imagination, and that,

The system of reflected colour in pictures.

But no one attributes the reflections of a picture to imagination.

CHAPTER VIII.

by parity of reasoning, we need no faculty of imagination to account for the transfigurations of poetry produced by simile and metaphor. Here is a story which is told in many different ways: it is told of Queen Elizabeth when her portrait was painted by Zucchero; it is told by Catlin of some Red Indians, whose likenesses he was taking. In each case the limner represented the nose as throwing a shadow on the face. In each case the sitter for the portrait objected to the shadow as a blur that altered and misrepresented the facts of the face. Let me ask two questions: Is it the force of imagination that enables the painter to perceive a shadow on the face, and leads him to imitate it? Is it through lack of imagination that Queen Elizabeth failed to see a shadow on her face, and objected to its being placed there in a picture? I follow up these questions with a third: Why should it be supposed that, whether in picture or in poetry, the transfer of the qualities of one object to another must require a special faculty of imagination? "All things are double one against another," says the son of Sirach; "and God hath made nothing imperfect." Why should the perception of this fact and the constant assertion of it in art be set down to imagination? The only explanation is, that this faculty of seeing double is supposed to be a sort of drunkenness, and imagination is sometimes used as a synonym for illusion.

Why should we attribute them to imagination when they appear in poetry.

CHAPTER VIII.

How the imagination sees wholes.

II. The imagination not only takes and makes like; it also takes and makes whole. The one process is clearly a step towards the other. The discovery of resemblance is an advance to the perception of unity. And as we have spent some time over that state of the mind in which it contemplates resemblance, we must now give our attention to that more complete grasp of thought in which we attain to the sense of unity and wholeness. The mind is never content with a part; it rushes to wholes. Where it cannot find them it makes them. Given any fragment of fact, we shape it instantly into a whole of some sort. In scholastic language which I shall presently explain, the mind discovers or invents for itself three sorts of wholes—the whole of intension, the whole of protension and the whole of extension. The intensive whole is the favourite of the lyrical mood; the protensive whole dominates in the epic; and the extensive whole is the very life and essence of dramatic art. But these phrases are enigmas, and the reader if he pleases may forget them at once and for ever. Throughout this treatise I have taken care not to trouble him with the jargon of technical language, and he shall not be troubled with it now. Technical language is too often the refuge of obscurity, and a make-believe of depth. The technicalities of philosophy are like the tattooing and war-paint of savages to affright the enemy. Stripped of its war-paint,

Invents or discovers three sorts of wholes.

the greater part of philosophy is tame enough, and fit for the understanding of M. Jourdain himself. What I have now to state about the way in which imagination seizes upon wholes is in reality very simple. Never mind about the names of the wholes. Only understand that in number they are three; and the point of the argument which I have to establish is, that when the mind leaps to wholes—leaps from the particular to the universal, from the accidental to the necessary, from the temporary to the eternal, from the individual to the general—we gain nothing by the supposition of a faculty called imagination which has the credit of making the leap. It can be shown that the very same sort of leap is made every hour in reason.

But it can be shown that the work of imagination in creating these wholes is not peculiar to itself.

The case of Peter Bell, for an example of the first whole.

We are told of Peter Bell, that "a primrose by the river's brim a yellow primrose was to him, and it was nothing more." This is characteristic of a man without the power of imagination, as people say generally—without the power of thought, as they might say more correctly. Now let us ask what is it that the man of imagination, the man of thought, sees more than Peter Bell in a primrose? He sees in it a type. It is not merely a fact; it is a representative fact. The primrose by the river's brim stands for all primroses—and more, for all flowers—and yet more, for all life. It comes to signify more than itself. By itself it is but a single atom of existence. Our thought sees in it the entirety

Peter does not see that the primrose is a type.

of existence and raises it into a mighty whole. This is what I mean by the whole of intension, which predominates in lyrical art, and in arts not lyrical when they rise in the early or lyrical period of a nation's life. The units of existence are intensified and exalted into things of universal existence,

> All things seem only one
> In the universal sun.

The typical whole takes many forms.

The tendency of the mind to see or to make these wholes shows itself in many ways; but in art it chiefly shows itself in the love of symbols and types, emblems and heraldic devices. Judah is a lion's whelp; Issachar a strong ass; Dan shall be a serpent by the way; Naphtali a hind let loose. According to this view, which most frankly expresses itself in the earlier stages of thought, everything in nature becomes a type of human nature. So we find in all young art that man and the world amid which he lived were placed on an equality. The beasts of the field, and the fowls of the air, and the fish of the sea, became the friends and confederates of man. He was as they were; and they were all alike. Not only so; trees and flowers could think and feel, and vegetable life was to human life but as the grub to the butterfly. The very stones had life; they were not dead but sleeping. All nature was sentient, and had its voices for man, who was, indeed, a superior being, but still a being on the same platform of existence

And involves in it the assertion of a peculiar kinship between man and nature.

CHAPTER VIII.

with all else. The man might one day become a beast, and the beast might one day become a man. The beast epic of the middle ages, the natural expression of this belief, was received less as an allegoric representation of human life than as a genuine description of a possible history. We can trace the faith, in all its stages of childish simplicity, boorish doubt, and final relinquishment, in the various legends of almost every literature belonging to the Indo-European tribes, where, in the first stage of the tendency, the beast-world is represented as equal—in many respects superior—to the man-world; in a lower stage the beasts are treated with less veneration and as inferior beings; in a still lower stage the sense of human superiority creates a feeling of dislike; we are taught to think, not simply of the stupidity, but also of the hatefulness of the animal kingdom; and, finally, we reach the position of Æsop, who, when he makes his lions, bears, and foxes talk and act, uses them palpably as the representatives of men. The forms, however, in which this love of type, this tendency to symbol manifests itself are innumerable, and their history is not what we have now to study.

But why should we suppose a special faculty to create types.

What concerns us now is to see clearly that the symbolism of art, however and whenever it appears—whether in the frank seizure of types, as in the earlier periods of art, or in the subtle suggestion of them, as in the more advanced periods, does not need the figment of a special faculty to produce it.

What is the nature of the whole which the mind creates in a type.

It is evident that in the determination of thought which raises a primrose into a type, the mind has added something which is not found in the fact. A yellow primrose after all is but a yellow primrose; and if the mind sees more in it, that more is an addition, a creation. Now, it is too often and too hastily assumed that this creation of the mind is a special property of fantasy; and people are the more ready so to think because the process by which we arrive at that creation is perfectly inexplicable. How do we come to know that this primrose is a type? What right have we to say that it may stand for all flowers? What reason is there in the endowment of it with the power of representing all life—and not least, human life? Critics are much too prone to go off in fits of wonder when they consider the working of imagination. This is the easiest mode of escaping from the difficulties of analysis, and the perils of explanation. In the present case there is a real and wellnigh insoluble difficulty before us; but a very little consideration will serve to show that it is nothing peculiar to a so-called faculty of imagination.

It is the same sort of whole as reason creates in generalization.

It is the grand problem of logic; it is the crux of reason. A type is but a name for the result of generalization; and generalization is a process of reasoning. Now, we never generalize without adding some-

CHAPTER VIII.

thing which is not in the facts, and which is a creation of the mind. Here is a well-known specimen of generalization: All men are mortal. Nobody doubts this: but when logicians proceed to analyze it they find themselves unable to explain satisfactorily how we reach from particular examples to the general conclusion. All we know of a surety is, that a certain limited number of men have died—what has become of the rest we know not. But suppose we know for certain that all men hitherto *have* died; how do we arrive at the conclusion that in future all men *must* die? Old Asgill, in the last century, seriously disputed the necessity of death passing upon all men. The leap to a generalization is a creature of the mind. From the earliest dawn of reason the mind is in the habit of taking these leaps. It may generalize well, or it may generalize ill, but generalize it must. The child burns its finger with the flame of a candle: straightway it flies to the conclusion that all fire burns. There is a correct generalization. Once is enough: it flies from the one to the all. But it also makes mistakes of generalization. It calls every man it sees, papa; it calls every bird, Polly; it calls the dog, puss; it runs to eat the snow for sugar. Right or wrong, it generalizes so continually that philosophers have raised a question whether knowledge in man begins in generals or in particulars.

And the generalizations of reason are quite as wonderful as those of imagination and not less inexplicable.

CHAPTER VIII.

Summary of the argument.

The argument then stands as follows: You wonder at the work of imagination when you see how it magnifies isolated facts into continental truths; you are amazed at its creativeness, and think that there must be something singular in the faculty, which, in a manner quite inexplicable, can effect such transformations. But, strange to say, this is the very work, and this the very marvel of reason. No man has yet been able to explain how, because this, that, or some other thing, has happened so many times, we are driven to the conclusion that it shall happen always. In both cases, the process of generalization is precisely the same. When imagination makes a seven-leagued stride from the one to the all, and from the part to the whole, it is no other than the usual stride of reason from the particular to the general. What is peculiar to imagination is not that it differs in this respect from the usual process of reasoning, but that it exhibits that process working automatically. Just as in the free play of thought, the mind tends to dwell on images of sight, whence one of the leading characteristics of imagination from which its very name is derived; so, in the same free play, the mind tends to generalize and totalize every individual fact that engages its attention: and hence another leading characteristic of that automatic energy which is commonly known as imagination.

CHAPTER VIII.

We never get beyond the conception of imagination as free play.

Here as before, then, we never get beyond the conception of imagination as the free play and unconscious movement of thought. There is nothing peculiar in it except that it reveals the instinctive tendency of the mind. That instinctive tendency to generalize on every possible occasion, which shows itself in the first dawn of childish reason, we learn to check as we grow older, and thought becomes more conscious. Then we become hard and prosaic, sticking to facts, in and for themselves, as mere facts. A child accepts every event as a matter of necessity, and it is often exceedingly difficult to convince the little soul — following the natural tendency of mind—that what has happened once may not or will not happen again. Experience comes with years and corrects the imperious tendency of the mind to believe in the uniformity of nature and the necessity of all things. The idea of accident enters, and, while a general belief in the certainty of nature remains, it no longer usurps the throne of absolute law. Perhaps the process goes even further, until at length in the mind's dotage certainty is banished from our expectations, the muse of history becomes the most incredible of Cassandras, and the whole world lies dead before us and around us, with men and women rattling over it like dice from a dice-box. And here we can see precisely the difference between the realism of childhood and poetry and the realism of dotage and prose. The child in everything perceives the element of necessity; the old man perceives but the element of contingency. In particulars the child sees the universal, the old man sees in particulars only the particular. Herein lies the difference between poetry and prose. It is the difference not between imagination on the one hand and reason on the other—but between reason on the one hand playing free and fast, and reason on the other going warily in fetters.

CHAPTER VIII.

—

The element of necessity which imagination supplies.

Much of what has been said about symbols in art, their meaning and their origin, will apply to that other form of generalization, described above as the whole of protension or duration. We have a natural tendency when we see a thing, to think of it not only as now existing but as having always existed, and as destined to exist for ever. The mind is unable to conceive either the beginning or the end of existence. When left to itself in free play it conceives an idea of life in which there is no death. One living thing may be transformed into another living thing, but there is no annihilation. It is just as in our dreams, where life appears to us as a series of dissolving views, a transmigration of souls, an incessant Protean change, without an end. We pass through innumerable avatars; we run the cycle of existence; but cycle is followed by cycle, and existence is indestructible. To die, in the old legends, is to be

The second kind of whole which the mind creates.

We raise the tempo-rary into the eternal.

CHAPTER VIII.

changed for a certain length of time into tree or stone, beast or bird, but never to be quite extinct. The primrose of our dreams is transmuted as we look on it, into a damsel or some other fair creature: it never dies. Wordsworth has a little poem—*We are Seven*—in which he takes note of this, our natural inability to compass the idea of death. The little child has lost one of her brothers, but still she says, "We are seven." Still to her mind the lost Pleiad remains one of the seven. And under the eye of heaven there is not a more touching sight than that presented by Oriental artists when they enter the tombs to protest against dissolution. Some of the elder races of the world arranged the homes of the dead as if they were homes of the living, with panelled walls and fretted ceilings, elbow chairs, footstools, benches, wine flagons, drinking-cups, ointment phials, basins, mirrors, and other furniture. By painting, by sculpture, by writing, they had the habit, as it were, of chalking in large letters upon their sepulchres, NO DEATH.

And cannot compass the idea of death.

The assertion of the continuity of existence makes epical art.

The assertion of the continuity of existence which the mind thus makes is the generating principle of epic or historical art, of all art, indeed, which has to do with the evolution of events; and is there any reason why, when the narrative poet pleases us with his pictures of the transmutations of life, we must call up a special faculty—fantasy—to account for those transmutations? It is no more than the ordinary process of reasoning by which, involuntarily, we connect every fact or thing that comes before us with causes and with effects. We may, with the greater poets, trace our facts to the gods; with Homer, show how the will of Zeus is accomplished in the slaughter of the Achaians; with Milton, how man's first disobedience leads to his fall. Or again, with the lesser poets and storytellers, we may show how the Beast, when Beauty gives him her hand, becomes a prince; how Daphne, pursued by the god, is transformed into a laurel. But what is there in all this metamorphosis of persons, of things, or of actions, which needs for its production a special faculty? When we come to analyze it, is there any real difference in thought between the transmutation of one personality into another, and the transmutation of one action into another? In either case the mind is actuated by one law, the law with which we are most familiar in thinking about causes and effects. We know we are compelled to think of a cause for every event, and that likewise every event suggests to us an effect. Why we are thus compelled to rush back to causes and to rush after effects we cannot tell. We only know the fact, and we are able to resolve it into this more general fact, that to think of a breach in the continuity of existence is beyond our power. We cannot

The transformations of poetry.

But do these transformations need for their production, a separate faculty?

CHAPTER VIII.

think of existence beginning; we cannot think of existence ending; we only think of it as passing from one form to another. This is the law of all thought, and nothing peculiar to a faculty of imagination.

The third kind of whole which the mind creates—that of extension.

And now a few words in conclusion about the third kind of whole which the mind creates, and which is best known as it appears in dramatic art. Not that the two other tendencies I have been describing are to be held as excluded from dramatic art. On the contrary, it appropriates them and turns them to account. But it has also a way of its own which may be described as constructive. The drama is, in a far higher sense of the word than can be applied to any mere narrative—it is in the highest sense of the word, constructive. There is the construction of character and all its traits; there is the construction of the personages in relation to each other; there is the construction of events into a consistent plot. The constructive skill required in a drama will appear all the more remarkable if we remember that the dramatist cannot plaister and conceal defects of construction by comment or description.

On dramatic construction.

The creation of character.

Now when, a single trait of character given, an artist builds upon it with endless details, many of them conflicting, an entire character, this, which in popular criticism is most frequently cited as evidence of the creative power and wholeness of work belonging to imagi-

CHAPTER VIII.

nation, is the result of a mental process not different in kind from that by which the comparative anatomist sees the perfect form of an unknown animal in one of its bones. When Professor Owen pictures for us some great saurian of the ancient world, we do not accuse him of drawing upon his imagination, because he reasons consciously at every step, and we can follow his processes. But when a dramatist or novelist raises before us a great complex character, finely moulded and welded into a consistent whole, we attribute his work to imagination, because it has been devised in unconsciousness, and neither he nor we can follow the process. It is not imagination in the sense of a special faculty that does the work, but imagination in the sense of the hidden soul, the ordinary faculties engaged in free, unconscious play.

On the truth of imagination.

In the free play of thought the mind may commit many errors; but there is one error of which we always absolve it, that of inconsistency, or a disregard of wholeness. We who know what ill names have been heaped on imagination, how it is represented often as the great source of illusion, may be perplexed sometimes to find that many an error, many a lapse from truth, is explained by the absence of imagination. How constantly do we hear it said, when a poet or an artist fails of truth, that he has no imagination, or a feeble one. In these cases it will be found

Where always allowed.

that the want of truth, and therefore the want of imagination, shows itself in a want of consistency or of construction. When in one of the beautiful windows of the Sainte Chapelle, in Paris, Isaiah is pictured reproving Mohammed; there may be want of truth, but not of imagination. If the history be wrong, the thought is right. When Goethe in the play presents Egmont as a bachelor, though at the time of the story he had a wife and children, there is a want of truth, but we do not call it a want of imagination. When the Greek sculptor gives us Laocoon naked, though as the priest of Apollo he must have been in his sacerdotal robes at the time of the serpent seizing him, there again is want of truth, but we do not complain of want of imagination. But when, in one of the mysteries enacted in Germany towards the end of last century, the Creator of the world was represented as an old gentleman in a wig, who groped about in the dark, and after running his head against posts, exclaimed in utter peevishness, "Let there be light," and there was light—the light of a candle; there was not only the absence of truth, but also that of imagination. When Domenichino, in a picture of Creation, put into the garden of Eden trees decaying with age and pollarded trees, there again was a defect of imagination as well as of truth. And, lastly, when Dryden made Eve in the garden a modern coquette, who, on Adam first offering her love, expressed a doubt as to his fidelity, whether he would always be true to her, and whether he would not be running after others; there once more was a lack of truth, and with it a lack of imagination. These falsehoods are offences against imagination, because they are offences against consistency, derelictions from the sense of wholeness. But in thus attributing to imagination the sense of wholeness, of fitness, of consistency—in attributing the lack of consistency to the lack of imagination—what do we really mean? Do we mean that imagination is a special faculty, which looks after consistency as no other faculty looks after it? and that only imaginative persons can be consistent? Surely not.

The wholeness of imaginative work to be explained on a very simple principle.

The wholeness that marks all the work of imagination is a very simple matter, to be explained on a very obvious principle. Imagination, I repeat, is only a name for the free, unconscious play of thought. But the mind in free play works more as a whole than in conscious and voluntary effort. It is the very nature of voluntary effort to be partial and concentrated in points. Left to itself the mind is like the cloud that moveth altogether if it move at all; and this wholeness of movement has its issue in that wholeness of thinking which we find in true works of imagination.

Summary of the argument.

But this lengthy argument must now draw to a close. I have, one by one, touched upon

CHAPTER VIII.

every feature of imagination which is supposed to be peculiarly its own, and I have shown that each, without exception, belongs to the general action of the mind. In the first place, the name of imagination is derived from one of the most evident facts connected with the free play of the mind—sensibility to images or memories of sight. Sight is the most lively of the senses, and we recur most readily in idea to the impressions derived through that sense. Next in free play, and according to the very notion of it, the mind wanders; it is, therefore natural to speak of imagination in this sense as a source of illusion. And so we go over the other tendencies of free play. The mind has a tendency to see likeness and to become like what it sees. The mind has a tendency to see and to create wholes. Moreover, all these tendencies herd together. They are separable and quite distinct; but in the free play of the mind, they generally appear in combination. The result is, that by the law of inseparable or pretty constant association, we come to regard all these uniting tendencies as a composite whole, one special faculty.* It is true

* For the fullest and clearest account of the law of inseparable association, see Mill's *Examination of Sir William Hamilton's Philosophy*, chapter xiv. It is really an important law, and it is the corner-stone of Mr. Mill's system of philosophy, which aims at overthrowing and displacing the established philosophy of Europe. Mr. Mill, however, complains that this, his leading principle, is not so much rejected as ignored by the great European schools of thought. "The best informed German and French philosophers," he says, "are barely

that, in the processes which we attribute to imagination, there is a specialty. It is a specialty, however, not of power, but of function; not of tendency, but of the circumstances under which the tendency is exerted. The nature of the work performed by imagination is not peculiar to itself. What is peculiar to itself is, that the work is done automatically and secretly. That

CHAPTER VIII.

aware, if even aware, of its existence. And in this country and age, in which it has been employed by thinkers of the highest order as the most potent of all instruments of psychological analysis, the opposite school usually dismiss it with a few sentences, so smoothly gliding over the surface of the subject as to prove that they have never, even for an instant, brought the powers of their minds into real and effective contact with it." Of the thinkers "of the highest order," who have made much of the law, I know only one—Mr. John Mill himself; and if it be a fact that it has hitherto been ignored, that would be the clearest of all proofs that until Mr. John Mill took it up, it cannot have been applied by any thinker "of the highest order." The truth, however, is that the law is nowhere ignored. It is a very simple and a very obvious law which cannot have escaped the notice of the blindest bat in philosophy. All that Mr. Mill has a right to complain of is that the chief European thinkers do not attach so much importance to it as he believes it deserves, and as it really does deserve. We all know the force of association in our ideas of things. We see things together; we learn to think of them as inseparably associated, and of their union as incapable of dissolution. Mr. James Mill uses the following illustration: "When a wheel, on the seven parts of which the seven prismatic colours are respectively painted, is made to revolve rapidly, it appears not of seven colours, but of one uniform colour—white. By the rapidity of the succession, the several sensations cease to be distinguishable; they run, as it were, together; and a new sensation, compounded of all the seven, but apparently a single one, is the result." That is precisely the case of imagination. In the free play of the mind, there are a number of tendencies which harmonize and unite; we come to regard them as a unity; and we dub that unity Imagination.

the work is automatic, or that the work is secret, does not alter its character, and make it different from reason, memory or feeling. Imagination therefore, can only be defined by reference to its spontaneity, or by reference to its unconsciousness. Regarding it as automatic, we define it the Play of Thought. Regarding it as unconscious, we define it the Hidden Soul.

THE SECRECY OF ART.

CHAPTER IX.

THE SECRECY OF ART.

CHAPTER IX.

Review of the previous argument.

WE OUGHT now to proceed at once to the consideration of pleasure. I began by showing that pleasure is the end of art. I brought forward a cloud of witnesses to prove that this has always been acknowledged. And after showing that all these witnesses, in their several ways, define and limit the pleasure which art seeks, we discovered that the English school of critics has, more than any other, the habit of insisting on a limitation to it, which is more full of meaning as a principle in art than all else that has been advanced by the various schools of criticism. That the pleasure of art is the pleasure of imagination is the one grand doctrine of English criticism, and the most pregnant doctrine of all criticism. But it was difficult to find out what imagination really is ; and therefore the last three chapters

CHAPTER IX.

were allotted to an inquiry into the nature of it. The result at which we have arrived is that imagination is but another name for that unconscious action of the mind which may be called the Hidden Soul. And with this understanding, we ought now to proceed to the scrutiny of pleasure. I will, however, ask the reader to halt for a few minutes, that I may point out how this understanding as to the nature of imagination bears on the definition with which we started—that pleasure is the end of art. Few are willing to acknowledge pleasure as the end of art. I took some pains to defend pleasure in this connection as a fit object of pursuit, and if I have not satisfied every mind, I hope now to do so by the increased light which the analysis of imagination will have thrown upon the subject.

And its bearing on the definition of art.

We started with the common doctrine, that art is the opposite of science, and that, as the object of science is knowledge, so that of art is pleasure. But if the reader has apprehended what I have tried to convey to him as to the existence within us of two great worlds of thought—a double life, the one known or knowable, the other unknown and for the most part unknowable, he will be prepared, if not to accept, yet to understand this further conception of the difference between science and art that the field of science is the known and the knowable, while the field of art is the unknown and the unknowable. It is a strange paradox that the

Art is the opposite of science.

Its field therefore is the un-mind should be described as possessing and compassing the unknown. But my whole argument has been working up to this point, and, I trust, rendering it credible—that the mind may possess and be possessed by thoughts of which nevertheless it is ignorant.

Known and the unknowable.

Now, because such a statement as this will appear to be a paradox to those who have not considered it; also, because to say that the field of art is the unknown, is like saying that the object of art is a negation, it is fit that in ordinary speech we should avoid such phrases, and be content with the less paradoxical expression—that the object of art is pleasure. The object of science, we say, is knowledge—a perfect grasp of all the facts which lie within the sphere of consciousness. The object of art is pleasure—a sensible possession or enjoyment of the world beyond consciousness. We do not know that world, yet we feel it—feel it chiefly in pleasure, but sometimes in pain, which is the shadow of pleasure. It is a vast world we have seen; of not less importance to us than the world of knowledge. It is in the hidden sphere of thought, even more than in the open one, that we live, and move, and have our being; and it is in this sense that the idea of art is always a secret. We hear much of the existence of such a secret, and people are apt to say—If a secret exist, and if the artist convey it in his art, why does he not plainly tell us what it is? But here

That statement however sounds too much like a paradox for ordinary use.

People do not understand how a secret exists which cannot be told.

CHAPTER IX.

at once we fall into contradictions, for as all language refers to the known, the moment we begin to apply it to the unknown, it fails. Until the existence of an unknown hidden life within us be thoroughly well accepted, not only felt, but also to some extent understood, there will always be an esoteric mode of stating the doctrine, which is not for the multitude.

Yet there are current phrases which may help us to understand the paradoxical definition of art.

Although at first sight it may appear absurd to speak of the unknown as the domain of art, and to describe the artist as communicating to the world, through his works, a secret that he and it will never unravel, yet there is a common phrase which, if we consider it well, may help to render this paradox less difficult of belief. Montesquieu has a profound sentence at which I have often wondered: "Si notre âme n'avait point été unié au corps, elle aurait connu; mais il y a apparence qu'elle aurait aimé ce qu'elle aurait connu: à présent nous n'aimons presque que ce que nous ne connaissons pas." I have wondered by what process of thought a man of the last century arrived at such a conclusion. It scarcely fits into the thinking of his time; and I imagine he must have worked it out of the phrase—Je ne sais quoi.* It was

Je ne sais quoi.

* Montesquieu's remark will be found in his *Essai sur le Goût*, where, indeed, he dwells so much upon the je ne sais quoi, as to make one nearly certain that by some subtle process of hidden thought, unknown to himself, it suggested the remark. The curious thing is, that he attempts to explain in measured language

in the last century a commonplace of French criticism and conversation, that what is most lovely, most attractive, in man, in nature, in art, is a certain je ne sais quoi. And adopting this phrase, it will not be much of a paradox to assert that, while the object of science is to know and to make known, the object of art is to appropriate and to communicate the nameless grace, the ineffable secret of the know-not-what. If the object of art were to make

CHAPTER IX.

If the ob-

the je ne sais quoi; and his explanation robs it of its richness of meaning. Nothing can be more flat; and one is puzzled to understand how the thinker who could make the remark which I have quoted above, should give us the following definition of the je ne sais quoi: "Il y a quelquefois dans les personnes ou dans les choses un charme invisible, une grâce naturelle, qu'on n'a pu définir, et qu'on a été forcé d'appeler le *je ne sais quoi*. Il me semble que c'est un effet principalement fondé sur la surprise. Nous sommes touchés de ce qu'une personne nous plaît plus qu'elle ne nous a paru d'abord devoir nous plaire, et nous sommes agréablement surpris de ce qu'elle a su vaincre des défauts que nos yeux nous montrent, et que le cœur ne croit plus. Voilà pourquoi les femmes laides ont très-souvent des grâces, et qu'il est rare que les belles en aient. Car une belle personne fait ordinairement le contraire de ce que nous avions attendu; elle parvient à nous paroître moins aimable; après nous avoir surpris en bien, elle nous surprend en mal; mais l'impression du bien est ancienne, celle du mal nouvelle: aussi les belles personnes font-elles rarement les grandes passions, presque toujours réservées à celles qui ont des grâces, c'est-à-dire des agrémens que nous n'attendions point, et que nous n'avions pas sujet d'attendre. Les grandes parures ont rarement de la grâce, et souvent l'habillement des bergères en a. Nous admirons la majesté des draperies de Paul Véronèse; mais nous sommes touchés de la simplicité de Raphaël et de la pureté du Corrége. Paul Véronèse promet beaucoup, et paye ce qu'il promet. Raphaël et le Corrége promettent peu, et payent beaucoup; et cela nous plaît davantage."

CHAPTER IX.

ject of art were to make known, it would not be art but science.

known and to explain its ideas, it would no longer be art, but science. Its object is very different. The true artist recognises, however dimly, the existence within us of a double world of thought, and his object is, by subtle forms, tones, words, allusions, associations, to establish a connection with the unconscious hemisphere of the mind, and to make us feel a mysterious energy there in the hidden soul. For this purpose he doubtless makes use of the known. He paints what we have seen, he describes what we have heard; but his use of knowledge is ever to suggest something beyond knowledge. If he be merely dealing with the known and making it better known, then it becomes necessary to ask wherein does his work differ from science? Through knowledge, through consciousness, the artist appeals to the unconscious part of us.

It is to the hidden soul, the unknown part of us, that the artist appeals.

The poet's words, the artist's touches, are electric; and we feel those words, and the shock of those touches, going through us in a way we cannot define, but always giving us a thrill of pleasure, awakening distant associations, and filling us with the sense of a mental possession beyond that of which we are daily and hourly conscious. Art is poetical in proportion as it has this power of appealing to what I may call the absent mind, as distinct from the present mind, on which falls the great glare of consciousness, and to which alone science appeals. On the temple of art, as on the temple of Isis, might be inscribed—"I am whatsoever is, whatsoever has been, whatsoever shall be; and the veil which is over my face no mortal hand has ever raised." ✓

CHAPTER IX.

This view of art supported by authority.

There are persons so little aware of a hidden life within them, of an absent mind which is theirs just as truly as the present mind of which they are conscious, that the view of art I have just been setting forth will to them be well nigh unintelligible. Others, again, who have a faint consciousness of it, may see the truth more clearly if I present it not in my own words, but in words with which others have made them familiar.

It is implied in Macaulay's criticism on Milton.

Here, for example, is what Lord Macaulay says of Milton and his art: "We often hear of the magical influence of poetry. The expression in general means nothing; but applied to the writings of Milton it is most appropriate. His poetry acts like an incantation. Its merit lies less in its obvious meaning than in its occult power. There would seem at first to be no more in his words than in other words. But they are words of enchantment. No sooner are they pronounced than the past is present and the distant near. New forms of beauty start at once into existence, and all the burial places of the memory give up their dead. Change the structure of the sentence, substitute one synonyme for another, and the whole effect is destroyed. The spell loses it power; and he who should then hope to conjure with it, would find

CHAPTER IX.

himself as much mistaken as Cassim in the Arabian tale when he stood crying, 'Open wheat, Open barley,' to the door which obeyed no sound but 'Open sesame.'" This is admirably expressed, with the fault, however, of attributing magic to Milton's poetry alone, while denying that magic belongs to poetry in general. The fact is, that all poetry, all art, has more or less of the same magic in it. We are touched less by the obvious meaning of the poet than by an occult power which lurks in his words. This is what I have been all along enforcing, that art affects us not as a mode of knowledge or science, but as suggesting something which is beyond and behind knowledge, a hidden treasure, a mental possession whereof we are ignorant. Given the magic words, given the magic touch, and not only Milton's poetry, but all good poetry and art will force the burial places of memory to render up their dead, will set innumerable trains of thought astir in the mind, fill us with their suggestiveness, and charm us with an indefinable sense of pleasure.

Only the same criticism applies to all poetry as well as to Milton's.

Precisely in this vein of thought sings Thomas Moore :

It is implied in Moore's verses.

> Oh, there are looks and tones that dart
> An instant sunshine through the heart:
> As if the soul that minute caught
> Some treasure it through life had sought;
> As if the very lips and eyes
> Predestined to have all our sighs,
> And never be forgot again,
> Sparkled and spoke before us then.

CHAPTER IX.

He is here referring to the action of love in that sense of it which suggested the well known sentence that the poet, the lunatic, and the lover, are of imagination all compact. Love, says Shakespeare, is too young to know itself. It belongs to the secret forces of the mind, and is connected with them by a freemasonry which mere consciousness may recognise but cannot penetrate. There is a passing glance, a sign, a tone, a word. In the lover as in the poet, it appeals not to the conscious intelligence, but to the secret places of the soul; it illumines them with an instant gleam, which allows us no time to see what passes there; it gives light without information; and the light as it vanishes leaves us with a vague sense of possessing, we know not where, some hidden treasure of the mind for which all our lives we have been searching.

Byron also refers to it.

Now let us turn to Byron for a change. He takes a gloomy view of the strange power of the mind which we are considering, but he dwells on its existence as a great fact. He refers to it again and again, but the best known passage in which he makes mention of it will be found in the fourth canto of *Childe Harold*, where he describes with much force the insidious return of grief:

> But ever and anon of griefs subdued
> There comes a token like a scorpion's sting,
> Scarce seen, but with fresh bitterness imbued;
> And slight withal may be the things which bring

CHAPTER IX.

Back on the heart the weight which it would fling
Aside for ever: it may be a sound—
A tone of music—summer's eve—or spring—
A flower—the wind—the ocean—which shall wound,
Striking the electric chain wherewith we are darkly bound;

And how and why we know not, nor can trace
Home to its cloud this lightning of the mind,
But feel the shock renewed, nor can efface
The blight and blackening which it leaves behind,
Which out of things familiar, undesigned,
When least we deem of such, calls up to view
The spectres whom no exorcism can bind,—
The cold, the changed, perchance the dead—anew
The mourned, the loved, the lost,—too many!—yet too few!

It is implied in Wordsworth's poetry.

Let me ring another change upon the same idea by next quoting Wordsworth. One of the most admired passages in his works, and frequently cited as a perfect embodiment of the poetical spirit, is the following from the poem on Tintern Abbey:

I have learned
To look on nature, not as in the hour
Of thoughtless youth; but hearing oftentimes
The still sad music of humanity,
Not harsh nor grating, though of ample power
To chasten and subdue. And I have felt
A presence that disturbs me with the joy
Of elevated thoughts; a sense sublime
Of something far more deeply interfused,
Whose dwelling is the light of setting suns,
And the round ocean, and the living air,
And the blue sky, and in the mind of man:
A motion and a spirit that impels
All thinking things, all objects of all thought,
And rolls through all things. Therefore am I still
A lover of the meadows, and the woods,
And mountains; and of all that we behold
From this green earth; of all the mighty world,
Of eye and ear—both what they half create,
And what perceive.

CHAPTER IX.

The meaning of some passages unintelligible without reference to the hidden soul.

What is the meaning of it? Does he simply mean that sunsets and other sights of nature are so beautiful as to afford him great pleasure? He says much more, which it is not easy to put into clean-cut scientific language. Any man of poetical temperament knows what it means, though he might be puzzled to express it logically. What is the presence which surprises the poet with the joy of high thought? What is that something in the light of setting suns which is far more deeply interfused than the five wits can reach, and is to be apprehended only by a sense sublime? Is it fact or fiction? It is but Wordsworth's favourite manner of indicating the great fact upon which all art, all poetry, proceeds. Nature acts upon him as Milton's words upon Macaulay, like magic. It appeals to his hidden soul, and awakens the sense of a presence which is not to be caught and made a show of. The light of setting suns, the round ocean, and the living air, arouse in him a demi-semi-consciousness of a treasure trove which is not in the consciousness proper. What that treasure, what that presence is, it would pose Wordsworth or any one else to say. All he knows is that nature finely touches a secret chord within him, and gives him a vague hint of a world of life beyond consciousness, the world which art and poetry are ever pointing and working towards.

But there

The poetry of Wordsworth abounds with

CHAPTER IX.

are many such passages in Wordsworth.

passages that vividly refer to the concealed life of the mind and the secret of poetry. Some of these were quoted in the last chapter, and I will now, even at the risk of becoming tedious, quote another, which is one of the finest descriptions of that which we are to understand by the know-not-what of art. I should like to cite every line of the Ode on Immortality, but restrict myself to the following verses, in which the poet raises the song of praise. It is not simply because of the delights of childhood and its simple creed that he gives thanks for the remembrance of his youth :

Another in the Ode on Immortality.

> Not for these I raise
> The song of thanks and praise ;
> But for those obstinate questionings
> Of sense and outward things,
> Fallings from us, vanishings,
> Blank misgivings of a creature
> Moving about in worlds not realized,
> High instincts, before which our mortal nature
> Did tremble like a guilty thing surprised ;
> And for those first affections,
> Those shadowy recollections,
> Which, be they what they may,
> Are yet the fountain-light of all our day ;
> Are yet a masterlight of all our seeing ;
> Uphold us, cherish us, and have power to make
> Our noisy years seem moments in the being
> Of the eternal silence ; truths that wake
> To perish never,
> Which neither listlessness nor mad endeavour,
> Nor man, nor boy,
> Nor all that is at enmity with joy
> Can utterly abolish or destroy.

What a Saturday

Now, it may be interesting to read the comment which a very intelligent critic makes

CHAPTER IX.

Reviewer says of it.

upon this in one of the weekly journals. He is obliged to confess that the passage reads like nonsense; it has no special meaning; but his heart responds to it, and he pronounces it perfectly beautiful. "There is no reason," he says, "why a confused state of mind should not be poetical. Indeed we may go further and say, that some of what is universally acknowledged to be the finest poetry, has scarcely any definite meaning whatever. In Wordsworth's great ode there are many lines comprising a kind of essence of poetry, but to which it is scarcely possible to attribute any distinct signification. The often-quoted passage about the 'fallings from us, vanishings, blank misgivings of a creature moving about in worlds not realized,' &c., are exquisitely beautiful, but are altogether without any special meaning. If we try to interpret them, to fix the idea embodied in them, it evaporates at once. The words are the right ones to awaken, for some reason, a set of pleasant associations, and to stimulate our imaginations; but as soon as we try to dissect and analyze them, to distinguish between the form of expression and the sense which it is intended to convey, we fail altogether. The words themselves are the poetry. It is like a mosaic work, which puts together a number of beautiful colours, without attempting to form any definite picture."

How far he is correct in his view.

The view which the critic here indicates, although not altogether correct, is well ex-

CHAPTER IX.

pressed; and, making allowance for some incautious phrases, the reader will find no difficulty in squaring it with the view of art contained in these pages. It is hard to say that Wordsworth's phrases have no special meaning which it is possible to fix in the terms of cold reason. The poet is describing, with all the clearness he can command, the know-not-what—the vanishing effects produced in his consciousness by the veiled energy of his hidden life; and by the bare mention of these vanishing effects (not as the critic says, by unmeaning words that are as the colours of a kaleidoscope) he appeals to an experience which all who can enjoy poetry must recognize, he brings back upon us strange memories, and through memory surprises us with a momentary sense of the hidden life, a sudden gleam as of a falling star that comes we know not whence, and is gone ere we are conscious of having seen it:

> Swift as a shadow, short as any dream,
> Brief as the lightning in the collied night,
> That in a spleen unfolds both heaven and earth,
> And ere a man hath power to say—behold!
> The jaws of darkness do devour it up.

Sir Edward Lytton gives expression to similar thoughts.

Since Wordsworth, the man who has shown the most abiding sense of a mystery surrounding human life and thought, of an energy which is ours, and yet is separate from conscious possession, is Sir Edward Lytton. It may be doubted whether he fully understands the nature of this mysterious energy—whether, at any rate, he understands it as fully as Wordsworth. Still, he is so impressed with its reality, that it has suggested to him more than one marvellous tale of a secret magic belonging to humanity; and even when he is not thinking at all of Rosicrucian mysteries, but merely describing ordinary flesh and blood, he refers to the mental gifts of his more poetic personages in terms which, without the key supplied by the theory of the Hidden Soul, are to most readers a perfect riddle. Take the description of Helen, in *Lucretia*. "There is a certain virtue within us," says Sir Edward Lytton, "comprehending our subtlest and noblest emotions, which is poetry while untold, and grows pale and poor in proportion as we strain it into poems." In other words—if I may interpolate my own explanation—which is poetry so long as it remains the know-not-what, and ceases to be poetry when it is defined into knowledge and becomes an item of science. "This more spiritual sensibility," Sir Edward proceeds, "dwelt in Helen, as the latent mesmerism in water, as the invisible fairy in an enchanted ring. It was an essence, or divinity, shrined or shrouded in herself, which gave her more intimate and vital union with all the influences of the universe—a companion to her loneliness, an angel hymning low to her own listening soul. This made her enjoyment of nature, in its merest trifles, exquisite and profound; this gave to her tendencies of heart all the delicious and sportive variety

His description of Helen.

CHAPTER IX.

love borrows from imagination; this lifted her piety above the mere forms of conventional religion, and breathed into her prayers the ecstacy of the saints."

Senior's criticism on this description.

I have not seen this passage as it stands in the original, and quote it from a critical essay of Mr. Nassau Senior. The comment which that hard thinker makes upon it, struck me as a capital example of one-eyed criticism. He introduces the passage by saying that Sir E. Lytton is apt to ascribe to his characters "qualities of which we doubt the real existence;" and he dismisses it with the declaration, "we must say that these appear to us to be mere words." The anonymous critic whom I quoted just now saw in the extract from Wordsworth meaningless phrases; but he allowed that the phrases had an influence on him, and suggested something very delightful to his mind. In Bulwer Lytton's description, Mr. Nassau Senior sees words without influence and without any hold on reality. What would such a man say to Shelley's account of poetry with which he closes his *Defence of Poetry?* "It is impossible to read the compositions of the most celebrated writers of the present day without being startled with the electric life which burns within their words. They measure the circumference and sound the depths of human nature with a comprehensive and all-penetrating spirit, and they are themselves perhaps the most sincerely astonished at its manifestations; for it is less their

He does not understand it.

Nor would he understand Shelley.

spirit than the spirit of the age. Poets are the hierophants of an unapprehended inspiration; the mirrors of the gigantic shadows which futurity casts upon the present; the words which express what they understand not; the trumpets which ring to battle, and feel not what they inspire; the influence which is moved not, but moves."

So far the definition of art as the Empire of the Unknown has been explained solely by reference to poetry.

In these various quotations I have been endeavouring, from as many points of view as I can command, to justify and make clear the paradox that whereas the theme of science is the known and knowable, that of art is the unknown and unknowable. But the quotations which I have been able to bring forward relate chiefly to poetry, and they ought to have the supplement of a few words on the other forms of art, showing that they too, music, painting, sculpture, not less than poetry, are what they are, and gain their peculiar ends, not as exhibitions of knowledge in one form or another, but as suggesting something beyond knowledge. This, however, is even more clear in the case of music than in that of poetry. There is no pretension in music to increase the store of knowledge, and so far it is to be regarded as the purest type of art. The glory of music is to be more intimately connected than any other art with the hidden soul; with the incognisable part of our minds, which it stirs into an activity that at once fills us with delight and passes understanding. We feel a

See the same definition as it applies to music.

CHAPTER IX.

certain mental energy quickened within us; faint far-away suggestions, glimpses of another world, crowd upon the uttermost rim of consciousness; and we entertain through the long movements of a symphony the indefinable joy of those who wake from dreams in the fancied possession of a treasure— they wot not what. Music being thus the most spiritual of the arts—having less connection than any other with knowledge and matter of fact; more connection than any other with the unknown of thought; we are for a moment reminded of the opinion of those who would make it the queen of the arts, as there are those on the other hand who would make metaphysics queen of the sciences. Into a discussion of that point which, after all, is of little importance, I shall not now be tempted to stray; but I wish to say, in passing, that when critics seek to measure a great musician like Beethoven with a great dramatist like Shakespeare, they are apt to run the comparison upon qualities which are incommensurable.

Music is the art which has more direct connection than any other with the unknown of thought.

Beethoven and Shakespeare compared.

The art of Shakespeare, be it observed, is complex. It is built on a vast expenditure of facts, on a wonderful exposition of knowledge. Through the splendid collision of facts, we learn to catch at something which is not in the facts; from the conquered world of knowledge we sidle into the unconquered world of hidden thought—"the worlds unrealized" of Wordsworth. But in any attempt to show the greatness of Shakespeare, the proofs are nearly all based on the greatness of his knowledge. It is only this kind of proof that we can logically construe. Who can take the measure of his influence in the hidden world of thought? We can measure his knowledge, we cannot measure all that is comprised in the know-not-what of his influence. Now if we try to put into comparison the menta' grasp of Beethoven with that of Shakespeare—what do we find? We find in Beethoven the great master of an art, which is not complex but simple—which acts powerfully and vitally on the unknown realm of thought, but not through the means, or at least very little through the means, of definite knowledge. The definite knowledge which Beethoven or any great musician puts before our minds as a means of gaining access to the hidden soul is very small; compared with that which Shakespeare sets in the glare of consciousness it is as nothing. The standard, therefore, of conscious comparison between the great musician and the great dramatist entirely fails.

The comparison impossible.

When we turn from music and poetry to painting and sculpture, there may be more difficulty in accepting art as in the strictest sense the opposite of science—the keeper of a secret which may be imparted but never known. Music is nothing if not suggestive, and all good poetry has a latency of meaning beyond the simple statement ot acts. But in the arts of

The definition applied to the arts of painting and sculpture.

The arts *f*

CHAPTER IX.

painter and sculptor exhibit the precision of science.

painting and sculpture there is the precision, the clearsightedness, the accuracy of science; and we admire so much the knowledge of the thing represented, which the artist exhibits, that we are less struck by the something beyond knowledge—the know-not-what which he suggests to the imagination. When the poet makes Perdita babble of the daffodils that come before the swallow dares, and take the winds of March with beauty, he displays a suggestiveness which outruns the whole art of painting. *Qui pingit florem, non pingit floris odorem.* How can a painter in the tinting of a daffodil convey fine suggestions of the confidence and power of beauty in a tender flower? The painter may give us "pale primroses," but how can he convey what Perdita means when she tells us that they die unmarried ere they can behold bright Phœbus in his strength? The painter's art is evidently tied to fact more strictly than that of the poet. We are all familiar with the manner in which truth of drawing, truth of colour, truth of perspective, truth of light and shadow, truth to the minutest hair and filament of fact—in one word, complete science is demanded of the artist who appeals to us through the visual sense; and his scientific mastery of the human forms, or dog-forms, or forms of whatever else is to be pictured, bulks so large in our esteem that we forget often the somewhat more than science which ought to be on his canvas or in his marble, and without

And the painter's art especially is very strictly tied to fact.

which his art is naught. If mere accuracy, if mere matter of fact, were all in all, then the artist would stand a poor chance in competition with the photograph and other mechanical modes of copying nature. It is the artist's business, by the capture of evanescent and almost impalpable expression, by the unfathomable blending of light in shadow, by delicacies of purest colour, by subtleties of lineament, by touches of a grace that is beyond calculation, by all the mysteries that are involved in the one word—tone—to convey to the imagination a something beyond nature, and beyond science—

CHAPTER IX.

But science is not enough.

The pictorial artist reaches to something beyond science.

> The light which never was on sea or shore,
> The consecration and the poet's dream.

If there be artists who content themselves with adhesion to bare fact, who are never able to transcend fact and to move the imagination, then we must think of them as of Defoe. We take an interest in what Defoe tells us, but it is not the interest excited by art. He sees things clearly and describes them sharply; but the complaint against him is that he has no imagination—that he never touches the hidden sense, which we have been trying to analyze. And as a man may tell a story well (it is done every day in the newspapers), and yet his clear story-telling is not poetry; so a man may paint a picture well, and yet his picture for all the clearness and fulness of knowledge it exhibits may not be art, because it wants that something which a great

The artists who adhere to bare fact—what are they?

Their art

CHAPTER IX.

wants the essential quality of art.

artist once described by snapping his fingers. " It wants, said Sir Joshua Reynolds, " it wants *that.*"

There is a famous saying of Shakespeare's Ulysses, " that one touch of nature makes the whole world kin ;" and in a sense very different from that which our dramatist had in his mind, it is frequently cited as the clearest expression of what art most gloriously achieves, and what the artist ought most steadily to pursue. Whoever will refer to the passage in the original, will see that Shakespeare meant nothing like what his readers divorcing the line from the context now see in it. The supposition is, that when we discover any one touch of nature our hearts are stirred into sympathy with all nature, and we rejoice in the felt grandeur of the bond which links us to the universe. It is a mistake, however, to suppose that any touch of nature will produce this effect, and that the artist has nothing to do but to render nature. It is only by touches of nature that he can move us, but he has to select his touches. Truth of touch is not enough, because every true touch is not in magnetic relation with the hidden life of the mind. The artist may fill his canvas with true touches; and Sir Joshua, snapping his fingers, may have to say—" It wants that."

But if the

If the essential quality of art may be expressed

CHAPTE IX. — **domain of art is the unknown and unknowable, how can it ever be the subject of science?**

by the pantomime of snapping one's fingers, and by saying, "'tis *that*," then there is good reason why in a previous chapter I should have refused to limit the scope of art to the true, to the beautiful, or to any one idea within the sphere of knowledge; but there may also seem to be fair grounds for challenging the possibility of a critical science. If the field of art be the unknown and unknowable, where is the room for science? Is it not likely that all our inquiries into the nature of art may end in no better result than the page-boy in one of Lilly's plays got out of Sir Tophaz? "Tush, boy!" cries the bragging soldier, Sir Tophaz, "I think it but some device of the poet to get money." "A poet!" says Epiton; "what's that?" "Dost thou not know what a poet is?" "No," says the page. "Why, fool," rejoins Sir Tophaz, "a poet is as much as one should say, a poet." If, however, there be aught of which a science is impossible there may still be room for scientific ignorance. Nay, more, Sir William Hamilton, who, notwithstanding Mr. Mill, will hold his place as the greatest thinker of the nineteenth century, maintained, though he did not originate the paradox, "that what we are conscious of is constructed out of what we are not conscious of,—that our whole knowledge, in fact, is made up of the unknown and incognisable," I do not insist upon this, although it is capable of distinct proof, because to render such a mystery in knowledge

CHAPTER IX.

The question answered by reference to biology, which is the science of something the essence of which is unknown.

plain to the popular mind would be too much of a digression. But it may be enough to say that if we cannot tear the secret from art, we can, at any rate, lay bare the conditions under which it passes current. There is a science of biology, and yet no one can define what is life. The science of life is but a science of the laws and conditions under which it is manifested. So, again, is it essential to the science of electricity that we should know for certain what is electricity? We know not what it is: we only see its effects; and yet relating to these effects of an unknown power there has been built up a great science. Again, we can trace the orbits of comets and reckon upon their visits, though of themselves, their what, their why, their wherefore, we know almost nothing. And so there may be a science of poetry and the fine arts, although the theme of art is the Unknown, and its motive power is the Hidden Soul.

END OF VOL. I.

LONDON: PRINTED BY WILLIAM CLOWES AND SONS, STAMFORD STREET AND CHARING CROSS.